Scotland for backpackers

Erica Brock

illustrations by
Violet Cooper

Reel Publishing
Edinburgh

Copyright © Erica Brock 1998

4th Edition

Published by   Reel Publishing
                        Suite 17 / 28 North Bridge
                        Edinburgh EH1 1QG
                        Scotland

Illustrations by Violet Cooper
Cover illustrated by Violet Cooper
Maps by Erica Brock, Violet Cooper and Susan MacKinnon

Printed by Bell & Bain Ltd, Glasgow

British Library Cataloguing-in-Publication Data
A catalogue record for this book is available from the British Library

ISBN   0-9524913-1-1

SCOTLAND for backpackers

ADDITIONAL WRITING and RESEARCH
by
Marian L McPetle   Richard Phipps
Jonathan Ledgard   Claire Hartley

Paul Wastney Len Costantini
Angela MacKintosh Diana Morgan
Susan MacKinnon Derek Alston

THANKS TO
Bruce Gorie Christine Peterson Gina Dolbey
Stephan Rappo   Michael & Cynthia Brock
Katherine Muir   Angela & Deidre   David Eccles
Mike Armstrong Mike Lillyman Mike Cooper Ruby
Peter MacMillan & Barbara Simmons

Written & researched, printed & published in Scotland

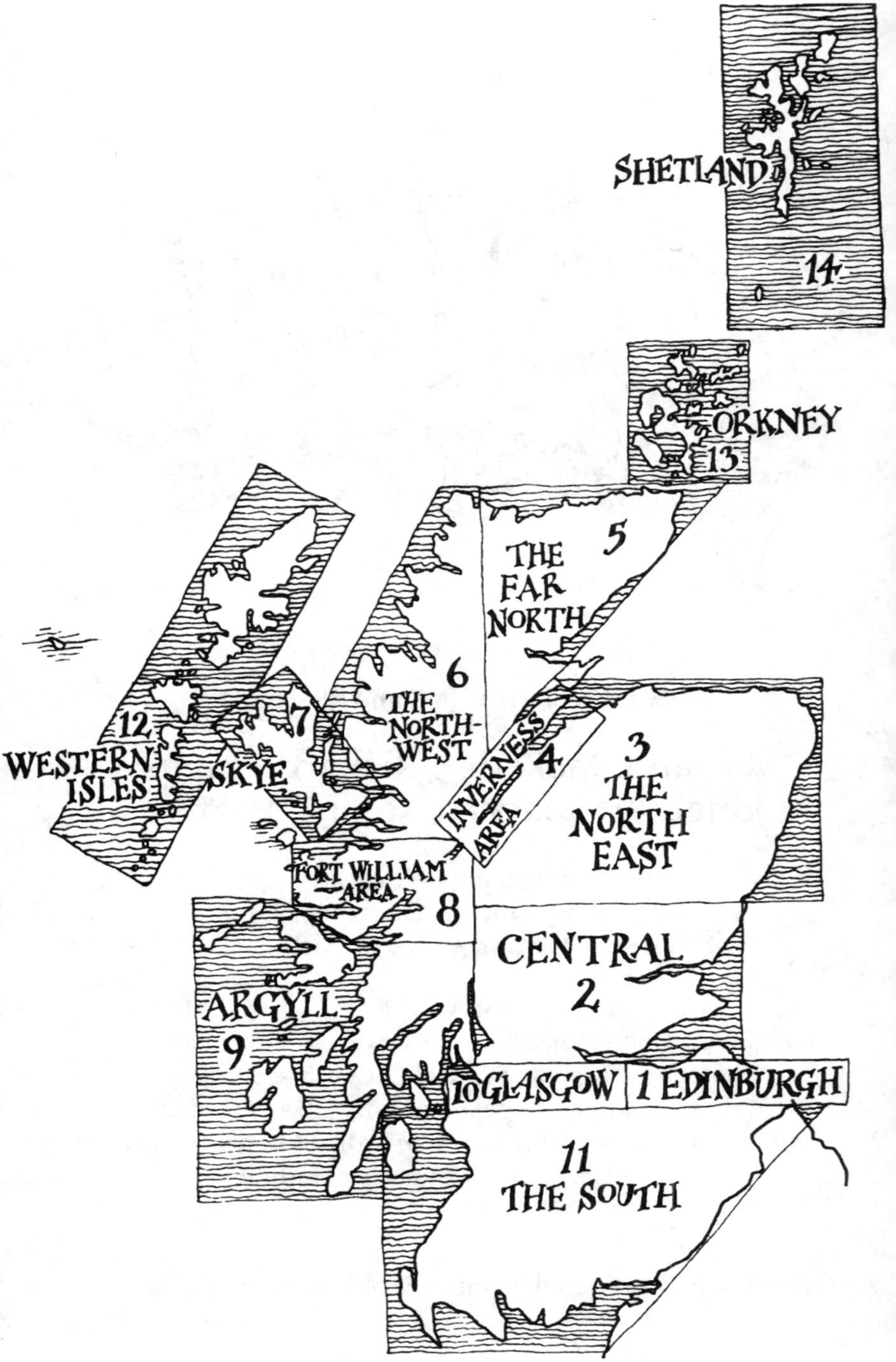

SHETLAND

14

ORKNEY

13

THE
FAR
NORTH

5

6

THE
NORTH-
WEST

INVERNESS AREA

4

3
THE
NORTH
EAST

7

SKYE

12
WESTERN
ISLES

FORT WILLIAM
AREA

8

CENTRAL
2

ARGYLL

9

10 GLASGOW

1 EDINBURGH

11
THE SOUTH

Contents

Key

C   century
HS   Historic Scotland
NTS   The National Trust for Scotland
SYHA   Scottish Youth Hostel Association
RSPB   Royal Society for the Protection of Birds
rtn   return

INTRODUCTION

Scotland has so much to offer the adventurous traveller.

Around every corner there seems to be something intriguing - a remnant of her dark and bloody history or a perfect landscape, wild and untamed. Mix this with a population that likes to enjoy itself (witness the pub any night) and you have a holiday full of promise. What's more, it's an easy country to explore with extensive transport, bountiful accommodation and best of all, friendly, helpful locals.

This book endeavours to show you the best of Scotland. We believe that we are more qualified than most in this respect as our writers and researchers have amassed a couple of hundred years experience of this country.
We hope you enjoy this book, we are sure you will find it useful and money saving.

Just one other thing - have a good holiday.

Edinburgh

Edinburgh, Scotland's magnificent capital, is one of the most physically beautiful cities in Europe. With its medieval character remaining, a trip to this historic burgh evokes powerful images of the past. Whether walking through its ancient, cobble-stoned streets or climbing to one of many vantage points to take in the skyline, this is a city that cannot fail to impress. Edinburgh provides so much scope for exploration. Lovers of history can delight in a long and complex saga telling the tragic tale of Mary, Queen of Scots, as well as the story of Deacon Brodie, the inspiration for Robert Louis Stevenson's 'Dr Jekyll and Mr Hyde'. Architecturally the city is a gold-mine with its earliest building dating from the 11thC. And for those with a penchant for nature, even you will not be disappointed, with the dramatic Holyrood Park and its peak, Arthur's Seat, providing a refreshing break from the bustle of city life. Although Edinburgh is a place to visit throughout the entire year, the city virtually explodes with activity during its international arts festival every August and at Hogmanay a vast legion of revellers choose Edinburgh's streets as *the* place to greet the New Year with a whisky and a kiss.

A Brief History

The exceptional landscape of the city centre resulted from glacial activity during the last Ice Age. Scotland was once covered by a thick sheet of ice and Edinburgh's shape was determined by a glacier moving eastwards. The ice met, but was broken by, a volcano's solid core (the castle rock) and went either side, gouging out the deep crevices of the Grassmarket and Princes Street Gardens. The land directly behind the core was largely untouched and remained as a kind of tail, later to become the world-famous Royal Mile. It is the castle rock's supreme defensive qualities that have always attracted peoples to the area. The Picts settled here using both the castle rock and Holyrood Park as strongholds, and the Romans too, although their major settlement was at Cramond on the River Forth. The region has changed hands many times and it probably received its name in the 7thC from the Gaelic 'Din Eidyn'. It remained just a small community until King Malcolm and Queen Margaret moved their court south from Dunfermline in the 11thC, and from that time Edinburgh grew and developed as Scotland's capital. Much later in the 16thC, Mary, Queen of Scots, lived in, and reigned from, the Palace of

7

Holyroodhouse, until her humiliating departure from Scotland. Her son James VI inherited the English throne from the childless Queen Elizabeth, thus uniting the English and Scottish crowns, and he quickly left for London. About 100 years later, in 1707, Edinburgh's parliamentary power was effectively taken away and transferred to Westminster in London with the Act of Union. (In 1997 the Scottish people voted for the return of a Scottish parliament and this will be set up in Edinburgh in the next few years.) Bonnie Prince Charlie spent several weeks in Holyrood Palace in 1745 on his way south in an attempt to reclaim the throne, but apart from this Edinburgh was largely ignored by the monarchy. The next significant period in Edinburgh's history is that known as the Enlightenment. During the 18th and 19thC an astounding surge of intellectual activity took place in the city. Writers, philosophers, innovators and inventors led the world and history has recorded their remarkable achievements.

The central city can be fairly neatly divided into two halves - the Old Town and the New Town. Due to unmanageable land to the north, Edinburgh was initially confined to the Old Town and southern area. Overpopulation along the Royal Mile eventually led to high-rise living and Edinburgh in the Middle Ages had the world's first skyscrapers some 13 storeys high. Rich and poor lived in the same buildings, the wealthy in the more central floors, the poor to the top and the bottom. These crowded conditions were of course uncomfortable and unsanitary and as soon as the

CALTON HILL

New Town development became available to them in the late 18thC, the wealthy of the middle floors left the Old Town in a hurry. The New Town became possible with the building of the North Bridge spanning the Nor' Loch - today Princes Street Gardens, but once a smelly marsh that has, thankfully, been drained. A competition was held for the design of the New Town and 23-year-old James Craig's winning entry, the basis for the New Town, is a historic monument to town planning. Looking at these beautiful buildings, the wealth and comfort of the original occupiers becomes quite obvious. As the New Town prospered, the Old Town slid into decline (indeed it was, until the 1950s, a slum area), however its historic buildings and unique character have been preserved and now are admired and valued by people from all over the world.

The Old Town

The Royal Mile

Edinburgh's historic thoroughfare forms the backbone of the entire city. A trek down it is essential and should be well and truly savoured. It's best and easiest to start at the castle at the top and make your way to the palace at the bottom. To see the Mile you should allow at least a couple of hours, if not days, as there are many attractions and diversions to explore. Various streets and closes (or lanes) leading off the Royal Mile deserve some of your time, so don't confine yourself to the main street.

Sitting on top of Castle Rock is Scotland's most visited attraction - **Edinburgh Castle**. Edinburgh's original buildings nestled up against this virtually impregnable fortress, and it has dominated the city for its entire history. The castle is magnificent from every angle, but perhaps at its best from Princes Street Gardens below, especially from beside the fountain. The oldest building within the castle still in existence today is St Margaret's Chapel, dating from the 11thC. The Scottish Crown Jewels are kept within the castle and there is an excellent exhibition to visit before seeing the jewels which were hidden within the castle for 110 years and forgotten until Walter Scott instigated the search for them. You can also now see the Stone of Destiny or Stone of Scone, which was returned to Scotland in November, 1996 (for more information about the stone see 'Scone'). Other things to see are the Mons Meg cannon, Mary, Queen of Scots' apartments where she gave birth to James VI, the Great Hall and the superb views of the city and the River Forth beyond. Look for the pet cemetery where officers' favourite dogs have been buried. Entry costs £6/£4.50, and once

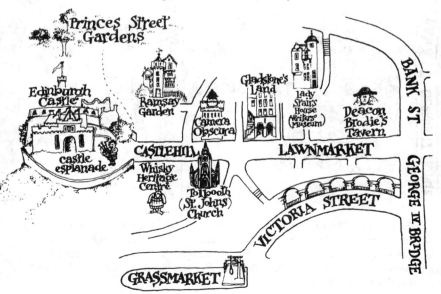

you're inside entertaining guides run tours regularly through the summer months. Afterwards you can explore at your leisure. It's open 9.30am-5.15pm (last ticket sold) in the summer and 9.30am-4.15pm in the winter (HS). Anyone who wants to visit the Scottish National War Memorial only can enter for free.

Edinburgh's celebrated Military Tattoo is held on the **Castle Esplanade** for three weeks during August while near the end of the Festival the castle is host to the splendid Bank of Scotland Fireworks Display. There are several monuments in the esplanade but the most intriguing is the Witches' Well, a small fountain which commemorates the unfortunate men and women (over 300 of them) accused and killed for practising witchcraft over the centuries. After you leave the castle you will soon arrive at **The Edinburgh Old Town Weaving Company**. They have an exhibition on the production of tartan and of Highland Dress through the Ages, but this is also a busy, working tartan mill where many different fabrics are being woven at the one time; £3/£2, and of course, you can buy all sorts of tartan in their shop afterwards. Across the street is **The Scotch Whisky Heritage Centre**, however, we suggest that you hold on to your £4.20/£3.50 entrance fee and go to a proper distillery up north.

For a quick detour, go to the left down Ramsay Lane for a look at the beautiful residences in **Ramsay Garden**.

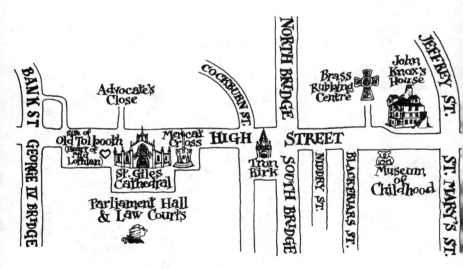

The **Camera Obscura** is an interesting visual, panoramic, 19thC novelty, all done with mirrors. Providing an excellent introduction to the city, it includes many old photographs and paintings of the streets of Edinburgh as well as a holography and pin-hole photography exhibition. There are excellent views from the top; £3.85/£3.10 (£3.95/£3.15 in July and August).

Gladstone's Land is a museum which depicts an authentic image of life in a tenement in the 17thC; £3/£2, NTS. Open April-October. Look for the James Court closes and wander into the courtyard (and perhaps have a pint in The Jolly Judge).

The **Writers' Museum** in Lady Stair's House, down Lady Stair's Close, commemorates Scotland's three most famous writers - Walter Scott, Robert Burns and Robert Louis Stevenson. It houses a collection of memorabilia rather than an introduction to their work, but there are many curious articles on display justifying a quick visit. The display on Stevenson is the most thorough and interesting. Free entry.

You'll see Deacon Brodie's Tavern on the left of the Lawnmarket, and the notorious character this pub is named after is worth a mention. A respected town councillor by day, he was the leader of a gang of thieves by night. Deacon Brodie was the inspiration for Robert Louis Stevenson's 'Dr Jekyll and Mr Hyde'.

Looking down Bank Street to the left, you can see the Bank of Scotland's head office - a splendid place to go and change your traveller's cheques.

From George IV Bridge to the right you can divert to **Victoria Street**, a picturesque street which winds its way down to the historic **Grassmarket.** This was a path many criminals took to meet their fate at the gallows (including the aforementioned Deacon Brodie) in front of a large and bloodthirsty crowd. Victoria Street and the Grassmarket today have many shops, restaurants and pubs to choose from. For many centuries a market was held there.

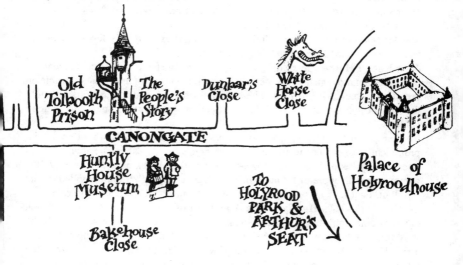

Back on the High Street, **St Giles Cathedral**, with its unusual crown spire, is the principal church of Edinburgh, and although not as famous as the castle or palace, has seen many crucial moments in history. It changed from being Catholic to a Protestant cathedral during the Reformation mainly thanks to John Knox, who's apparently buried under the car park. A relaxed walk through St Giles is pleasant - look out for the Thistle Chapel tucked away to the side. Out on the High Street (just outside the west door of the cathedral) brass-lined stones can be seen, marking the outline of the old Tolbooth Prison. The Tolbooth is mainly known for its role as a jail but it was also a tax collection point for the government - either way, not a popular establishment with the locals. Tradition continues today to spit upon the site of the front door - the heart-shaped stonework of the **Heart of Midlothian** - for good luck.

Parliament House is inside Edinburgh's law courts, just to the side of the cathedral. The Parliament Hall's ceiling is truly magnificent, and below it you can see lawyers pace the length of the hall in deep discussion, keeping moving to prevent you eavesdropping. Afterwards, why not take in a murder trial? (Ask at the desk for which trials are open to the public.)

The **Mercat Cross** just beyond the Cathedral marks the Old Town's busy central point where people met, goods were sold and announcements were made. The cross that stands today was reconstructed in the 19thC but retains the shaft of the 16thC cross.

The **Tron Kirk** holds a special place in Edinburgh's heart and memory. Open all summer as a visitor centre, it is around this kirk that people traditionally gathered at Hogmanay. It takes its name 'Tron' from the weighing beam which once stood near it. For something a bit different head down Chalmers' Close to the **Brass Rubbing Centre** located inside Trinity Apse. Trinity Apse was built from the stones of the demolished Trinity Church and is tucked away down this quiet close. It's free to enter, but if you want to try some brass rubbing prices range from 40p to about £10, depending on the brass plate you choose.

The **Museum of Childhood** is full of toys and games, but sadly few of them you can play with. Good for a quick look. Free entry.

John Knox's House offers a detailed exhibition on the famous and fiery preacher of the Protestant movement. This picturesque building is one of the most noticeable on the High Street; £1.95/£1.50. Theatre performances and exhibitions are held throughout the year at the adjoining **Netherbow Art Centre** - their cafe is good value too.

Further down there's the magnificent looking **Canongate Tolbooth** with its prominent clock. Once the prison and court-house for the Canongate area, it is now home to **The People's Story**, a down-to-earth museum looking at the history of the common (real) people of Edinburgh. There's an engaging 20-minute video on the top floor, then several rooms below packed with information. It's free to enter.

Directly opposite is **Huntly House Museum** (also free), a 16thC house, which depicts Edinburgh's history, displaying many artefacts from many eras. Possibly the most important exhibit is the deerskin upon which thousands signed their names in 1638. This, the National Covenant, was a bid to protect the Protestant faith from the plans of the Catholic monarch, Charles I. Be sure to find the basement room with the old-fashioned shop-front figurines.

One of the Royal Mile's best-preserved closes, **Bakehouse Close**, can be reached through the arch beneath Huntly House.

A well-kept secret of the Royal Mile is the 17thC garden in **Dunbar's Close**. The gate is not locked and at the back it's a quiet place to relax on a sunny day. Another close to visit, at the foot of the Royal Mile, is the attractive **White Horse Close**. It is now residential but was once the place where the stagecoach arrived from London. The **Palace of Holyroodhouse** is of major historical importance. King David I founded Holyrood Abbey in 1128, having encountered a vision on the site. As a stag was about to attack him, a cross appeared between the animal's antlers. David clasped the cross in his hands and the stag fled. This holy cross, or holy rood, gave the area its name. The palace beside the ruined abbey was mostly built around the year 1500. A comfortable residence for the reigning monarch, it was only in times of danger that royalty would move to the castle. Mary, Queen of Scots, resided at Holyrood for six years during her reign. Inside she saw her friend David Rizzio murdered by her husband, when she was six months pregnant. Here, too, she argued long and hard with the disapproving Protestant and misogynist John Knox. Later, in 1745, Bonnie Prince Charlie enjoyed five weeks here socialising and generally whooping it up - good to know he had some fun before his defeat at Culloden.

The present queen comes to stay for a week each June, during which the Palace is closed to the public. The Palace at the very least must be seen from the outside, but sadly during the summer the entrance price at £5.30 and the official Palace guide-book at £3.70 make a visit outrageously expensive. You don't have to buy the guide book, but without it the fascinating history of the Palace is almost entirely unexplained. During winter guided tours of the palace are included in the entrance price.

Also in the Old Town

The **Royal Museum of Scotland** on Chambers Street has such a magnificent interior that the large selection of exhibits within the museum are almost irrelevant. £3/£1.50 (or you can buy a £5 annual pass). Across the road from the west end of Chambers Street is the cute statue of **Greyfriars Bobby**, the Skye Terrier who kept watch over his master's grave for many years in the nearby Greyfriars Kirkyard.

Greyfriars Kirk and Kirkyard will always be important in Scottish history as it was here the National Covenant was signed in 1638. This agreement was a vow to retain the Protestant faith. Covenanters were persecuted and forced to worship secretly for many years afterwards.

The New Town

People have lived in the New Town of Edinburgh since around 1770 when the North Bridge was built. The New Town allowed the city to expand, and today it is the busy financial and commercial centre of the capital of Scotland. There are fewer tourist attractions open here, but it is important to see the other half of Edinburgh's city centre. Before venturing over to the busy thoroughfares of Princes Street and George Street, it's a good idea to wander into the delightful **Princes Street Gardens**. The eastern side has the **Scott Monument**, the elegant memorial to Sir Walter Scott (and his dog). At the other end of the Gardens, below the majestic profile of Edinburgh Castle, is a grand fountain. These extensive gardens are divided by the

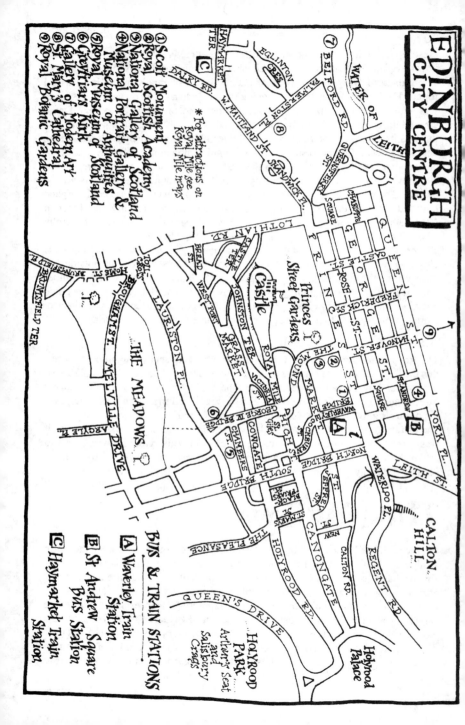

EDINBURGH CITY CENTRE

① Scott Monument
② Royal Scottish Academy
③ National Gallery of Scotland
④ National Portrait Gallery & Royal Museum of Antiquities
⑤ Royal Museum of Scotland
⑥ Greyfriars Kirk
⑦ Gallery of Modern Art
⑧ St. Mary's Cathedral
⑨ Royal Botanic Gardens

* For attractions on Royal Mile see Royal Mile maps

BUS & TRAIN STATIONS

Ⓐ Waverley Train Station
Ⓑ St Andrew Square Bus Station
Ⓒ Haymarket Train Station

man-made **Mound** (the earth dug up in the building of the New Town was piled into the Gardens, then the Nor'Loch, to create a path or road across to the Old Town).

Princes Street is the major shopping street of Edinburgh and were it not for the magnificent view of the castle you get every time you walk out of a shop it would be a commercial street just like any other. Busy, especially on a Saturday, you should stick to the pavement beside the Gardens for a more relaxing walk.

Charlotte Square is viewed by some as the New Town's greatest achievement. The buildings on the north side of the square were designed by the renowned architect Robert Adam, and one of these buildings, the **Georgian House**, has been restored in the style of an 18thC residence and is open to the public. It is an elegant and meticulous display, though pricey at £4.20/£2.80, and open April-October, NTS. Unfortunately the park in the square is closed to the general public.

On St Andrew Square, at the other end of George Street, the banking hall of the Royal Bank of Scotland head office is good for a wee look.

Museums and Art Galleries of the New Town

The most impressive attractions of the New Town are its art galleries and museums. The **National Gallery** on the Mound is open all year and contains many of Scotland's, and indeed the world's, most treasured works of art. Rembrandt, Degas, Raphael, Titian and Rubens are all displayed here in this beautiful 19thC building. Look for Canova's sculpture 'The Three Graces', which cost us taxpayers over 7½ million pounds! Open 10am-5pm, Sundays 2-5pm. Free entry.

The **Royal Scottish Academy**, also on the Mound and facing Princes Street, opens for several exhibitions throughout the year but is closed between exhibitions. Entrance prices vary, only occasionally free. (The area of the Mound beside the galleries comes overwhelmingly to life during the Festival when all the jugglers, buskers and street-traders of the world converge here. Don't miss it.)

The **Scottish National Portrait Gallery** and the **Museum of Antiquities** are housed in the same magnificent building on Queen Street, quite close to the bus station. The entrance hall alone is astounding enough, with an extensive mural depicting episodes and characters from Scotland's history. The Portrait Gallery contains an excellent permanent exhibit on the Stewart dynasty as well as a great collection of Scotland's most famous faces. The Museum of Antiquities is to the left of the entrance hall. Relics of the past dating from as far back as the Stone Age shed light on Scotland's many different civilizations. Look for Edinburgh's guillotine, the Maiden, introduced to Scotland by the Earl of Morton who eventually lost his life on it. The gallery and museum are free.

The **Scottish National Gallery of Modern Art** on Belford Road (not strictly in the New Town, but just outside it) has a fine collection of 20thC art including Matisse, Magritte and Picasso, as well as much work by Scottish artists. Look for JD Fergusson's and Samuel Peploe's colourful paintings as well as John Bellany's outstanding compositions. In the gardens are several sculptures to admire. The gallery has a fine cafe with good food. Free entry.

Further from the city centre, but easily accessible by bus, is **Edinburgh Zoo** on Corstorphine Road. With a large penguin colony, the daily Penguin Parade at 2pm from March to October is a must. It's a zoo with a modern and humane attitude; £6/ £4.40.

Edinburgh Walks

Edinburgh is a city for walking so don't even think of catching a bus.

Once you've walked the length of the Royal Mile and wandered through Princes Street Gardens, head for **Calton Hill**. This excellent vantage point is easy to get to and is free. There are various monuments and attractions on the hill. The most imposing is the 19thC copy of the Parthenon (known as Edinburgh's Disgrace as it was not completed due to lack of funding), and the most unusual is the Edinburgh Experience, a show with 3D glasses provided. The £2/£1.20 entrance fee is probably worth its novelty value. Open April-November everyday, weekends in winter.

From Calton Hill you can see the magnificent Salisbury Crags and Arthur's Seat in **Holyrood Park**, a place for explorers and admirers of fine views. There are several paths to take within the park, although the ultimate destination for most people is the peak of **Arthur's Seat** (823 ft), from where there's a commanding view of the entire region. Walking from Holyrood Palace to the top takes only about 45 minutes.

JOHN KNOX

John Knox was the most influential character of the Scottish Reformation, a movement which reached its major turning-point in 1560. Within Scotland, disillusionment with the Catholic church had reached its peak - clergymen lived a corrupt life with the church financing their many excesses. Their godliness under question, the time was ripe for revolution. John Knox proved himself a powerful orator and his speeches inspired mass destruction. Catholic churches were stripped of their despised symbols of idolatry, and Catholicism was eventually abolished as the religion of Scotland. This was all well and good except that the ruling monarch, Mary, Queen of Scots, was herself a Catholic and had no intention of renouncing her faith. Such was Knox's standing, he berated Mary for celebrating Mass, Catholic worship being a punishable crime at the time. Knox will also be remembered (not fondly) for writing a paper directed at the 'monstrous regiment of women', but implementing free education for all classes was perhaps his most significant and far-sighted contribution.

Other outstanding features of the park are the dramatic **Salisbury Crags,** or cliffs, and an easily ascended path (the Radical Road) leading around the crag-face. If you're totally averse to climbing of any description then grab some bread and feed the ducks at either St Margaret's or Dunsapie Lochs or even further at Duddingston Loch. Holyrood Park is so quiet and peaceful, it's hard to believe there's a thriving metropolis so close by.

Another path runs along the **Water of Leith,** which starts in the Pentland Hills outside the city, and flows to the Firth of Forth at Leith. A good starting point in the city is near the West End at the **Dean Village** and then heading east toward Leith. This walk could include a visit to the beautiful **Botanic Gardens** on Inverleith Row. You'll need a city map for all this or you'll never find your way home.

If you're in Edinburgh for an extended stay you should consider visiting the **Hermitage of Braid** and **Blackford Hill** to the south of the city, or go to the village of **Cramond** where there are several walks you could take. Catch a bus to Cramond Brig first of all, and then walk along the burn to the village. From there you can either walk across (at low tide) to **Cramond Island** or take Scotland's shortest ferry crossing and walk via a coastal path to **Dalmeny House.**

Day Trips from Edinburgh

It's an easy 40-minute train ride (off-peak day return £5.30) heading north-east along the coast to the quiet, affluent town of **North Berwick.** Take a quick steep walk up Berwick Law, the conical volcanic hill one mile south of the town. There's a lovely view from the top, with a whale's jawbone forming an arch - a sad reminder of the once rampant whaling industry. Strolling west for a couple of hours along the white sandy beach you'll come to **Gullane Beach.** You can hitch or bus back to Edinburgh from here. In the other direction, 3 miles along the coastline, is the brilliant ruin of **Tantallon Castle.** It's built in the red sandstone of the area and perched upon the sea cliff; £2.30/£1.75, HS.

Further round the coast is **Seacliff,** a picturesque bay popular with daring bathers and picnickers - but not so popular with motorists as it costs 50p to get into the car park. From the bay keep going (west) round the coast to find the harbour or take a path up the slope and seek out the ruined old house.

Just north-west of Edinburgh is **South Queensferry.** The town's most remarkable feature is its unbeatable view of the magnificent **Forth Rail Bridge.** Construction of this bridge, completed in 1890, was a major feat of Victorian engineering. South Queensferry itself is a lovely town, with some quaint buildings, shops, pubs and ice-cream stands. The energetic could walk across the Forth Road Bridge to North Queensferry (take the bus or train back). If you have time, catch a ferry to **Inchcolm Island** in the Firth of Forth. There's an interesting Abbey and of course fantastic views. The ferry costs £7.50/£5.75 (tel:(0131) 331 4857 for sailing times), Easter-October, and includes entrance to the Abbey, HS. Regular local buses go to South Queensferry from St Andrew Square bus station (day-return £1.90). Trains go from Edinburgh to nearby Dalmeny (off-peak day-return £3.20).

An almost perfect example of a 17thC Scottish town, **Culross** (pronounced kyoo-ross), with its cobble-stoned streets and many restored buildings, is a delight. The

Palace, the **Town House** and the **Study** are open Easter-September and cost £4.20/ £2.80, NTS. Afterwards take a stroll up the hill to Culross Abbey, parts of which date back to the 13thC. For lunch or coffee try the Dundonald Arms. Getting to Culross is not easy by public transport - you need to catch a Citylink bus to Dunfermline, which is north of the Firth of Forth, then a Fife Scottish bus west to Culross - but, it's worth every effort.

Dunfermline itself is of major importance as it was once the capital of Scotland. You can visit the impressive remains of **Dunfermline Abbey** - founded in the 11thC and where Robert the Bruce was buried; £1.80/£1.30, HS. The 19thC steel mogul-turned-philanthropist, Andrew Carnegie, is the town's most famous son and the **Andrew Carnegie Birthplace Museum** in Moodie Street tells his fascinating story; free. A day-return bus ticket to Dunfermline costs £3.70.

Last, but certainly not least, is **Linlithgow Palace** - one of Scotland's most superb ruins and the birthplace of Mary, Queen of Scots. As you admire and explore this truly great building, it's easy to imagine the luxury of former royal court life; £2.30/ £1.75, HS. Afterwards, take a walk around the loch or have lunch in the town. Linlithgow is 18 miles west of Edinburgh and is quick and easy to get to by train (off-peak day return £4.50).

TOURIST INFORMATION

i Edinburgh's **Tourist Information** is at 3 Princes Street, above Waverley Train Station and two minutes' walk from St Andrew Square bus station, tel:(0131) 473 3800. Opening hours are-

> April and October - Mon-Sat, 9am-6pm; Sun, 11am-6pm.
> May, June and September - Mon-Sat, 9am-7pm; Sun, 11am-7pm.
> July and August - Mon-Sat, 9am-8pm; Sun, 11am-8pm.
> November-March - Mon-Sat, 9am-6pm; Sun, 10am-6pm.

There is another Information desk at Edinburgh airport, tel:(0131) 333 2167, whose opening hours are longer-

> April-October - Mon-Sat, 8.30am-9.30pm; Sun, 9.30am-9.30pm.
> November-March - Mon-Fri, 9am-6pm; Sat, 9am-5pm; Sun, 10am-5pm.

Guided Tours of Edinburgh

Edinburgh has several walking tour companies providing a wide choice including historical, ghost, pub and literary tours. If you're looking for a spooky experience it is possible to go down into Mary King's Close, an old close underneath the City Chambers where plague victims were sealed within and left to die. Otherwise you could visit the Vaults, underneath South Bridge, a large vaulted cellar concealing some supernatural tales. Of course, you don't have to take a tour that visits these places - they simply take you down there to scare the living daylights out of you (hopefully). **Auld Reekie Tours**, tel:(0131) 557 4700. This company has several tours to choose from - historic, ghost, witch and even pub tours; £6/£5 or £4/£3. Tours depart from the Tron Kirk.

The Cadies-Witchery Tours, Castlehill, tel:(0131) 225 6745. The Witchery's spooky night-time trips have been going for years and are great fun. Dracula, or someone who looks like him, takes you around. Tours depart from outside the Witchery restaurant near the castle; £6.50.

Mercat Ghost and History Walks, tel:(0131) 661 4541. Historical tours by day (informing you of the life of Mary, Queen of Scots) with ghost-and-ghoul tours in the evening. There are more of these well-researched tours operating in the summer. Phone ahead for details. Tours start near the Mercat Cross along the Royal Mile; £5/£4 for daytime tours, £6/£5 for evening ones.

Robin's Edinburgh Tours, tel:(0131) 661 0125. Similar to the above company but starting from outside Tourist Information on Princes Street; £5/£4/£3 daytime tours, £5/£4 evening tours.

Macallan Scottish Literary Pub Tour, tel:(0131) 226 6665. This company takes a literary look at Edinburgh recounting the exploits of Robert Burns, Walter Scott, Robert Louis Stevenson and others. There are plenty of opportunities to buy a drink on this tour - not included in the price, however; £6.50/£5.50. Tours depart from the Beehive Inn in the Grassmarket.

Open-top coach tours run regularly and have many jump-on, jump-off stops on its route. The **Edinburgh Classic Tour** costs £5.50/£4.50 and **Guide Friday** costs £7/£5.50 (includes discount tickets to other attractions). The bus journeys officially start at Waverley Bridge outside the train station, however, you can jump on at any point on the route. Good if you're in a real hurry or to get the lie of the land, otherwise the city centre is best explored by foot.

ACCOMMODATION

Finding a bed in the summer doesn't have to be a nightmare, but arrive as early in the day as you can (if you're coming in the Festival in August, make that in the morning, or preferably book ahead). Through the rest of the year, availability's unpredictable, with some weekends being very busy.

OLD TOWN HOSTELS

High Street Hostel, 8 Blackfriars St, tel:(0131) 557 3984, £9.90/£10.90. Edinburgh's first independent hostel has an excellent reputation and is in a great central location, just off the Royal Mile. The hostel has plentiful facilities with friendly and helpful staff. Open 24 hours. Train station 5 minutes. Bus station 10-minute walk. Pre-paid reservations - by post, by telephone with a credit card or you can book through sister hostels, Inverness Student Hotel, Fort William, Oban and Skye (Kyleakin) Backpackers (and vice versa). Free walking tours of the Royal Mile.

Royal Mile Backpackers, 105 High St, tel:(0131) 557 6120, £9.90/£10.90. Small and intimate hostel providing luxurious backpacker accommodation right on the Royal Mile. From Princes St, cross North Bridge, turn left and it's about 100 yards on the left. 24-hour access.

Castle Rock Hostel, 15 Johnston Terrace, tel:(0131) 225 9666, £10/£12.90. Central new hostel with a relaxed atmosphere and unbeatable views looking up at the castle. Open 24 hours. Internet access and movies every night on a big screen.

Edinburgh Backpackers, 65 Cockburn Street, tel:(0131) 220 1717, £10/£15, open all year. A centrally located hostel with a comfortable, laid-back atmosphere. Open 24 hours.

Brodie's, 12 High Street, tel: (0131) 557 8800, £9.50. This is the Go Blue Banana tour company's hostel but individual travellers are welcome. Very central.

Cowgate Tourist Hostel, 112 The Cowgate, tel:(0131) 226 2153, £10/£15, early July to mid-September only. These student flats convert into tourist accommodation for the summer. Good central location. No curfew.

SOUTHSIDE HOSTELS

Iolaire Guest House, 14 Argyle Place, tel:(0131) 667 9991, £9/£11. Dorms and twin rooms. Twenty minutes' walk from the centre, but Iolaire's pleasant, relaxing and great value. Credit card phone bookings. 24-hour access. Catch a local bus to South Clerk Street and then walk (10 minutes), otherwise catch a taxi from the centre (about £3).

SYHA Bruntsfield, 7 Bruntsfield Crescent, tel:(0131) 447 2994, £8.60/£11.10, open all year. A hostel in a quiet location about 30 minutes walk south of the city centre. Curfew 2am. Local buses leave from Princes Street at the Scott Monument - ask for Bruntsfield Place.

NEW TOWN HOSTELS

SYHA Eglinton, 18 Eglinton Crescent, tel:(0131) 337 1120, £11.50/£14, includes breakfast, open all year. The hostel has a grand exterior and cheery staff, but is often booked out with groups. Curfew 2am. Close to the West End. Haymarket train station 4 minutes' walk. Bus station 25 minutes' walk. Numerous local buses leave from Tourist Information to Haymarket.

Belford Youth Hostel, Belford Rd, tel:(0131) 225 6209, £9.50/£15. A church converted into a hostel is a novel idea - unfortunately churches have good acoustics not conducive to sleep. 30 minutes' walk from the main bus station, 10 minutes from Haymarket train station. 24 hour access.

Princes Street West Backpackers Hostel, 3 Queensferry Street, tel:(0131) 2262939, £9.50/£13. It's about a 20 minute walk from Tourist Information to the end of Princes St for this hostel. Open 24 hours.

Princes Street East Backpackers Hostel, West Register St, tel:(0131) 556 6894, £9.50/£11. Central, near the bus and train station and close to all the shops on Princes St. 24-hour access.

CAMPSITES

Little France Caravan & Camping Park, Old Dalkeith Road, tel:(0131) 666 2326, £9 for 2 people, open April-Sept. 3 miles south, catch a bus from Princes Street.

Silverknowes Caravan Site, Marine Drive, tel:(0131) 312 6874, £5.50-£6.50, open April-September. North of the city centre by the River Forth.

There are many **B&Bs** scattered all over the city, but one area with a high concentration is around Minto St and Mayfield Gardens. Gilmore Place at Tollcross and Pilrig St off Leith Walk also have quite a few.

FOOD

Takeaway

Baked potato or fish and chip shops are about the cheapest way to fill that empty stomach. The ever-popular **Baked Potato Shop** in Cockburn St has tatties with lots of delicious vegetarian fillings. The amount you get for about £2.50 is excellent value. For a pricey but delicious choice of sandwich fillings go to the delicatessen **Di Placido** on the Royal Mile, near the Museum of Childhood. There are also many pizza and kebab takeaways - **Pizza Paradise** in the centre of town on South Bridge, near the Tron Kirk, is open till 5am.

Sitting in at Lunchtime

Pub lunches are usually great value and are on offer all over the city. **Deacon Brodie's** and **The World's End** on the Royal Mile and the **City Cafe** on Blair St have all been tried and tested (many times). **The Last Drop** in the Grassmarket has a good deal for backpackers and students - £2.50 for a main meal. **The Arches** on the corner of Drummond St and South Bridge is quite good value, too. Apart from the pubs, many restaurants have a cheap lunch menu which in the evening would be much more expensive. Try **Bar Napoli** in Hanover St or the Mexican **Pancho Villas** on the Canongate (Royal Mile), but there are many more.

The **University Students' Union**, inside the Teviot Row building on Bristo Place, do probably the fullest plate at the cheapest price. About £3 for a main course, open until 6.30pm. **The City Restaurant** on Nicolson St serves basic Scottish food at basic prices. During the day department stores on Princes St serve food in their cafeterias, usually at good prices.

In the Evening

The list of restaurants in Edinburgh is impossible to mention in full, but for a rough guide most of the less expensive will have main courses for about £4-£5. There aren't many places that are especially cheap but all listed below are recommended.

Kebab Mehal in Nicolson Square is a takeaway and restaurant with excellent Indian food. Amazing value and open to midnight.

Pierre Victoire is in 3 locations around central Edinburgh (Victoria St, Union St, Grassmarket) and has reasonably priced French food. They enjoy great popularity and rightly so.

There's no shortage of Italian restaurants. **Beppe Vittorio** on Victoria St serve reasonably-priced meals and house wine in a pleasant atmosphere. **Bar Napoli** on Hanover St are fair with their pricing while **Dario's** on Lothian Rd is open until 4 or 5am. **Gordon's Trattoria** on the High St has a very friendly atmosphere and cheeky staff.

For Mexican food, try **Pancho Villas** on the Canongate or **Viva Mexico** on Cockburn St (though it's much more expensive). The **Buffalo Grill** on Chapel St (at the end of West Nicolson St) is a popular restaurant for steak-lovers.

Vegetarian

Although most restaurants will have something vegetarian on the menu, there are quite a few that are exclusively so. During the day (till 6pm) the **Cornerstone Cafe** beneath St Johns Church at the west end of Princes St, serves healthy and cheap vegan and vegetarian food, as does **Helios Fountain** in the Grassmarket (closes at 6pm). **Bann's Vegetarian Cafe** in Hunter Square next to the Tron Kirk in the centre of town has tasty food and won't break your budget. Open till 11pm.

The **Kalpna** on Nicolson St (officially St Patrick Square) has the best vegetarian curries around, and **Black Bo's** on Blackfriars St is simply superb but this is getting into more expensive territory.

Scottish

You'll have to dig a bit deeper into your pocket for local fare, sadly. **Dubh Prais**, 123b High St, has delicious food as does **Stac Polly** on Grindlay St. **Wee Windaes** on the High St has several Scottish dishes on the menu.

Haggis, 'chieftain of the puddin' race', according to Robert Burns, is of course an essential ingredient in your Scottish holiday. It is widely available in most food-serving bars and hotels and also in some restaurants. If you see haggis in a chip shop, give it a wide berth.

Cafes

Cafe Florentin on St Giles Street, near the cathedral, is a fashionable spot to sit and write some postcards. Open from 7am-midnight and till 2am at weekends. An alternative is the popular **Elephant House** on George IV Bridge, open until 10pm, or **Gustos Cafe** at 105 High Street which has a good view overlooking the busy Royal Mile. **Number One Brasserie**, on the corner of Chambers St and South Bridge, is another city centre cafe to check out and if you're missing your computer at home you can e-mail or 'surf' at one of Edinburgh's internet cafes - try **Web 13** in Bread St or **Cyberia** in Hanover St.

NIGHTLIFE

Old Town Pubs

Drinking in the pub is a venerable institution in Scotland. No holiday here is complete unless you include quality drinking time devoted to soaking up the atmosphere of these fine establishments.

The Grassmarket has a good concentration of pubs making it a hugely popular spot for drinking and socialising. People have been drinking and socialising here for centuries and although there's no one pub in particular to recommend, the atmosphere is cheerful and lively in almost all of them and very busy at the weekend.

At night the Cowgate comes alive with some of the best bars in town. **Bannerman's**, is in an old cellar at the bottom of Niddry St, and across the road is the **Bare Story** and the **Living Room**. The **Green Tree** is nearby and serves a good pint too. The Cowgate continues along into Holyrood Rd and there you'll find the **Holyrood**

Tavern, a characterful studenty bar not usually as busy as the others.

Up on the Royal Mile, **Ensign Ewart** near the castle is perfect for a relaxed drink (sometimes they have music) and tucked away down James Court is the **Jolly Judge** - go there, it's a good pub. **Jock's** on the High St, the **World's End** further down the High St at the St Mary's St intersection, and the **Scotsman's Lounge** at the top of Cockburn St, are all cosy and friendly places.

Behind the Tron Kirk in Hunter Square is the **Tron** also known as the **Ceilidh House**. It's a comfortable bar that seems to suit all types and often has folk musicians playing away in the corner downstairs. The **City Cafe** opposite in Blair St is the trendy place to be seen, as is **EH1** on the corner of Cockburn St and High St, open until 1am.

After 1am the places you are most likely to find a drink are **Bertie's** up a lane off Candlemaker Row, **Sneeky Pete's** on the Cowgate, just under the George IV bridge, the **Royal Oak** on Infirmary St and **Whistlebinkie's** in Niddry St. They're not necessarily the best pubs but they're open, so they're understandably very busy. Beware - some bars are open until 3am, but licensing restrictions means that you must be inside by 1.30am.

New Town Pubs

The New Town may have less student-orientated establishments but there are some fine bars here.

Both the **St James Oyster Bar** on Calton Rd (just off Leith St) and the **Queen St Oyster Bar** on Queen St are good fun and with a down-to-earth feel. On Hanover St is **Milne's Bar** which is usually buzzing. Once a meeting point for Edinburgh's literati, it's now just a meeting point.

L'Attache on Rutland St is a basement cellar with a unique character. There's music from Sunday-Thursday, open 7pm till 1am. Also try the **West End Oyster Bar** on West Maitland St which sometimes has live music.

At Haymarket, a good mix of people gather at **Ryrie's**. It's an old fashioned pub that never changes and doesn't need to.

If you're staying at the Eglinton or Belford youth hostels at the weekend, the exceptionally plain **West End Hotel** on Palmerston Place bursts into life with music and rowdy folk.

There are some establishments pub connoisseurs must seek out. The **Cafe Royal** is on West Register St just up from Princes St, and is one of Edinburgh's most elegant drinking holes. **Bennets Bar** on Leven St near the King's Theatre also has a spectacular interior, while the **Canny Man's** at 237 Morningside Rd is filled to the brim with absolutely everything (including difficult management).

At the other end of the spectrum, the **'Diggers'** (officially the **Athletic Arms**) in Angle Park Terrace is a spartan, functional sort of bar but renowned for serving the best pint (of eighty shilling) in Scotland. Similar, but more central, is **Mathers** in Queensferry Street, close to the West End - real coal fire in winter. Three excellent bars down in Leith are the **Shore Bar** (on the Shore), the **Waterfront** (Dock Place) and **Leith Oyster Bar**, (Burgess St).

Live Music

Many bars offer free live music from rock bands to solo folk musicians. These are hard to list, though, as the venues and the frequency often change from month to month. It's best to read 'The List' (on sale in newsagents) or the 'Gig Guide' (which is free and available in many pubs and some hostels) for more precise information. There are a few however which are consistent, namely:-

Tron Ceilidh House in Hunter Square - frequent folk sessions.
Royal Oak, Infirmary St - late night folk, 11pm-1.30am.
Ensign Ewart, Castlehill - relaxing folk music at the weekends.
Ryrie's, Haymarket Terrace - Thursday and Sunday nights.
L'Attache, Rutland St - Sunday to Wednesday nights.
Whistlebinkie's, Niddry St - late-night music every night.
Stones, Frederick St - rock music most nights.
Cas Rock, West Port - rock music at the weekends.

Clubs

Edinburgh's club scene is hard to pin down as it's constantly changing. Many places have a different theme and name every night so it's best to check 'The List'. Naturally, clubs are cheaper and not so crowded during the week.

> THE LIST is a fortnightly events magazine for Glasgow and Edinburgh available in newsagents for £1.90. Detailed listings and reviews include films, music, theatre, dance, comedy, art and clubs. Both informative and interesting reading, Edinburgh folk couldn't live without it.

Cinemas

The **ABC** cinema on Lothian Rd, tel:229 3030, and the **Odeon** cinema on South Clerk St, tel:668 2101 show all the latest mainstream releases. The **Filmhouse** on Lothian Rd, tel:228 2688, and the **Cameo** on Home St, tel:228 4141, are successful independent cinemas providing a more diverse choice in films from all over the world. Afternoon matinees are the least expensive, with some Filmhouse matinees costing only £2.70/£1.50. The **Dominion** on Newbattle Terrace, tel:447 4771, is an option for those staying at the Bruntsfield hostel and although the **UCI** on Kinnaird Road, tel: 669 0777, and the **ABC Multiplex** in Wester Hailes, tel:453 1569, have a huge selection of films, they are a long way from the centre of town.

Comedy Clubs

Edinburgh has a few regular comedy nights and details can be found in the List magazine. The **Tron Ceilidh House** in Hunter Square and **Christie's** on West Port, are both recommended and cost about £3 or £4.

Theatres and Concert Halls

The largest venue for concerts and large theatrical ventures is the **Playhouse Theatre** on Greenside Place, tel:557 2590. Here you'll find the likes of Shirley Bassey and 'Grease'. The beautiful **Usher Hall** on Lothian Rd, tel:228 1155, occasionally has rock artists but most concerts are classical and certainly that suits the environment best. The **Queen's Hall** on Clerk St, tel:668 2019, is a busy musical venue in a smaller hall. The **Edinburgh Festival Theatre** on Nicolson St, tel:529 6000, is now a major venue for opera, ballet and drama. The **Royal Lyceum Theatre** in Grindlay St, tel:229 9697, is a reliable dramatic venue with productions year-round. The **King's Theatre** on Leven St, tel:229 1201, presents popular productions mostly touring. The **Traverse Theatre** in Cambridge St, tel:228 1404, is an adventurous and experimental venue with an excellent reputation. **Theatre Workshop**, Hamilton Place, tel:226 5425, is also not afraid of experimenting, but the theatre is on a much smaller scale than the Traverse.

Ceilidhs

Scottish folk-dancing has really come back into fashion - you don't have to know the steps, just copy what everyone else does. The **Assembly Rooms** on George St, tel:220 4349, occasionally has ceilidhs and are consistently good, usually £6/£4. The more people the merrier, so get a group going. The ceilidh bands with a name at the moment are the Tartan Amoebas and the Robert Fish Band, so if you see them advertised, buy a ticket - quickly.

Shopping

The street with the major department stores and the largest selection of clothes shops is Princes St (crazily busy sometimes). The Royal Mile has the tourism trade pretty much sewn up when it comes to tartan, whisky, woollens and shortbread. For bargain shopping you might find something along South Bridge, and for antique and less commercial shopping, there is Victoria St and the Grassmarket. Cockburn St has a diverse selection of shops including Whiplash Trash and the independent record shop, Fopp.

Second-hand Shops

For an impressive and wide range of second-hand clothing head straight for **Armstrong's** in the Grassmarket, or to their original shop on the Cowgate. At the top of Blackfriars St on High St is the **PDSA** charity shop and way up South Bridge there are a few more charity shops to choose from. Books are sold second-hand at **Castle Books**, 204 Canongate, but you might not need it as there are so many bargain bookshops these days selling new books at really low prices - **Bargain Books** and **Bookworld** are on Princes St.

Supermarkets

The most central supermarkets are **Safeway** inside the St James Centre, at the top of Leith Street, **Marks & Spencers** at 53 Princes St and **Tesco**, 94 Nicolson St. For those staying near Bruntsfield, there's **Scotmid** at 5 Leven Street, and for those near Haymarket there's **Somerfield**, 114 Dalry Road.

the Edinburgh Festival

The last three weeks of August sees Edinburgh's city centre surrender itself to the immense pressure of the world's largest arts festival. The atmosphere completely changes as the streets fill with people from all corners of the earth. What began as a high-brow affair to add a bit of sparkle after World War II has now become a mad chaotic frenzy of the dramatic arts. It's mayhem but it's wonderful and here is some information to help you make some sense of it - and hopefully save you a few pennies.

The Festival is actually a mixture of many separate festivals all running concurrently. By far the biggest is the **Fringe** with hundreds of theatre companies booking venues and turning up from around the world. The **Edinburgh International Festival** (the original) offers the likes of classical concerts and high quality drama. Then there are a number of smaller festivals which have all jumped on this fabulous band-wagon - the **Jazz Festival**, the **Book Festival**, the **Film Festival** and probably some more, all adding extra flavour to a marvellously varied assortment of entertainment. Finally the **Edinburgh Military Tattoo** is all military bands and parades and held 6 nights a week in the Castle Esplanade.

BEWARE - a lot of Fringe shows are just plain crap. It's important you never ever go to a show that has not been recommended to you by, at the very least, one person. The Scotsman, Guardian and Independent newspapers and the magazine The List all review hundreds of shows throughout the Festival, often with free ticket offers inside. The best way to find good shows is, of course, to ask people, but make sure they're not in the show they're recommending. Never buy a ticket from some sweet-talking leafleteer.

If you're short of funds there's always something for free, mostly in the form of street entertainers. The Mound is the best place for this unless you're here on Fringe Sunday when thousands of people head for Holyrood Park. The magnificent fireworks display from the castle is held during the last week of the festival with most people watching from Princes Street. Accommodation during the Festival is a bit of a nightmare so book as far in advance as possible or commute from Glasgow.

Useful Addresses

WAVERLEY TRAIN STATION, Waverley Bridge, tel:0345-484950 (24-hour service). Edinburgh's main station (the smaller one is Haymarket). Left luggage facilities, toilets and showers (both cost), information desk in main hall.

BUS STATION, St Andrew Square, tel:0990 505050 (phone service 8am-8pm, daily, but the bus station office is open 9-5pm Mon-Sat). Left luggage facilities. Local buses and national coaches leave from here. Buses to the airport leave from Waverley Bridge.

POST OFFICES

The main post office is tucked away inside the St James Centre at the top of Leith Street and is open 8.30am-5.30pm Mon-Fri, 8.30am-6pm Sat. Other central offices are at 46 St Mary's St, 4 West Maitland St, 7 Hope St (all open Mon-Fri and Saturday mornings) and 40 Frederick St (open Mon-Fri). All have a poste restante service. For information telephone 0345 223344.

BANKS

Bank of Scotland (main branch), The Mound, at the top. Open 9am-5pm, M,T,Th,F; 10am-5pm, Wed.

Royal Bank of Scotland (main branch), 42 St Andrew Square. Open 9.15am-4.45pm, M-F. One Royal branch (142 Princes St) is open Saturdays 10am-1pm.

Clydesdale Bank, (main branch), 29 George St. Open 9.15am-4pm, M,T,W,F; 9.15am-5.30pm, Thurs.

Barclays Bank, (only branch), 1 St Andrew's Square. Open 9.30am-5pm, M,T,W,F; 10am-5pm, Thurs.

Lloyds Bank, (only branch), 113 George St. Open 9am-5pm, M,T,Th,F; 9.30am-5pm, Wed.

National Westminster Bank, (only branch except sub-branch at Edinburgh University), 80 George St. Open 9am-5pm, M,T,Th,F; 9.30-5pm, Wed.

FOREIGN EXCHANGE

When the banks are closed there are several places that exchange money, however their commission rate is usually higher.

Tourist Information, 3 Princes St. See Tourist Information listing for opening hours.

XChange, 207 High St, tel:220 0080. Open 9am-6pm Mon-Sat, 10am-6pm Sun.

Waverley Train Station, Waverley Bridge, tel:557 2784. Open 7.30am-9pm every day (7am-10pm in summer).

Thomas Cook, 79 Princes St, tel:220 4039. Open 9am-5.30pm Mon-Sat, Thursday 10am-5.30pm.

American Express, 139 Princes St, tel:225 9179. Open 9am-5.30pm Mon-Fri, 9am-4pm Sat.

TRAVEL AGENTS

Edinburgh Travel Centre specialise in student and youth travel - there are three branches; 92 South Clerk St, tel:667 9488; 196 Rose St, tel:226 2019; Bristo Square, tel:668 2221.

Campus Travel, 53 Forrest Rd, tel:225 6111, telesales:668 3303.

TRAVELLING AROUND SCOTLAND FROM EDINBURGH

Go Blue Banana, 16 High St, tel:556 2000.

Haggis Backpackers, 7-9 Blackfriars St, tel:557 9393.

MacBackpackers, c/- Castle Rock Hostel, 15 Johnston Terrace, tel:225 9666.

For more information about these companies see **Getting Around Scotland**, Chapter 17.

CAR RENTAL

Listed here is a rough price guide. Most companies will let you rent a car provided you have a current driver's licence, however the minimum age varies so check first. Also check for any hidden charges.

Condor Self Drive, 45 Lochrin Place, tel:229 4548. £19.95 daily/£125 weekly however they sometimes have special offers so ask about these. U.K. drivers must be at least 21 years, non-U.K. drivers must be 23 years. 20% off with the voucher at the back of this book.

Arnold Clark, Lochrin Place, tel:228 4747. £18-£30 daily/£100-£168 weekly. Drivers must be at least 23 years of age.

Melville's, 9 Clifton Terrace, just opposite Haymarket train station, tel:337 5333. £18 daily/£99 weekly. Minimum driver's age - 23 years.

BICYCLE RENTAL

Edinburgh Cycle Hire, 29 Blackfriars St, tel:556 5560. 21-speed mountain and hybrid bikes £10-£15 a day, 10 & 15 speed city bikes £7.50-£10. Edinburgh sightseeing bike tours, weekly and group rates, cycling holidays, tandem bikes, transportation, repairs and sales. Rent-a-tent £5 a day. Deposit required. 10% off with voucher at the back of this book.

Central Cycle Hire, 13 Lochrin Place, Tollcross, tel:228 6333. £10 a day, £15 for a mountain bike. Deposit required.

Sandy Gilchrist Cycles, 1 Cadzow Place, Abbeyhill, tel:652 1760. Mountain bikes £15 daily/£60 weekly. City bikes £8 daily/£35 weekly. Deposit required.

TAXIS

City Cabs, tel:228 1211.
Central Radio Taxis, tel:229 2468.

CAMPING SHOPS

Graham Tiso's have a large shop on Rose Street and in the Old Town there is the Camping and Outdoor Centre on South Bridge.

 Hitching from Edinburgh - see **Hitching**, Chapter 17.

The Edinburgh National Telephone Code is (0131)

2.Central Scotland

Between the waters of the Forth and the mountains of the Highlands, lies a gentle landscape full of historical intrigue. Here there are marvellous remnants of darker times when Scottish armies fought for independence, Highlanders raided for Lowland cattle, feuding lords sided with kings against rivals and Covenanters fought the Crown. Strolling around the battlements of Stirling Castle or down the ruined aisle of St Andrew's Cathedral is a stroll through a thousand years of bitter, brutal struggle which defined Scotland as a nation. Here lie many castles, palaces, streets and villages where deeds gruesome, brave, honourable and treacherous, were done.

Ironically, today it is this area's peacefulness and prettiness, not just its murky history, that makes it such an attractive place to visit.

Stirling

Stirling Castle stands proudly atop a volcanic outcrop creating the city's distinctive skyline. This towering fortress has played an important role in Scottish history. For many years a royal residence, it has overlooked some of Scotland's most significant and sensational battles. As a gateway to the Highlands, Stirling made an ideal place to fight off the marauding English. As well as the Castle, exploring the curious streets of the old town and visiting the nearby Wallace Monument, Stirling makes either a great day-trip from Edinburgh or Glasgow, or as a first stop as you begin your conquest of the Highlands.

Stirling Castle rivals Edinburgh's in its beauty, dramatic position and historical importance. The permanent royal residence during the 15thC and 16thC (Mary, Queen of Scots, was crowned here in 1543), the Castle became a military outpost in later years. Today it provides a great insight into Royal Scottish history. The Palace, the Great Hall, the Chapel Royal and the Regimental Museum all look onto the cobbled courtyard - but don't miss the kitchen, tucked away toward the back. Admirable even as it stands (so don't let this deter you) Stirling Castle is continually undergoing restoration due to be completed by the year 2000. The views from the Castle make it obvious why Stirling was so strategically important. To the north-east across the meandering River Forth, you'll see on the hilltop the Wallace Monument while below the castle to the south-west can be seen the King's Knot, a geometrically-shaped mound which was once (around 1630) a magnificent garden. There's also a free 20-minute audio-visual display at the Visitor Centre outside on the Castle Esplanade and with few restrictions on where you can wander it is much better value than its nearby rival, Edinburgh Castle. Entrance costs £4.50/£3.50 (this also includes entrance to Argyll's Lodging), open all year, seven days a week; HS.

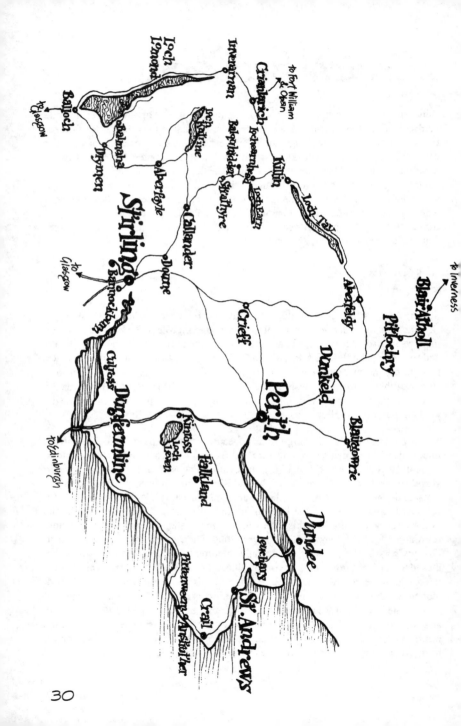

The old town is the most interesting part of Stirling. Well-preserved buildings line the cobble-stoned streets which wind their way up to the Castle, with probably the most impressive route up Spittal Street. The grand-looking SYHA hostel with the facade of an old church is about half way and further on, the **Church of the Holy Rude**. This was the principal church of Stirling for over 500 years and saw the crowning of James VI in 1567. On the right of the church there is a great cemetery with a rock outcrop in its centre, from which you can see for miles on a clear day. On the left of the church is the Guildhall, or Cowane's Hospital. Built between 1639-49, it is now, especially in summer, the venue for ceilidhs (check with Tourist Information). Up Castle Wynd on the left is **Mar's Wark**, the shell of a Renaissance town house,

built around 1569, that was almost destroyed in the 1745-6 Jacobite uprising. Just before the castle esplanade, is **Argyll's Lodging**, a brilliant 16thC Renaissance mansion; £2.50, or £4.50/£3.50 for a ticket which includes entrance to the castle.

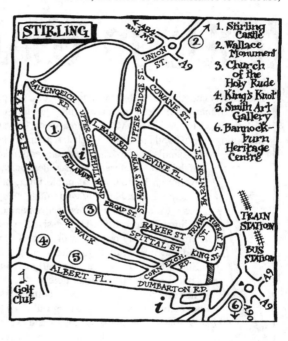

The former commercial activity of the Old Town centred around Broad Street, St Mary's Wynd and St John Street. The **Tolbooth** and **Mercat Cross** still stand there today. Stirling's old town wall can be followed along Back Walk to stairs returning up to Guildhall.

After exploring the city centre your next major objective is to walk, cycle, drive, bus or hitch your way to the other prominent feature of the Stirling landscape, the **Wallace Monument.** This unique structure on the hill of Abbey Craig was built in honour of Scotland's most important hero, William Wallace. Fighting for the freedom of all Scots against the English army of King Edward I, he was most successful at Stirling Bridge in 1296. An excellent audio-visual display at the monument tells the story of Wallace's life, while climbing the 246 steps up the spiral staircase to the top, with its magnificent views of the castle and the winding path of the River Forth, is an exhilarating experience not to be missed. Admission is £2.50 and is open all year but usually weekends only in January and February. (Near the monument is a new statue of Wallace which bears a striking resemblance to Mel Gibson - funny that.)

Two miles south of Stirling's town centre is the **Bannockburn Heritage Centre** located near the site of the Battle of Bannockburn. Here, Robert the Bruce triumphantly defeated the English army in 1314 and there is an impressive monument to Bruce depicting him astride his horse. The centre nearby has a modest exhibition and costs £2.40/£1.60, NTS.

William Wallace

The fiercely courageous William Wallace is Scotland's greatest national hero, the first of many in the long and continuing fight for Scottish independence. Wallace lived in the late 13thC, at a time when Edward I of England was attempting to turn Scotland into an English region. Wallace was convinced of Scotland's right to her own throne and freedom and unlike most of the nobles, refused to swear allegiance to the English throne. Although he was not of noble birth, he managed to gather together a sizeable army who fought many battles but Wallace was most successful and is best remembered for the Battle of Stirling Bridge in 1296. The massive English army's only option to cross the River Forth was at the narrow Stirling Bridge. Wallace and his men waited for them on the other side. Lack of knowledge of the area and various unwise decisions led to the English army's total defeat. Wallace was knighted and named 'Guardian of the Kingdom of Scotland' but his army ultimately was not strong enough to keep the English forces at bay. Wallace was branded an outlaw and eventually captured, taken to London and sentenced to death. He was hung, drawn and quartered and his head impaled on London Bridge. He was accused of, though not allowed to defend himself against, the charge of treason. This wrongful accusation was directed at a man who had never sworn allegiance to England, only to his home of Scotland to which he was never a traitor. (See Wallace Monument, **Stirling**.)

The **Smith Art Gallery and Museum**, just up Dumbarton Road from Tourist Information, has a series of changing displays, and provides a welcome respite from any chill winds. Closed Mondays; free.

Stirling's **Tourist Information** is on Dumbarton Road, tel:(01786) 475019, but there is another office up on the Castle Esplanade. Both are open all year.
If you're coming by train from Edinburgh for a day-trip it costs £6.60 for an off-peak day-return (by bus it costs £6.50 but the service is much slower).

Guided Tours of Stirling

Stirling Tours and Guiding Services (**STAGS**) in Broad St, tel:(01786) 446044, provide walkman-tours all year (everyday in summer, three days a week in winter) for £2.50. The commentary is about an hour long but you can stop and start as you please. There is also an open-top jump-on jump-off bus tour from May to September for £5/£3.50, which will take you across to the Wallace Monument.
The **Stirling Heritage Company**, tel:(01786) 447150, run ghost walks twice a night for £5/£3 (Tuesdays-Saturdays from June to September, occasionally in winter) as well as re-enacting in the old town centre some of Stirling's important historic events (free) on most days in July and August.

Stirling's university keeps the nightlife reasonably vibrant year-round. Two good pubs are **Behind the Wall Too** (corner of King's Rd and Corn Exchange Rd) and the **Hogshead** (on Baker St) which buzz on Fridays and Saturday nights and have pub lunch menus at very reasonable prices. The **Barnton Bar and Bistro** on Barnton St has good food and coffee in attractive surroundings.

Stirling SYHA, Spittal Street, tel:(01786) 473442, £11.50/£14, includes continental breakfast. Grade 1, open all year. Very clean, great kitchen, and each room has its own shower, toilet and basin...but the walls are paper thin. They have an annexe in Union St open 1/7-31/8 with single rooms, £12.50/£14.
With no independent hostel in Stirling you may consider the hostels in Callander (see Callander) and Crieff (see Perth accommodation).
Silver Birch Campsite, Cornton Rd, tel:(01786) 474503, just a mile or so north of the castle. Open April-October, £5.50-£8.50 per tent. Catch a local bus to Cornton from the bus station. There are many **B&Bs** for around £15-£17.

 Hitching from Stirling - see **Hitching**, Chapter 17.

WEST OF STIRLING

Callander, situated on the Highland/Lowland divide, can be an excellent base for the exploration of the beautiful surrounding area, the Trossachs in particular. Despite suffering from an abundance of tourists in the height of summer, Callander still retains a pleasant and comfortable atmosphere. Its long, straight main street devotes itself to tourism with many shops, coffee shops and hotels strung along it.

The **Rob Roy and Trossachs Visitor Centre** in the town square will probably be your first port of call as **Tourist Information** is situated there, tel:(01877) 330342, open daily March-December (January & February weekends only). The exhibition on the life and times of the notorious Rob Roy MacGregor is entertaining and informative and costs £2.50/£1.75.

Running parallel to the Main Street but at a much more leisurely pace is the River Teith. Ideal for fine, easy walking - don't forget to take some bread for the ducks.

There are several walking paths out of Callander. You can head up to the Crags, taking a detour to the Bracklinn Falls; serious hillwalkers can attempt the difficult Ben Ledi (2882 ft).

For those who like easy walks on flat ground, there is a superb trail alongside Loch Lubnaig leading to Strathyre which is about 6 miles away. Cycling along this abandoned railway-line is even better, not to mention faster, and once you get to Strathyre you can have a beer in the hotel there. You could also continue another four miles to Balquhidder to see Rob Roy's grave. Bicycles can be hired in Callander from **Wheels**, Manse Lane, tel:(01877) 331100, £10 full/£6 half day.

 Trossachs Backpackers, Invertrossachs Road, tel:(01877) 331200, £10/£12.50 including breakfast. Dormitory and twin rooms available.

Auchenlaich Caravan Park, tel:(01877) 330811, near the Heather Centre, 1 mile east of the town centre. Open April-October, £5.50 a tent.

North of Callander and deeper into the Highlands, under the slopes of grand old Ben Lawers, sits the lovely village of **Killin**. As well as plenty of shops and pubs it has a visitor centre in the Old Mill which, for £1, offers a good value introduction to local history and legends. The best thing about Killin, however, is the wonderful **Falls of Dochart**, where the river tumbles and churns over rocks and boulders and squeezes through the arches of the quaint old bridge - all the better for really heavy rain.

There are some delightful quiet country roads that you should walk, cycle or drive along. By the mill find the turning to Auchlyne (Craignavie road). This riverside road leads through quiet, pastoral scenes - don't forget to shut the gate. The mile-long road down to Loch Tay is another delight to stroll. If you have a car or some low gears on your bicycle, find Glen Lochay (left over the bridge from the Lochay Hotel). When you get to what appears to be the end of this road, take the turning heading north and uphill. Unmarked on any road map this road climbs over the hill and dramatically arrives in the next glen, Glen Lyon. You can then return to Killin in a circular route, turning right at the Bridge of Balgy, but only for very fit cyclists.

 The visitor centre in Killin also doubles as **Tourist Information**, tel:(01567) 820254. Open March to October, and weekends in February.

 For budget accommodation there is the **SYHA hostel**, tel:(01567) 820546, Grade 2, £6.10/£7.60, open 27/2-30/10, plus weekends in winter.

Sheiling Campsite, Aberfeldy Road, tel:(01567) 820334, open April-October, £3.50.

THE TROSSACHS AND EAST LOCH LOMOND

This area can't be rated highly enough - its only drawback is its summertime popularity, a victim of its own success. A footpath runs the whole length of Loch Lomond's eastern shore (part of the West Highland Way). Mid-way is **Rowardennan SYHA** which can also be reached by a small road or by boat from Inverbeg, tel:(01360) 870259, Grade 1, £7.75/£9.25, open 30/1-30/10. It's in an unbeatable lochside situation with a lush lawn to lie on, a small beach if you fancy a swim and a nearby pub. (The hostel has a small shop but you are best to stock up in advance.) From Rowardennan you can either continue walking north or south or head east to lovely Loch Ard.

Cycling is also a great way to explore the Trossachs by the quiet eastern shores of the loch or along the **Glasgow-Killin Cycleway** which connects with other scenic cycle routes around **Loch Katrine** and **Loch Ard** (pick up the leaflet).

St Andrews

Even if St Andrews were without a 12thC cathedral, a 13thC castle and a 15thC university, people would still flock here, for this attractive town is world-famous as the 'home of golf'. Compact enough to be covered in a day-trip, it is also a deserving place for a longer stay.

Comprising only three main streets, it's difficult to get lost in, and the wynds which lead off these main streets are one of the joys of the town, full of detail and history. In contrast, the young university population keeps the nightlife bubbling. No one knows precisely when golf was first played at St Andrews but it was at least as far back as the reign of Mary, Queen of Scots (16thC). Anyone with a handicap can play on the Old Course and next to the golf courses (there are five of them) is the West Sands beach where the opening sequence of the film 'Chariots of Fire' was shot.

The history of St Andrews is so complex and central to that of Scotland that it can scarcely be done justice here. According to legend, it was in the 6thC that the monk St Regulus, guided by God, buried the bones of the apostle Andrew here. The location became an important place of pilgrimage, and to receive the faithful a great cathedral was built and an Archbishop installed. The town prospered as the centre of the Scottish church and as a focus for intellectual pursuits. St Andrews had pressed hard for a university throughout the 14thC, and in 1410 the Pope, the only person who could give permission for a university, gave his consent. The university prospered until the Reformation, when John Knox preached in the city and had Archbishop Beaton murdered in the ensuing trauma. The castle was destroyed, the cathedral pulled down, the university left to decline.

It was in this period of decay and apathy that golf was born and grew to dominate the life of the city. The university continued, but it was not until the mid-19thC that the city prospered again. It became the seaside resort of the gentry and life revolved around study, occasional swimming in the sea and, of course, golf.

Nowadays St Andrews pushes back the boundaries of the surreal - you can have lunch in a restaurant built 600 years ago with a student of laser physics (St Andrews has pioneered some of the most advanced lasers in the world), then step out and see a jet fighter from nearby Leuchars aerodrome cutting over the ruined Cathedral.

St Andrews Cathedral stands on the edge of the sea, today a magnificent ruin. Its demise came in 1559 after a furious sermon by John Knox when the cathedral was ransacked, its icons destroyed and thrown into the sea. Open all year, £1.80/£1.30. The **Visitor Centre** describes the Cathedral's development. If you are interested in history then the excellent display is essential; otherwise the atmosphere of the crammed graveyard and ruined cathedral (where King Robert the Bruce once rode his horse down the aisle) will be enough. For those without vertigo, a climb up **St Rule's Tower** is a must. Open 9.30-6pm, Monday-Saturday in summer and until 4pm in winter.

The ruins of the **Castle** sit on a rocky promontory overlooking the sea and dates from 1200. Look for the mines dug under the main walls during the 16thC siege in

an effort to collapse the walls. Also make sure you see the bottle dungeon which served as one of the more brutal prisons in medieval Scotland. Included in the castle's £2.30/£1.75 entrance price is the Castle Museum, a sleek, modern building. If you are here at night take the path down below the castle (always open) to the castle sands and watch the waves rolling in. A combined entry ticket to the cathedral and the castle costs £3.50/£2.70.

The university and the town have grown together and are thoroughly entwined. On North Street see the chapel of St Salvator's, built in 1450, and the

quadrangle. The gates to the quad are original. On the pavement outside can be seen the letters PH, which stand for Patrick Hamilton, a student of the university who spoke out against the Catholic church in the 16thC and was burned to death in front of his fellow students. Walk beyond St Salvator's quad to the elegant seashore road, The Scores, where many of the university buildings now sit, perched beside the sea and close to the castle. Perhaps the loveliest part of the university is St Mary's campus on South Street. It is dominated by grassy gardens and an ancient oak tree. Flanking South Street is the Parliament Hall, where the Scottish Parliament used to meet.

Everyone who lives here at one time strolls along the ancient stone pier (below the Cathedral). The pier has no name but is an important feature of St Andrews. The most colourful student tradition takes place here too, as after Sunday service the students in traditional red gowns walk precariously along the upper ledge in a tradition dating back many years.

The **Botanical Gardens** make a fine walk on a sunny day. The gardens are free and open 10am-7pm, Monday-Saturday. Walk along Bridge Street beyond the burn, up the hill and first right on Canongate. The **St Andrews Museum** in Kinburn Park on Doubledykes Road is a free museum detailing St Andrews historic past; open all year. **St Leonard's Chapel** of St Leonard's College is one of the most beautiful medieval kirks in Scotland, notable for its elegant simplicity. It is open most weekdays - if not, see one of the university porters who will try and arrange to open it. The **Crawford Arts Centre** on North Street often has interesting exhibitions. The gallery is linked to the high-powered university Art History department and is especially known for promoting young Scottish artists.

Golf

St Andrews is to golf what Mecca is to Islam. The reason there are 18 holes on every golf course is because St Andrews had 18 holes and everyone followed suit. Sitting astride the 18th green and the 1st tee is the red stone clubhouse of the Royal & Ancient. This is the most important golf club in the world because it approves all rule changes. Sean Connery had to wait a decade before he was made a member. Forget about peering in the windows, though, as not only is it rude, but a large caddy might appear and clobber you! Just behind the R&A is the **British Golf Museum**. The £3.75/£2.75 entrance fee is good value for enthusiasts and makes use of state-of-the-art audio-visual technology. Open all year but closed on Tuesdays and Wednesdays in winter.

If you want to play, the good news is that you can, and at reasonable fees. The only real problem comes when you want to play the Old Course. The cost, at £72, will deter most budget travellers, and to play you must either book months in advance or enter into a ballot system, where prospective players put their names down by 2pm the day before. Fear not, however, if you don't make it - there are four other golf courses which will accommodate you, with prices ranging from £16-£31. If time is a problem you could play the 9-hole course for only £7. Make sure you warm yourself in the **Jigger** pub afterwards.

Central reservations for all St Andrews courses - tel:(01334) 475757. Golf clubs can be hired for £15 here or go to the best golf shop in town (and probably in Scotland), **Auchterlonies**, in Golf Place and hire clubs for £10.

i St Andrews' **Tourist Information** is located at 70 Market St, tel:(01334) 472021, and is open all year. (Open until 5pm, except June and September - 6pm, and July and August - 7pm. Closed on Sundays in winter.)

Apart from walking, the easiest way to get around St Andrews and the surrounding countryside is by bicycle. You can hire them during the summer months from **Spoke's of St Andrews**, 77 South St, tel:(01334) 477835, mountain bikes are £10.50 a day.

Guided tours

During the summer an immense choice of walking tours operate, including city, university and ghost tours - it's best to go to Tourist Information and get the up-to-date times. Running year-round is a historical tour every Wednesday at 11am, leaving from Church Square, £2.50, and some evenings there's Mr Lindskill's **Witches Tour**, tel:(01592) 642383, £5/£4 (more frequent in summer).

Food

Brambles wholefood cafe on College Street provides a filling lunch and serves excellent cakes for tea. **Merchants House** on South Street is in a wonderful setting with original medieval ceilings. They serve hot food at lunchtime. The **Babur** on South Street is in the evenings a delectable but pricey Indian restaurant, but at lunchtime lays on a buffet lunch at a reasonable price. The **Victoria Cafe** on St Mary's Place is a breezy bohemian cafe opposite the New Students' Union - good cappuccino and croissant sandwiches. The **New Students' Union**, a modern cube building at the golf course end of Market Street, has a cafe which sells basic student fare at low prices. A large lunch will cost only a few pounds and the bar is subsidised. Sometimes they will ask for student ID on the door, but very rarely. The **Old Students' Union** in North Street adjacent to the university chapel has less variety but serves excellent and really cheap bacon rolls.

Nightlife

As a golfing town there are naturally many '19th holes'. The best are the **Jigger** which is attached to the Old Course Hotel; **Ma Bell's** on the Scores (also does bar

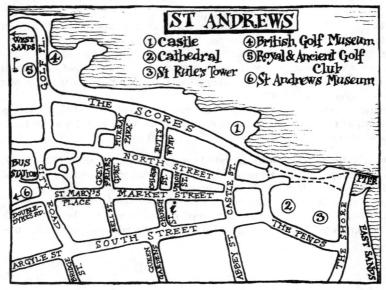

lunches); **Bert's Bar** on South Street opposite St Mary's College; and the **Central Bar** on Market Street.

In the town itself there is no budget accommodation, though you might consider staying at the independent hostel/bunkhouse 8 miles south - **The Bunkhouse**, West Pitkerie, near Anstruther, tel:(01333) 310768, open all year, £6.50/£8.50. No. 61 buses go several times a day and will drop you right at the front door. After 5.30pm the No. 65 bus to Leven stops at Anstruther and the bunkhouse is only a mile away. If it's getting dark, however, phone the bunkhouse and they might be able to come and pick you up (from Anstruther).

There is also a SYHA hostel at Falkland (see **Falkland**).

Cairnsmill Campsite, Largo Rd, tel:(01334) 473604, 1 mile from St Andrews' town centre along the A915 road; £3.50 for one person, £6.50 for two, £7.50 for three, etc. Use of indoor swimming pool included. Open April-October.

Otherwise book a **B&B** at Tourist Information.

If you want to get a feel for academic life here try the summer courses, such as Scottish history, tel:(01334) 473429, and stay at university accommodation for reduced rates.

Getting to St Andrews

The nearest train station to St Andrews is four miles away at Leuchars. A single from Edinburgh to Leuchars is £7.40 (return £12.20, day return £9.50) to which must be added the cost of the bus to St Andrews - buses go every half hour or so. The best way to get here (failing your own car) is by the Fife Scottish bus service from Edinburgh's bus station at St Andrew Square - two buses an hour all day. Single £5, return £10, day return £7.50. Students get a reduction.

ST ANDREWS AREA

THE EAST NEUK

St Andrews may be the jewel in the crown but it is set in one of the most delightful and quaint corners of Scotland. The coastline south of St Andrews, known as the East Neuk (neuk is Scots for corner), is dotted with vibrant and picturesque fishing towns and makes an excellent cycling day-trip.

In medieval days these villages were the main sea-trading ports with the continent and some of that seafaring spirit lingers on, even though today the lobster boats seldom reach out beyond sight of the coast.

Crail is perhaps the most idyllic and attractive of all the towns and there is an excellent view of the town from the end of the pier. After you've slowly meandered through the old streets near the harbour, take the easy walk that heads east out of town along the coast. There is a small free **Museum and Heritage Centre** within Crail's **Tourist Information**.

The next village of the East Neuk is **Anstruther**, another pretty resort. Here, there is the **Scottish Fisheries Museum** - a bit dated but of interest to those of a maritime persuasion; £3.20/£2.20, open all year. Tours out to the **Isle of May** allow you to see the old 17thC and new 19thC lighthouses on the island as well as a grey seal colony and many seabirds, including puffins. Tours run from May-September, weather permitting, tel:(01333) 310103, price £12/£10.

Near Anstruther is a bunkhouse for backpackers (see St Andrews' accommodation).

Crail and Anstruther are the main points of interest for the visitor but **Pittenweem**, with its crammed harbour and thriving fish market, and the more sedate **St Monans**, both deserve a look in. Elie, Largo (the birthplace of 'Robinson Crusoe') and Lundin Links are also good stops along the East Neuk trail.

Falkland

Its historic royal palace puts the beautiful town of Falkland squarely on the discerning tourist's map. **Falkland Palace** is a splendid example of 16thC architecture. Rich in history, it contains Britain's oldest real tennis court dating from 1539 and makes an enlightening diversion for an hour or two. Mary, Queen of Scots visited many times and took the opportunity to hunt game in the forest that was once around here. The price is £4.80/£3.20, open April-October, NTS. Falkland itself is an ancient and well-preserved town with many buildings dating to the 17thC making it a very pleasant place to stroll around.

MARY, QUEEN OF SCOTS

Mary became Queen of Scots at the ripe old age of one week. While her mother took care of affairs at home, Mary was brought up in France and returned to Scotland at the age of 18 (and already a widow). She proved herself a fair and intelligent ruler but perhaps unwise in taking Lord Darnley as her second husband. Darnley, in a fit of jealousy murdered, with Mary present, her secretary and personal adviser (make of that what you like), David Rizzio. She never forgave Darnley for this and a year later Darnley himself was murdered. The queen, after too short a period of mourning, married Bothwell who was implicated in the killing of Darnley. The people of Scotland were outraged - more at the improper hasty marriage than the murder - and Mary was forced to abdicate. Eventually she fled to her English cousin Queen Elizabeth I looking for protection. Instead, Elizabeth imprisoned Mary for 19 years and finally had her head chopped off.

There is a **SYHA hostel** (unfortunately not one of the 17thC houses) in Falkland at Back Wynd, tel:(01337) 857710, Grade 3, open 20/3-3/10, £4.65/£6.15.

Not only can you explore Falkland from this base but you can catch the bus to St Andrews for a day-trip - St Andrews has no youth hostel so this makes a cheap alternative.

Ten miles south-west of Falkland (close to the Edinburgh - Perth motorway road) is the memorable **Loch Leven Castle,** situated on a small island in the loch. Here Mary, Queen of Scots, was imprisoned for eleven months in 1567 before charming a son of the household to help her escape. He threw the keys into the loch and they were retrieved 300 years later. A small boat will take you from the pier in the town of Kinross across to the castle, open April-September, £2.80/£2.10, HS.

Dundee

Bonnie Dundee on the banks of the Silvery Tay is in a fabulous location - on the Tay estuary with the Sidlaw Hills rising up in the north. Unfortunately the city is not nearly as attractive as its surroundings. The 1960s architects ruined the skyline with their tower blocks, and you get an idea of the offerings in Dundee when the tourist office promotes the public swimming pool as one of their major attractions. On the other hand, you can't get more down-to-earth than Dundee, so if you are detained here, appreciate it as somewhere tourists hardly ever go.

The major attraction is the ship **RRS Discovery**. This was Captain Scott's vessel for his first trip to Antarctica and there is an awesome audio-visual display next door in the **Discovery Point Visitor Centre**; £4.50/£3.45 (entrance to ship included). Close by, at the Victoria Dock, you will find the Frigate **Unicorn**, the oldest British-built warship afloat (1824), with an exhibition of guns, models and displays; £3/£2.

The **McManus Galleries** on Albert Square has several exhibits and is free to enter, while nearby, the Howff Graveyard has interesting tombstones. The **Barrack Street Museum** houses a local wildlife and natural history display and a New Art and Nature Gallery; free.

Guide Friday run a jump-on jump-off bus service around Dundee from June to September, £2.50/£2.

On a fine day, try a walk to the top of Law Hill for a superb view over the River Tay and see the sweep of the Rail Bridge alongside the remains of the old bridge, destroyed one stormy winter night in 1879. Seventy-five passengers on a train which was crossing at the time were killed.

There are plenty of cheap cafes in Dundee's city centre and good friendly pubs.

 For accommodation try the White House, 208 Broughty Ferry Road, tel:(01382) 455788, or approach **Tourist Information**, 4 City Square, open all year, tel:(01382) 227723, for a list of **B&Bs**.

 Hitching from Dundee - see **Hitching**, Chapter 17.

Perth

The city of Perth sits on the banks of the River Tay. Its delightful location means plenty of good, easy walking and nearby Kinnoull Hill provides commanding views of the area. Perth may not have many buildings of major historic interest but this royal burgh has some interesting stories to tell. James I was assassinated here in his bedroom at Blackfriars and Robert III observed the MacKintoshes and the MacKays slay each other in the Battle of the Clans. Walking around the town centre can be pleasant but try and do your city centre walking after 5pm as the streets are very busy during the day (remember in summer it stays light until 10pm). Your first impressions of Perth as you exit either the train or bus stations may not be the most favourable, so try and save your judgement till later.

An easy walk over the river makes a perfect introduction to picturesque Perth. To begin, simply head over Perth Bridge and turn right. If you continue as far as the railway bridge, you can get onto **Moncrieffe Island** - just for a walk or maybe a round of golf. On the city side, head north along the **North Inch**, the site of the bloody Battle of the Clans in 1396.

Kinnoull Hill, just a mile east from the city centre, has a choice of excellent woodland walks - easy, difficult, short or long. Ask Tourist Information for their leaflet, 'Kinnoull Hill Woodland Walks'; even though the different walks are signposted it's easy to get lost. The best place to start your walk is at the Quarry Car Park on Corsiehill Road.

When choosing your route make sure you include on it **Kinnoull Tower**. This tower, along with Binn Tower (which can be seen from this viewpoint), was built in imitation of Rhineland castles in the 1800s. Cyclists can't use the paths on Kinnoull Hill, but you can cycle in nearby Deuchny Wood.

Perth has a modest range of museums and galleries. To the north of the centre is **Balhousie Castle** and the **Black Watch Museum**. The Black Watch military regiment was established by the government in the early 18thC to help bring some control to the Highlands. They were called the Black Watch because of their uniform's dark tartan and the 'watch' they kept over the Highlanders. The museum's full of pictures and memorabilia of their greatest battles; free. For an insight into the local history of the area (and various other topics) **Perth Museum and Art Gallery** on George Street makes an interesting and pleasant way to spend an hour or so; free. Inside the **Old Perth Water Works** on Marshall Place (in its own right a unique building) is a collection of Scottish artist J D Fergusson's impressive work; free.

Guide Friday operate a jump-on jump-off bus service around Perth and out to Scone from June to September, £4.50/£3.

Perth's **Tourist Information** is located at High St, tel:(01738) 638353, open all year.

From the bus and train stations, the **Perth SYHA** is in the opposite direction from the city centre and Tourist Information, so if you want to save yourself an even longer walk with your luggage, ask for directions first. A Grade 1 hostel with little atmosphere (closes at 11.45pm); 107 Glasgow Road, tel:(01738) 623658,

£7.75/£9.25. Open 27/2-30/10, Fridays and Saturdays in winter.

There is no independent hostel in Perth, however, if you are travelling by car an alternative is the **Braincroft Bunkhouse** in Crieff about 12 miles away (tel:01764-670140, £7/£9, open all year).

There is a campsite about a mile from the centre of town, further up Glasgow Road, the **Cleeve Caravan Park**, tel:(01738) 639521, £2.10 per person plus £1.60 per tent, open April-October. Several **B&Bs** are situated along the road to the SYHA.

Hitching from Perth - see **Hitching**, Chapter 17.

For well-priced daytime snacks, meals and coffee, head for **Betty's Coffee Parlour**, in George St (just behind Tay St), or the trendier **Strangeways Cafe Bar** in Skinnergate (just behind George St), but in the evening **Willows Coffee Shop**, in St Johns Place, provides tasty meals. For a drink, try the oldest pub, which was established in 1665, **The Ship Inn**. Their daytime meals are incredibly cheap - however no guarantee as to the quality. The pub that has to be at the centre of Perth's night life is the **Twa Tam's** in Scott St. There's music on most nights (sometimes costs) and they're open late - until midnight or a bit later. Of course this is no use if you're staying in the youth hostel which closes at 11.45pm. Anyway, it has a good lively atmosphere and a beer garden for when the weather's fine. On Sundays they serve a full 'Scottish' breakfast for about £3.

A bus from Edinburgh to Perth costs £4.40 single and £7.30 return.

ROBERT THE BRUCE

The post unheld, Robert the Bruce, of noble birth, declared himself King of Scots in 1306. The English king Edward I immediately came north with an army and swiftly defeated Bruce in battle, forcing him to flee. During his months in exile, while hiding in a cave, he was inspired by watching a spider trying over and over again until it succeeded in making a web. He returned from hiding to try again.

Bruce's arrival again prompted the English king north but Edward I died en route, allowing Bruce the freedom to reclaim the Scottish castles that were in English hands. He captured them all except Stirling and over this final and crucial stronghold the Battle of Bannockburn was fought in 1314. Edward II's 20,000 men were soundly defeated by 7,000 Scots and Bruce's right to the throne was confirmed. Scotland was independent and remained so until 1707.

King Robert the Bruce ruled for 23 years in all, one of Scotland's great and heroic leaders. His son David II became king upon Bruce's death in 1329.

Scone

Scone (pronounced Skoon), two miles north-east of Perth, has played a crucial role in Scottish history, for it was here that Scots monarchs were crowned and the Scottish parliament was held. During the coronation ceremony the king was sat upon the Stone of Scone (or Stone of Destiny), a stone which has an interesting story. In biblical times it was alleged to have been used by Jacob as a pillow but it eventually came to Scotland in the 9thC. After many coronations this revered relic was then stolen by the English king, Edward I, and taken to London's Westminster Abbey where it remained for 700 years (except for a brief period in the 1950s when it was recovered by some Scottish students). The Stone of Destiny was finally returned to Scotland in November 1996. However, it was not returned to Scone but to Edinburgh Castle. You can see a copy of the stone at Scone where it sits upon **Moot Hill**. This hill is a large mound of earth believed to be created from soil that was brought in the boots of lords who came to Scone to swear loyalty to the king (they had to stand upon soil from their own land to do this). Moot Hill is within the grounds of **Scone Palace**, a pre-16thC palace (enlarged in the early 19thC). Though small, it is packed to the brim with valuable items as well as an interesting display on the kings and queens of Scotland. Entry is £5.20 for the palace and grounds, £2.60 for the grounds only, which contain many pleasant walks and are patrolled by some menacing peacocks. Open 10/4-15/10. Just a few local buses leave Perth each day to Scone (ask at the bus station or Tourist Information), otherwise take Perth's Guide Friday jump on - jump off tour.

ROB ROY

Rob Roy MacGregor is famous in Scottish folklore as a loveable but fiercesome rogue. On the one hand he was a respected Highland cattle dealer and land-owner and on the other a cattle-raider and blackmailer. One of his many exploits inadvertently led him into trouble with the powerful Duke of Montrose, an ally of the government. Rob Roy was outlawed in 1713 and spent seven eventful years evading the authorities. His many raids on the wealthy Duke's properties was a source of amusement to all but the Duke himself. Talk of his exploits were wide-spread and Rob Roy became a legend in his own time. After some years he settled back down to live a long and prosperous life as a cattle dealer in Balquhidder, where his, and his wife Mary's, graves can be seen today.

Dunkeld, Pitlochry & Blair Atholl

These three towns sit at the heart of beautiful Perthshire and a stop in at least one, if not all, is highly recommended. The walking around here, both easy and difficult, is glorious with many side roads, forest trails and an old, seldom-used road for the most part linking the towns. Cycling is very enjoyable too.

Dunkeld

Dunkeld is a charming wee town on the banks of the silvery Tay. The quaint High Street with its ornate central Cross and buildings dating mainly from 1692, leads quietly up to the gates of the small but impressive 13thC cathedral; a cathedral filled with intriguing snippets of Scottish history. You'll find the lawn which slopes gently down to the riverbank a marvellous place to sit and watch the occasional salmon leap or trout taking a fly, while the current slowly eases its way towards the arches of Dunkeld's very impressive bridge.

The **Cathedral** as it stands today, consists of the striking ruins of the 15thC nave and the restored choir from the 13thC, but the Cathedral's site has been of religious significance since Celtic times. Within the choir, behind the carved oak screen, you will find the tombstone and armoured effigy of the notorious 'Wolf of Badenoch'. He lived in the 14thC as the Earl of Buchan and Lord of Badenoch, and by abandoning his wife Euphemia for the beautiful Mariotta, upset the church and was excommunicated. (In return, the Wolf and his cronies burned the towns of Forres and Elgin and plundered their churches.) To the side of the choir, the chapter-house museum contains various historic items including a pre-9thC Pictish obelisk. The cathedral suffered damage during the Reformation and again in 1689 when it and most of the village was burnt to the ground. This resulted from a fierce battle between Covenanters (defending the well-established Protestant faith) and the Catholic highlanders.

From the Cathedral grounds can be seen Thomas Telford's bridge, spanning the river to Birnam. It was built in 1809 and the people of the area were obliged to pay a toll (at a booth still there today) to finance its construction. The locals never approved of this and the toll gate was flung into the river on several occasions - after almost sixty years they figured the Duke of Atholl had been reimbursed more than enough. In 1868 disenchantment led to rioting and finally the toll was abolished.

These days the town of Dunkeld is thankfully a restful backwater by-passed by the busy A9 road with plentiful opportunities for walking. If you cross the bridge and head downstream you will soon come to the **Birnam Oak**, so old that it's on crutches. The tree is famous because the three witches in Shakespeare's 'Macbeth' predicted he would continue to rule until 'Great Birnam Wood to high Dunsinane hill shall come against him'. Whilst Macbeth sat confidently 12 miles away at Dunsinane,

Malcolm's men were preparing for attack disguising themselves as trees using leaves and branches from Birnam Forest. The Birnam Oak is the only tree remaining from that era.

Another walk is to the waterfall at **The Hermitage**, with its enchanting bridge over the dark rushing waters of the River Braan. Past the waterfall (look out for red squirrels playing above), the walk continues in various directions and if you find Ossian's Cave, carry on in that direction to a track leading up the hill through the pine trees for some splendid views. To get to The Hermitage you can just walk north along the main A9 road. There is, however, a more peaceful walk - start on the A9 but look out for the sign on your left pointing to Inver, a quiet road along the other side of the Braan.

There are many other lovely walks - to Birnam Hill (starts at the back of the train station), Loch of the Lowes (with the chance of seeing ospreys), and Rumbling Bridge (also reached by the Inver Road).

i **Tourist Information**, The Cross, tel:(01350) 727688, open March-October, sells maps which detail the town's heritage trail and walks in the area. Their free video also makes a fine introduction to this historic village. You could hire a bike from **Dunkeld Mountain Bikes**, tel:(01350) 728744, just under the bridge, in front of the Atholl Hotel. They are a bit expensive at £13 for a full day, £7 for three hours, but they provide maps and will recommend different routes. Bar food is available in several hotel bars, and Dunkeld has a few well-stocked shops.

Without a youth hostel, Dunkeld accommodation comes in the form of **B&Bs** or a campsite. The **Invermill Caravan Park** is not far and easy to get to - when you come out of the train station, don't cross the main A9 road, turn left and walk to the road heading to Crieff. Take this road and then the Inver road on the right to Invermill. £7 for 2 people with a tent or ask for a caravan which sleeps 4 (minimum let 2 nights), tel:(01350) 727477, open April-October.

A bus from Edinburgh to Birnam (for Dunkeld) costs £6.10 single.

Pitlochry

Pitlochry, set in a wide glen, is an excellent base for exploring the beautiful Perthshire countryside. There's so much to do and see here and lots of walking opportunities. The town centre is bustling, a bit too touristy in summer perhaps, but get away from the main thoroughfare and you'd never know it was there.

If you're interested in doing some walking, head straight for Tourist Information on the main road, and invest 50p in a pamphlet called 'Pitlochry Walks'. This outlines six varied walks.

You can wander down to Loch Faskally, a mile north of the town centre, either to feed the ducks (bring some old bread with you), or hire a rowing boat and go exploring (the most perfect thing to do on a sunny afternoon). Otherwise, if you walk alongside the loch, through the woods you'll find the **Pass of Killiecrankie**. This was a fiercely fought over gateway to the Highlands in past times. There is a visitor centre near the end of the Pass detailing the Battle of Killiecrankie. In this battle the government troops were totally defeated by the Highlanders and the **Soldier's Leap** (which you should stroll down to) refers to a terrified government soldier's jump across the gorge. This visitor centre also has displays highlighting the local flora and fauna, plus a cafe nearby.

Back in Pitlochry, at the dam across the River Tummel, is a fish-ladder for the salmon with an underwater viewing panel for fish-watching enthusiasts. If you see a salmon going up it, get excited - it doesn't happen that often. If you want to see them jump, however, it's better to look at the point where the ladder meets the river (spring and autumn are the best times). From here you can either follow the public footpath around the other side of Loch Faskally, or head along to the **Pitlochry Festival Theatre** (year round, high-quality productions) and back over the wobbly suspension bridge. The Black Spout Waterfall also makes a great excursion. Curling is a winter sport, invented in Scotland, and Pitlochry has an indoor curling rink in Lower Oakfield. Pop in and see if there's a game on, it's free to look.

The **Blair Atholl Distillery** in Pitlochry is easy to get to but charges £3 for a tour (with one free drink and a £3 voucher redeemable against the purchase of a bottle of Malt included). Instead you could go to the smallest distillery in Scotland, the **Edradour Distillery**, a couple of miles out of town. It's delightfully quaint, enjoys an excellent reputation and is free (one drink included).

• **Tourist Information** is on Pitlochry's main road, tel:(01796) 472215. Open all year and from May to September stays open until 8pm.

Pitlochry SYHA in Knockford Road, tel:(01796) 472308, is one of the more comfortable SYHA hostels. An easy place to stop for a couple of nights, £7.75/£8.85, open all year.

The **Milton of Fonab Caravan Park**, just half a mile out of town, costs £5.50/£8.50 a tent. They also rent out caravans which might be economical between many people, tel:(01796) 472882.

High quality mountain bikes can be hired from **Escape Route** on West Moulin Road, tel:(01796) 473859, for £14 for a full day and £8 for a half-day. Cycle helmets, toolkits, maps and route advice included.

West of Pitlochry

To the west of Pitlochry lies some very peaceful countryside. **Loch Rannoch,** situated at the very centre of Scotland is, even at the height of summer, like the eye of a storm, a tranquil refuge from tourism. On the south shore of the loch is the dark wood of Rannoch, as beautiful a forest as you could wish for with an abundance of red squirrels, deer and ancient twisted trees. The road ends at Rannoch's train station, an old quaint and slightly incongruous meeting point for these two modes of transport - in the middle of nowhere and going in completely different directions. This is the sort of place you find Scottish holiday-makers with ruddy cheeks and clanking frying pans hanging from their rucksacks. At the station drop in for a cup of tea and a slice of cake at the delightful cafe on the platform.

Between Pitlochry and Loch Rannoch be sure to stop at the dramatic **Queen's View** overlooking Loch Tummel. South of this loch and over the pass into the next glen sits Kenmore, a picturesque village at the east end of Loch Tay. In the churchyard of the nearby village of **Fortingall** is Europe's oldest tree, a small dainty yew, 2-3,000 years old. Fortingall is also the alleged birthplace of Pontius Pilate.

Blair Atholl

And so, on to Blair Atholl. It's much quieter and the major landmark of the town is **Blair Castle** - yes, it's the big white thing on the hillside. It's a splendid castle that is one of the most popular in Scotland, £5.50/£4.50, plus £2 to park your car (so drivers you should park your car in the village and take the long, lovely walk to the castle up the avenue), open April - October. The castle's situated in extensive grounds that you can walk through and explore (this is recommended).

The town of Blair Atholl is fairly small with a couple of bars and a couple of local museums. Bicycle hire at £10 (full day), £6 (4 hrs) and £4 (2 hrs) is available at **Atholl Mountain Bikes**, Old School Park (open at Easter and from May to October at this address; at other times phone (01796) 473553). They recommend certain cycle routes, the best of which would have to be through the castle estate to the **Falls of Bruar** (a 12-mile round trip) - get their leaflet which details the route. **Glen Tilt** is another good route for cyclists, although it and Bruar Falls make good destinations for walkers too. The Blair Castle Caravan Park takes bookings for pony-trekking, and on the castle estate ponies too, tel:(01796) 481263. A one-hour trek for beginners costs £7, with other treks for more experienced riders. Phone in advance to see which treks are available on which days, Easter-August only.

Blair Castle Caravan Park, tel:(01796) 481263, which you enter at the main road along from the castle entrance, is open between Easter and October; £6.50/£8 a tent.

There are several **B&Bs** in Blair Atholl.

3.The North-East

Many visitors come to Scotland and head in a great rush towards the west coast - but this is all the better for those who choose the rich and beautiful region of the north-east. Here there is an abundance of castles, whisky distilleries and quaint villages set against the backdrop of the Grampian and Cairngorm mountains. It's almost inexplicable that so many backpackers choose to stay away.

The large city of Aberdeen lends the area a cosmopolitan feel with its international connections due to the oil of the North Sea. Magnificent castles (too many to choose from, actually) are scattered everywhere, but near Stonehaven is the best, and perhaps the best castle ruin in Scotland - Dunnottar Castle.

The rivers Spey and Dee have brought the region much prosperity. The pure water of the Spey's tributaries, essential for the making of a delicious malt whisky, has led to the creation of the distilleries here, while the patronage of the Royal Family of the river Dee, particularly at Balmoral, has given the river's banks the name Royal Deeside. Aviemore, just south of Inverness, is the activity nucleus of the north-east and here you can walk, climb, windsurf, sail or, in winter, ski to your heart's content.

Royal Deeside

Beginning at a pool deep in the Cairngorms, the sparkling clear water of the River Dee carves its way seaward through the scenic grandeur of Deeside. Quintessentially Scottish villages line the riverbank and all have a royal connection, as this is the region Queen Victoria fell in love with and where she built her holiday 'home' - Balmoral Castle. The area has many walks, ranging from gentle strolls to demanding treks through the mountains, and other outdoor pursuits include fishing, pony-trekking, hang-gliding and skiing.

Braemar

For a place with such a well-known name, Braemar is surprisingly small. World-famous for the Braemar Royal Highland Gathering (which the Queen always attends), its other major attraction is Braemar Castle.

Braemar's Highland Games in September attracts large royal watching crowds. By attending, Queen Elizabeth continues a tradition that stretches back to the Scottish King Malcolm's patronage in the 11thC. The Games were founded to recruit soldiers, especially bodyguards for the chieftains.

To attend the Games you must book well in advance, contact Mr W. Meston, Coilacriech, Ballater, AB35 5US, tel:(01339) 755377. The Games are held on the first Saturday in September, and tickets range from £5 to no more than £17.50.

Braemar Castle was built in the 17thC and sits less than a mile out of town. £2.50/£2 is not much to pay for this historic structure, a private residence, furnished throughout. Open Easter-October (closed Fridays). The other castle in the village is **Kindrochit Castle**, Balnellan Road, much older and in a ruined state; free.

Explaining the history of the area and all its links with royalty, is the **Highland Heritage Centre** right beside Tourist Information on Mar Road, open daily from 10am-6pm; free. From the village are several signposted

Throwing the Hammer

walking routes that should keep you busy for days. Tourist Information have a booklet for sale detailing them.

Alternatively, you could hire a bike and cycle 6 miles west of the village to the **Linn of Dee**, a picturesque spot where the river suddenly narrows and gushes through a small gorge. The Brig o' Dee, a few miles east of Braemar, also makes a pleasant trip.

Cycles can be hired from the **Mountain Sports Shop** in Invercauld Rd, tel:(01339) 741242, for £14 a day.

The friendly **Tourist Information** office on Mar Rd, tel:(01339) 741600 is open all year. Although small, Braemar village has a bank, a grocer, hotel bars and plenty of craft/tourist shops.

 'Rucksacks' Braemar, 15 Mar Rd, tel:(01339) 741517, open all year, no curfew, £7/£8.

Braemar SYHA, Corrie Feragie, Glenshee Rd, tel:(01339) 741659, Grade 1, £7.75/£9.25, open all year.

Inverey SYHA, 5 miles west of Braemar along the road to the Linn of Dee, no telephone, open 15/5-3/10, £4.65/£6.15.

Remember that when the Highland Games are on you must book in advance to ensure a bed is available.

Balmoral

Balmoral Castle is the Royal Family's holiday home and has been since Queen Victoria's reign. The castle was built by Victoria and her patronage of the Highlands had a great impact on how Scotland was viewed by the English, who had long considered it the primitive backwoods of Britain. Victoria made the Highlands fashionable. What attracted royalty here is plain to see - the estate is magnificent (and large). You can visit the castle grounds and special exhibitions in the ballroom and carriage hall from 10/4-2/8, before the Royals arrive; £3.50. There is also pony-trekking which costs £15 for 2 hours.

Crathie Kirk, where Princess Anne was remarried, is on the small hill just opposite Balmoral's **Tourist Information**, which is open April-October. You can also visit the **Royal Lochnagar Distillery** for a tour and a tasting of their produce, something Queen Victoria certainly approved of; £2 to enter and open all year.

Ballater

Ballater is at the very centre of Royal Deeside. It's a pretty town, although at times there are too many tourists. The best time to visit here is in October when autumn is blazing gold in the mountains. The royal touch is everywhere - even the newsagent here appears to be by 'Royal Appointment'. Ballater **Tourist Information**, tel:(013397) 55306, open Easter-end October.

Banchory

The closest of the Deeside towns to Aberdeen is Banchory which makes it an ideal destination for a day-trip. It's a quiet place, very prettily situated beside the River Dee. You can watch salmon leap the falls here - head to the Bridge of Feugh, south of the town. Three miles to the east of Banchory is **Crathes Castle**, a grand 16thC tower house with delightful grounds - one of the best castles in the north-east. Castle only £2/£1.30, castle and grounds £4.80/£3.20; open April-October. Further east is **Drum Castle**, £4.20/£2.80, open Easter-October, NTS.

Although there are plenty of **B&Bs** there's no hostel in town; however about 5 miles north-west is the **Wolf's Hearth** at Tornaveen by Lumphanan, tel:(01339) 883460, £9.50/£11 a night and very cosy, open all year.

Remember that buses through Royal Deeside are infrequent.

Aberdeen

Aberdeen, the 'Granite City', is a place about which opinion differs radically. Many tourists are simply struck by the greyness of the city centre (there's no escaping it), rush for the next bus out of town and wonder why their guide-book ever recommended they go there in the first place. Others will appreciate the grandiose 19thC buildings made of the local stone, get a glimpse of the diversity beneath the city's surface, and find the beautiful (and more colourful) Old Town.

Aberdeen is the third largest city of Scotland and after oil was discovered in the North Sea in the 1970s it became the European capital of the oil industry (don't be put off by this as there are no refineries or oil slicks around - it's a neat and tidy city). Billions of pounds each year have been made in oil revenue but the money goes straight down to Westminster and London, and Scotland sees only a small proportion of it. Aberdeen, however, has lived well off the oil industry to become a city of affluence with a low unemployment level.

Aberdeen's central district can be roughly divided into three sections.

Old Aberdeen

The most attractive area is Old Aberdeen to the north of the city. Start your walk at Spital Street, then along the High Street, the Chanonry and on as far as the Auld Brig of Balgownie which spans the River Don.

The University of Aberdeen was founded in 1494 and of its original buildings, it is the elegant and eye-catching **King's College Chapel** on the High Street that has survived. Inside you will see some of Scotland's finest medieval wood carvings, and next door there is a visitor centre for the university and the Old Town. Free to enter.

St Machar's Cathedral on the Chanonry is open to visitors and has a unique heraldic ceiling. Although what we see today was built in the 14th and 15thC, a church was founded here in AD580 and Aberdeen grew around it.

Be sure to continue your walk to the **Brig of Balgownie**, a major highlight of this historic burgh. It is a gorgeous 14thC bridge with a 62-foot wide arch in excellent condition.

City Centre

The buildings of the city centre contrast sharply with those of the old town. They're rather scary at first but they grow on you. To soften the austerity of these structures the city has been extensively decorated with flowers, which is quite stunning through the summer months.

The main thoroughfare of Aberdeen is Union Street with all the major chain stores along it; turn off at Union Terrace and into the gardens for relief from the hustle and bustle.

For information about the early days of Aberdeen visit the **Tolbooth Museum** on Union Street. It makes a good introduction to the city and is free to enter.

You cannot fail to be impressed by the magnificent and intricate granite edifice of **Marischal College**. You can enter the courtyard by an archway on Broad Street, and inside is the Mitchell Hall, home to the interesting **Marischal Museum**; free.

Provost Skene's House is just off Broad Street in Guestrow. This was built in the 16thC and is now a museum with furnished period rooms and local history displays; free.

The **Kirk of St Nicholas** is located in the very centre of town and is worth a wander into. Once whole, it was divided during the Reformation so now there is the East church and the West church with a vestibule linking the two. The bells of St Nicholas are heard regularly throughout the city.

The **Aberdeen Art Gallery** on Schoolhill has an impressive collection of art from the 18th-20thC with an emphasis on contemporary work; free.

On Shiprow is the **Maritime Museum** located inside Provost Ross's House. This

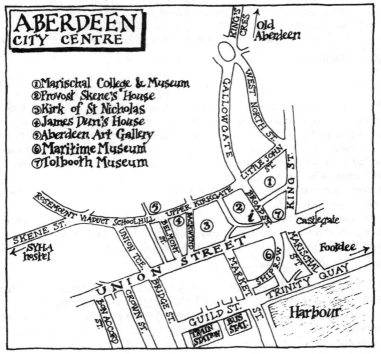

museum is probably the most relevant to Aberdeen's history with information about the early days of the harbour, the shipbuilding industry and today's profitable era of oil and gas; free.

The Harbour

After the Maritime Museum, take a look at the harbour. It is a massive and busy place but what you should aim for is Footdee (pronounced Fittee), a planned and picturesque fishing village of the 19thC. From here you can walk the Beach Esplanade - but wrap up well, as there's often an icy wind coming off the sea.

A visit to Aberdeen's fish market is not for everybody but can be a captivating place. The best time to wander around is early, about 7am, so you have to be keen. It's close to the train station on Market Street.

i **Tourist Information** is on Broad St, tel:(01224) 632727, and open all year with a bureau de change.

Aberdeen SYHA, 8 Queens Rd, tel:(01224) 646988. Grade 1, late access, £8.60/£11.10, open all year. Don't look forward to it too much. With little choice in budget accommodation you'll probably have to stay here anyway. From town, walk west along Union St until it runs into Albyn Place then on a mile to Queens Rd, or catch one of the many buses.

Hazelhead Campsite, Groats Rd, tel:(01224) 647647. Open April-Sept, £3.50-£7 a tent. About three miles west of the city centre.

Craighill Campsite, Stonehaven Rd, tel:(01224) 781973. Open all year, £5-£6. There are B&Bs along Bon Accord St and Crown St, however, they're not cheap.

 Hitching from Aberdeen - see **Hitching**, Chapter 17.

Food

There are many restaurants to serve the expense accounts of oil executives, but for people on a budget finding good food can present difficulties.

Students should go to the university's **Students Union** (take your student ID card) on the corner of Upperkirkgate and Broad St, which has cheap food during the day. For Italian food buffs try **Poldino's** on Little Beaumont St and for bistro types the **Wild Boar** on Belmont St has wholesome food at good prices.

Serving a tasty lunch menu is **The Lemon Tree** on West North St, including vegetarian meals; open 12-3pm.

After a long walk by the sea, fish and chips are in order and there is perhaps no better place in Scotland to sample this heart-stopping delicacy than at **Ashvales** at 46 Great Western Rd, the same end of town as the youth hostel.

Pubs and Entertainment

Especially recommended are the **Blue Lamp** on Gallowgate and the popular **Prince of Wales** on St Nicholas Lane, behind Union St. There's plenty happening at the **Student Union** on Upperkirkgate which has several bars and usually music from Thursday-Saturday. Sometimes the bands might cost but if so, it's only about £3. It's always open until midnight and until 2am from Thursday-Saturday. Take a student

ID card. **The Lemon Tree**, tel:(01224) 642230, is Aberdeen's most exciting live music, theatre, dance and comedy venue - there is music or comedy most nights in the cafe theatre (this will cost) and free jazz on a Sunday afternoon. Theatre and dance performances are held in the 150-seat theatre. Aberdeen hosts an Alternative Festival from 8-17 October, for details contact tel:(01224) 635822.

The price of a single bus ticket from Edinburgh to Aberdeen is £12.50.
A recommended day-trip out of Aberdeen is to **Stonehaven** to see Dunnottar Castle (see 'Castles of the North-East'). The bus costs just £4.40 return.

THE COAST - ABERDEEN TO INVERNESS

Quite different from Aberdeen and the rolling farmland is the long coastline from Aberdeen north to Fraserburgh and then west to Inverness. It's fair to say that this coastline is unspectacular compared with that of the west coast, but it has its own charms, particularly found in fishing villages like Cullen and Pennan and the elegant towns such as Banff. Each aspect of the north-east has its own flavour and though fisherman and farmers both use Aberdeen's cultural and shopping resources, they feel themselves to be separate communities with their own identities. There is nowhere in Scotland where you can see the farming or the fishing cultures as clearly as in the north-east.

Along the coastline heading north of Aberdeen toward Peterhead you could stop to see the beautiful sandy beaches around Balmedie, the endless dunes of Newburgh or the grand cliffs of the Bullers of Buchan.
Peterhead is by no stretch of the imagination a pretty town but it is rich from fishing. It is the largest white fish port in Europe, with the busiest fish market to match. If you are from Germany or Italy the chances are that the fish you have grown up on have been landed at Peterhead. The town does have the **Arbuthnot Museum** which traces not just the history of fishing in Peterhead but also of the old whaling days. It's very much a workaday town indifferent to tourism but there is still a **Tourist Information**, tel: (01779) 471904, open April-October.

Fraserburgh is similar to Peterhead, having even less to offer the tourist, so continue along the coast to **Pennan**. This idyllic village is a must for anyone driving or cycling along the coast. As you wind down the steep cliff road and see how tightly the small community hugs the coast you can see why it was once the refuge of smugglers. The film 'Local Hero' was shot here and Pennan's red telephone box had a starring role.

Prince among north-east coastal towns, **Banff** stands above the pale sands of Boyndie Bay. Banff remains one of the great, undiscovered towns in Scotland and worthy of comparison with its Canadian namesake. It was rebuilt extensively in the 18thC. Its most important building is **Duff House** designed by William Adam. This splendid building is now home to a collection of fine paintings. Open daily in summer except Tuesdays and from Thursday-Sunday in winter, £2.50/£1, HS. It's a pleasant walk along the sands to the fishing village of Whitehills. Banff **Tourist Information**, tel:(01261) 812419, is open April-October.

Castles of the North East

The north-east of Scotland must rank with Bavaria and Austria as the best place in the world to see castles. They are splendid and plentiful. Choose your castles carefully, though, as it is possible to have too much of a good thing. Here are some of the best in the region.

It is impossible to exaggerate the magnificence of **Dunnottar Castle**, just 1½ miles south of Stonehaven. Built on a promontory with a 160-foot drop to the sea, Dunnottar has taken the brunt of the North Sea's vicious winds and today stands a ruin - but what a ruin! It's no wonder that Zefferelli chose it as the setting for his film of 'Hamlet'; £3, open all year (closed weekends in the winter).

In complete contrast, **Craigievar Castle** stands within extensive grounds almost exactly as it did in the 17thC upon its completion. A tall and splendid tower house about 10 miles north-west of Banchory. Sadly it's £5.80/£3.90 to enter (remember a YHA membership card will get you in for half price), open May-Sept, 1.30pm-5.30pm, NTS.

Fyvie Castle is one of the greatest examples of Scottish baronial architecture. If you see only one castle Fyvie makes an excellent choice. Eight miles south-east of Turriff; £4.20/£2.80, open Easter-Oct, 1.30pm-5.30pm but 11am-5.30pm in July & August, NTS.

Crathes Castle, see Banchory, Deeside.

Castle Fraser, about 10 miles north of Banchory, is similar to Crathes and Craigievar Castles. £4.20/£2.80, same hours as Craigievar.

Excellent ruined castles are **Balvenie** (see Dufftown) and **Huntly**. Huntly Castle, in a beautiful setting, has superb heraldic adornments above the entrance and fireplaces. £2.30/£1.75, closed Thursday pm and Friday in winter, HS.

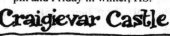

Craigievar Castle

56

Portsoy is another of this coastline's attractive towns. The long lanes of 17thC houses have been restored beautifully and are much used in film and advertising shoots. If you want even more pleasant harbour towns (perhaps you're travelling by boat), try Cullen, Portknockie, Findochty and Lossiemouth.

The town centre of **Elgin** sadly reveals little of its amazing past. Although the medieval street plan remains, the town is now a modern busy centre for the surrounding rural communities. The major attraction in Elgin is the **Cathedral**, a superb ruin with a long and violent history. Both the 'Wolf of Badenoch' and Oliver Cromwell did their best to destroy it but fortunately much of the original 13thC building still stands. It was thought to be an exceedingly beautiful cathedral when complete; £1.80/£1.30 to enter, and open every day but not Thursday afternoons or Fridays in winter, HS.

As one of the few places in this region to have budget accommodation, you might need Elgin as your base to get to the many whisky distilleries inland. **Saltire Hostel**, Plusgarden Rd, tel:(01343) 550624, £7.50/£6, open Easter-September. For **B&Bs** contact **Tourist Information**, 17 High St, tel:(01343) 542666, open all year.

SPEYSIDE

Scotland's fastest flowing river, the River Spey, flows to the coast at Spey Bay. World-renowned for its whisky, the Speyside district is the home of some of the most famous distilleries, Glenfiddich and Glenlivet amongst them. A long-distance footpath, the Speyside Way, runs alongside the more northern part of the river and at Aviemore and the Lecht are two of Scotland's popular ski centres.

Dufftown is considered a must on every whisky-lover's itinerary as the home to the world-renowned Glenfiddich Distillery. The town was founded in 1817 by James Duff and at the centre of its four main streets is the attractive Clock Tower. Once the town jail, it is now home to a small free local history museum as well as Dufftown's **Tourist Information**, tel:(01340) 820501, open Easter to October.

Glenfiddich Distillery is just one mile north of Dufftown. This distillery is a favourite with the coach tour companies so don't be surprised when you see bus loads of pensioners being dropped off for their free dram of whisky. Glenfiddich's visitor centre is a professional operation and, being one of the largest exporters of whisky in the world, it has to be. It's free to enter, open all year and has an audio-visual show on the whisky-making process. Conducted tours are available.

Across the road from the distillery, and hidden behind trees, is the considerable ruin of **Balvenie Castle**, a 13thC moated fortress. It has a long and dramatic history and like so many other castles, Mary, Queen of Scots, stayed there. Only £1.20/90p to enter, open April-September, HS.

Ben Rinnes, 2759ft, south-west of the town, is a good destination for hillwalkers. **Still Life Studio** not far from the Clock Tower, has a range of lovely artwork by local starving artists specialising in Scottish wildlife, whisky and local scenes.

There is no hostel but 2 B&Bs are **Nashville**, 8a Balvenie St, tel:(01340) 820553, and **Mrs Robertson's**, 11 Conval St, tel: (01340) 820818.

The Whisky Trail

With such a high concentration of distilleries it was inevitable that they should all band together to promote a 'Trail'. Of course visiting seven distilleries, each with an hour-long guided tour, can get pretty tiresome so it's best to choose just a couple. These are what you can choose from -

Cardhu - Knockando, Moray, tel:(01340) 810204.
Glenfarclas - Ballindalloch, Banffshire, tel:(01807) 500257.
Glenfiddich - Dufftown, Banffshire, tel:(01340) 820373.
Glen Grant - Rothes, Moray, tel:(01340) 831413.
The Glenlivet - Glenlivet, Banffshire, tel:(01807) 590427.
Strathisla - Keith, Banffshire, tel:(01542) 783044.
Tamnavoulin-Glenlivet - Tamnavoulin, near Tomintoul, Banffshire, tel:(01807) 590442.

Cardhu, Glenfarclas and Glenfiddich are open all year, daily in summer, Monday-Friday in winter. The rest are only open from Easter to October (roughly). Most distilleries now charge for their guided tours (£2-£4, but this usually includes a discount voucher of a few pounds if you buy a bottle of their whisky) - but Glenfiddich is still free.
The International Scotch Whisky Festival is held throughout Speyside and in Edinburgh in October.

·Whisky Distillery·

Tomintoul (pronounced Tom-in-towel) is a small and friendly town with a long, long main street and two hostels. It can make a good base for walkers, whisky-samplers and skiers. An easy 4-mile walk called the 'Tomintoul Country Walk' starts to the south of the village and takes you through beautiful Glen Avon.

i In the centre of town on the Square is **Tourist Information**, tel:(01807) 580285, open April-October, which also contains Tomintoul's free **Museum**.

 Tomintoul Bunkhouse, The Square, tel:(01343) 548105, £7, open all year. **Tomintoul SYHA**, Main St, no telephone, open 15/5-31/10, Grade 3, £4.65/£6.15.

Unfortunately there is very little public transport available in this area.

The **Lecht ski-slope** is good for beginners and only 4 miles south of Tomintoul. See **'Skiing Around Scotland'**.

 A new hostel in this area is **Speyside Backpackers**, in Grantown-On Spey, 16 The Square, tel:(01479) 872529, £8.50 a night, open all year.

STRATHSPEY AND BADENOCH

The busy route from the Lowlands to Inverness cuts through some fine glens below desolate mountains. Where the valley floor widens out meadows appear, the River Spey slows down and the sights and sounds of rural habitation can be perceived.

Newtonmore, in the heart of the highlands, is a pleasant traditional Scottish country town, with granite houses on the main street and a smattering of small shops, a bank, pubs and a gentle, easy air. When with the locals ask them about Newtonmore's shinty team.

 The town has many **B&Bs** and budget accommodation at the bright and pleasant **Newtonmore Independent Hostel**, Main St, tel:(01540) 673360, £8.50, open all year. There's also the **Spey Bridge Caravan Park**, ten minutes walk south of the village, tel:(01540) 673275, open Easter to mid-October, £3-£5.

From Newtonmore the A86 road branches out westward on a lovely route through Glen Spean to the west coast.

Nearby the River Spey meanders through highland pastures and flood plains downstream to **Kingussie**, a busier but still appealing version of Newtonmore.

i Around Kingussie there are many pleasant walks and **Tourist Information** in King St, tel:(01540) 661297, open May-September, can give you information on these. An easy one is to **Ruthven Barracks**. For climbers the challenging Creag Bheag at 1593ft provides views up and down the Spey valley. The **Highland Folk Museum** is of some interest, but the kind of place your teacher might have taken you for a school trip; £3, open March-October.

 You can stay here at **The Laird's Bothy** which is on the High St, tel:(01540) 661334, £8 a night, open all year.

One idea is to hire a bike in Kingussie (from **Service Sports**, High St, £10 a day, £6 a half day) and head out past the barracks on the B970 road towards Feshie Bridge. This is a delightful, twisting tree-lined country road with not too many hills (for car drivers it also makes a pleasant alternative route to the A9).

Near Feshie Bridge on the road signposted to Achlean (the second Glen Feshie Rd) is the **Glen Feshie Hostel**, in a peaceful location, tel:(01540) 651323; £8 including free porridge, open all year. Accommodation is also available near Kincraig on the B1952 at the **Kirkbeag Cabin**, tel:(01540) 651298, £8.50/£9.25, open all year. The cabin sits right next to a church (now a guesthouse).

Continue past Feshie Bridge and you'll find more gentle highland scenery. Spare a thought for the masses on the frantic A9 road across the valley, who've passed by all this. Beyond here lies the busy town of Aviemore, but first you can side-track past Coylumbridge to Loch Morlich (this road ends at the ski tow). Near the loch you can find accommodation at the **Loch Morlich SYHA** hostel, tel:(01479) 861238, £7.75/£9.25, Grade 1, open all year.

AVIEMORE

Aviemore panders to tourists in the adventure holiday mould, and with some abysmal modern architecture it can leave a poor first impression, but what it lacks in tartan trimmings it makes up for in designer day-glo. It's a vibrant, fun place and unless you're terminally lazy you'll feel virtually obliged to take part in some sort of healthy, character-building, sweaty outdoor sport.

· Squirrel ·

• Drop into **Tourist Information**, on the main road, tel:(01479) 810363, open all year, and you'll find a whole bevy of leaflets on, well let's just try and list them all - rock-climbing, abseiling (repelling), hillwalking, mountaineering, sailing, windsurfing, rowing, canoeing, white-water rafting, downhill skiing, cross-country skiing, skating, curling, cycling, mountain biking, bungee-jumping, marked walks, pony-trekking and orienteering. There are also more placid ways to pass the day such as fishing on the famous River Spey, taking a trip on the steam train, or for those of you who like to cheat your way to the top, climbing the 4,000ft mountain Cairngorm by chairlift - you can even eat your lunch near the top at the Ptarmigan restaurant.

Aviemore's mainstay, however, is the skiing which usually takes place from December until May and is actually very cheap compared with some countries. There are many ski-runs varying from very easy to suicidal, so there's something for everybody. See 'Skiing Around Scotland'.

Aviemore SYHA, tel:(01479) 810345, Grade 1, £8.60/£11.10, open all year. **Loch Morlich SYHA**, is 7 miles away- see 'Strathspey & Badenoch'.
Aviemore is on the Edinburgh/Glasgow - Inverness bus and train routes.

SKIING AROUND SCOTLAND

Skiing here is great fun. All the snobs go to the Alps or other posey places like the Pyrenees or Aspen, which leaves Scotland with the real people. You may see what looks like state-of-the-art fluorescent ski suits whizzing past but they are as likely to have 'Cleansing Dept' written on the back as any fancy designer label. What's more, Scotland's slopes are for true men and women - there's no pampering in the form of snow-making machines, so if it hasn't snowed in a while you ski on ice and you just enjoy it. Likewise the weather enhances the challenge, no guaranteed blue skies here, mate, just full-on weather. You need warm clothes at first but you soon heat up - make sure you take a woolly hat, sunglasses and gloves - any kind will do.

Aviemore is perhaps the best known (as it is easily accessible by public transport from the lowland cities and Inverness), and makes an excellent place to fall on your backside and generally make a total fool of yourself. The slopes are a bus ride from town (£2.20 single/£3.60 return, buses go about 6 times a day). Hire the skis at the slope rather than in town - as you can imagine, this saves so much hassle knocking people's teeth out on the bus. Skis, sticks and boots cost £13 a day but you need to leave a deposit - either a passport, credit card, driver's licence or £80. All-day lift-passes cost from £8 (for beginners) to £17; morning or afternoon only passes cost £12. Beginners can either ski outside the base station (depending on snow conditions), take the chairlift to the beginner's slopes at the top, or if you're feeling confident get a one-way lift ticket (£5) to the first stop and 'ski' back down. The Cairngorm Chairlift Company base station, tel:(01479) 861261, provides, apart from ski hire, plenty of facilities including a very reasonably priced canteen, a pub and shops. They sometimes offer free lift passes if you work for a few hours clearing tables in the canteen. Phone ahead and ask.

The other slopes are at **Glenshee**, in Perthshire, tel:(013397) 41320, the **Lecht**, near Tomintoul, tel:(01975) 651440, **Glencoe**, tel:(01855) 851226, and the new and much acclaimed **Aonach Mor**, 4 miles outside Fort William, tel:(01397) 705825. Aonach Mor prices are on a par with Aviemore and again you can hire skis, boots and sticks at the base (they don't hire ski-suits, however, so if you want one, hire it in Fort William).

If you want to know the ski forecast, don't phone up the various advertised 'Ski Hotline' 0898 numbers (they're very expensive), just phone the ski-slope companies the day before or first thing in the morning.

Don't worry about accident insurance, this is all covered by the National Health Service - helicopter flight too.

Blair Atholl to Aviemore by Glen Tilt then the Lairig Ghru
Distance: 39 miles, 63 km (16-20 hours - 2-3 days)
Map: O.S. Landranger 43, 1:50,000 and O.S. Outdoor Leisure 3, 1:25,000

If you fancy a few days walking and camping out in the wilds of Scotland, then an excellent recommendation would be to walk from Blair Atholl to Aviemore. Heading north the feeling of remoteness gradually increases as all signs of civilisation are left behind while the country becomes more desolate and the looming mountains more rugged. The trek will take you beneath Ben Macdui, the second highest mountain in Scotland, and the Cairngorm plateau, a fragile arctic environment which has been designated as an area requiring special protection.

The route is also convenient for those who depend on public transport to get around as Blair Atholl and Aviemore are well served by rail and coach services from Edinburgh and Glasgow. Both places also have those facilities which are vital to all backpackers, these being, in order of importance: a choice of pubs, a campsite with showers and grocery shops. Another advantage to this route is that there is a bail-out point at the halfway stage. If you find that your blisters have swollen up to resemble golf-balls or the weather looks set to rain for a further week then you can head for Braemar, civilisation and coffee shops.

Blair Atholl to White Bridge by Glen Tilt
Distance: 19 miles, 31 km (8-10 hours)
Map: O.S. Landranger 43, 1:50,000

This walk from Blair Atholl to White Bridge is mostly easy except for one area of fords which walkers need to be warned about before setting off. The Geldie Burn and Bynack Burn fords are likely to get your feet wet even on the finest day but can become quite dangerous and maybe even impassable during severe wet weather. The wreckage of a bridge testifies to the fury these rivers sometimes reach. There is a big warning to this effect at the Linn of Dee but none if approaching from the direction of Blair Atholl.

Warnings aside, this is a comfortable one and a half day hike, (also achievable during one long day), which is straight-forward to follow and has gentle inclines rather than steep climbs. The scenery is excellent throughout the route, especially the higher reaches of Glen Tilt which is littered with waterfalls and the high, open moorland beyond where there is an excellent view of the Cairngorm Mountains.

Blair Atholl to Aviemore Walk

BRAEMAR

TO DERRY LODGE

LINN OF DEE

TO LAIRIG GHRU

RIVER DEE

WHITE BRIDGE

CARN LAITH

GELDIE BURN

ALLT AN SEILICH

BUACHAILLE BREIGE

CHAPAN GARBH

BYNACK LODGE (ruin)

MEALL TIONAIL

ALLT GARBH BUIDE

LOCH TILT

ALLT A' GHLINNE MHÓIR

FALLS OF TARF

BRAIG COIRE NA CONLAICH

RIVER TILT

MEALL GHARRAN

BEINN A'GHLO

CARN ACHLAMAIN

FOREST LODGE

GLEN TILT

AIRGIOD BHEINN

ALLT DIRIDH

MARBLE LODGE

CAIRN LIATH

RIFLE RANGE

N

KINCRAIGIE FARM

BLAIR CASTLE

CAMP SITE

TENDERBRIDGE

STATION

BLAIR ATHOLL

63

From the castle campsite at Blair Atholl head east and cross over the River Tilt on the road bridge. There is a footpath along this side of the river which takes walkers through a beautiful avenue of birch trees and some gushing stretches of river rapids. All too soon the path joins the road at the Old Bridge of Tilt, follow the Glenfender road uphill, past a sign 'To Deeside by Glen Tilt', and continue on the road for another half mile to where the track starts proper at Kincraigie Farm.

At this stage you will have gained some considerable height, the River Tilt will be far below and you might be able to hear the sound of gunfire from the rifle range across from the other side of the glen. Follow the track through the edge of forest plantations and back onto the River Tilt, continue along to Marble Lodge and cross the river here. The path stays close to the river all the way past Forest Lodge to the Falls of Tarf. The Tarf Water is crossed by the wonderfully ornate Bedford Memorial Bridge, erected in 1886 after a young Englishman was drowned trying to cross the river near here.

After the falls the river forks and the path now clings to the steep west bank of the Allt Garbh Buidhe until the end of the glen is reached and enters a wide expanse of high and open moorland. The river here disperses into an array of peaty streams, the path is a little faint over this peaty land but soon becomes distinct again when it heads to slightly higher ground on the west side of this wet ground.

Follow the path along and down to the Bynack Lodge ruin then negotiate fords at the Bynack Burn and Geldie Burn and follow the track past the forest plantation to White Bridge. This is the point in the route where you must decide whether to continue on to the Lairig Ghru and Aviemore or make tracks for the relative comfort and civilisation of Braemar. If Braemar is your option then follow the track east along the River Dee to the road at the Linn of Dee which is 10 km from the town.

Walkers heading to Aviemore by the Lairig Ghru should cross the White Bridge and take the path which heads north-west.

White Bridge to Aviemore by the Lairig Ghru
Distance: 20 miles, 32 km (8-10 hours)
Map: O.S. Outdoor Leisure 3, 1:25,000

In past centuries the Lairig Ghru mountain pass was used by drovers to herd cattle from Inverness to markets in the lowlands and by crofters who carried eggs in a basket on their head from Aviemore to Braemar. Today's traffic on the Lairig Ghru consists of hardy walkers enjoying the solitude and magnificence of this rough mountain terrain. The only eggs you are likely to see will be in the pack-lunches of these walkers.

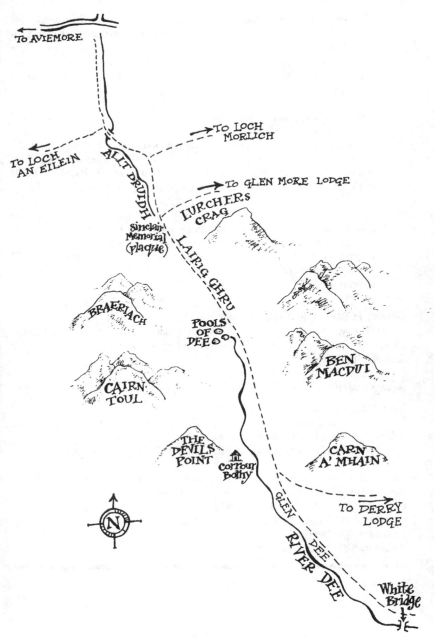

TO AVIEMORE

TO LOCH MORLICH

TO LOCH AN EILEIN

ALLT DRUIDH

TO GLEN MORE LODGE

LURCHERS CRAG

Sinclair Memorial (plaque)

LAIRIG GHRU

BRAERIACH

POOLS OF DEE

BEN MACDUI

CAIRN TOUL

THE DEVILS POINT

Corrour Bothy

CARN A' MHAIN

N

GLEN DEE

TO DERRY LODGE

RIVER DEE

White Bridge

From the White Bridge take the path which heads north-west along the east bank of the River Dee. The path continues for about 9 km towards the southern end of the Cairngorm plateaux and the Devil's Point, which appears from this viewpoint as a 1000m pyramid of rock. At the base of the Devil's Point is the Corrour Bothy which is a basic hut with a fireplace but sadly there is no wood to burn.

This is also the point where walkers from Braemar via the Linn of Dee and Derry Lodge enter the Lairig Ghru. The path becomes strewn with boulders which means good practice for those wishing to develop their hopping skills. The path ascends gently to the top of the Lairig Ghru where the River Dee suddenly disappears beneath a massive pile of rocks and boulders. The Pools of Dee, which are slightly above this point, signify the source of the river.

From now on it's downhill all the way to Aviemore, go past the now demolished Sinclair Memorial Hut and into the forest. The path is well sign-posted and continues in a north-westerly direction all the way to Coylumbridge. When you get to the road turn left (west) and walk the final 2 km into Aviemore where you can contemplate your next action-packed adventure.

Getting to Blair Atholl and Aviemore:
There is a regular coach and train service to Blair Atholl from Edinburgh and Glasgow via Stirling and Perth. These same services also continue north to Aviemore and on to Inverness.

Accommodation:

Blair Atholl Caravan Park (see Blair Atholl).
There are reasonable rough camping spots throughout Glen Tilt particularly at the Falls of Tarf then further on at the Bynack ruin.
Braemar SYHA, Braemar Bunkhouse and Inverey SYHA (see Braemar).

There are no good camping places on the Lairig Ghru path but there are good spots near the Derry Lodge Bothy (O.S. Sheet 43 Ref: 042934).
Corrour Bothy (O.S. Sheet 43 Ref: 981958).
Glen Morlich SYHA (see Strathspey and Badenoch).
Coylumbridge Campsite.
Aviemore SYHA (see Aviemore).

4. Inverness Area

Set around the shallow, salty waters of the Moray Firth and the deep, pure waters of Loch Ness is a thriving and picturesque area where the rich farmlands typical of the east meet the hillside crofts of the west. The sea laps gently up to quiet villages, busy towns and along rocky shores which give way, sometimes, to sandy beaches. Inland, the wild mountains roll down past lochs and rivers to this gentle coastline. The area is also well known for its castles and remarkable wildlife and these combined with comparatively mild weather and low rainfall make the area ideal for exploration.

Inverness

The River Ness, after its short journey from the famous loch, meets the sea at the busy and prosperous Highland town of Inverness. With its grassy banks below old stone buildings, the river gives the town a grand and spacious feel, while the views of the nearby hills and distant mountains serve as a reminder of the beautiful countryside over which Inverness rules as the capital of the Highlands. Its proximity to Loch Ness inevitably fills the town with keen Nessie-hunters while the locals simply look on their monster-searching visitors with an air of bemusement. The town centre, with its network of streets and alleys, is at times overwhelmingly busy with shoppers and strollers enjoying the bustle, but despite the crowds the people still keep their genuine Highland friendliness. If it gets too much for you, just nip down to the riverbank or up to the castle and enjoy the atmosphere in peace. If you're travelling in the Highlands, you'll find the town virtually unavoidable as it has many essentials to offer. For example - vast supermarkets to stock up in, a range of banks, good budget accommodation, extensive bus and train connections and, especially desirable in winter with those long, dark evenings, Inverness has a nightlife - theatre, cinema, live music, nightclubs and many pubs.

Around the centre there are a variety of buildings to visit. Although **Inverness Castle** is relatively youthful, dating from 1834, it is from this vantage point that Inverness can best be admired. Outside is a statue of Flora MacDonald, Bonnie Prince Charlie's faithful ally and during the summer months you can enter a small part of the castle to see the **Castle Garrison Encounter**, which takes a soldier's eye view of the Battle of Culloden; £3. The **Town House** on Bridge Street can be entered for a look at its many elegant features, but remember these are the local council offices and some rooms may be in use. On the pavement outside is the 'Clach Na Cuddain', a stone where women carrying water from the river would sit their buckets for a rest. There is a free **Museum and Art Gallery** behind the Town House, which has social and natural history exhibits of the Highlands as well as visiting displays. If you have an interest in folk music, head across the river to **Balnain House** in Huntly St, open daily; £2.50/£2. Inside is an excellent museum taking a modern approach to a traditional subject - it may be your one and only chance to play the bagpipes. It is often the venue for many professional performances, usually £3-£5 - phone ahead for details, tel:(01463) 715757. They have a good cafe and a free music session every Thursday night with the possibility of more sessions during the summer.

Walks

There are some great walks from the centre. The one along the **Ness Islands** is a must and is very short and easy. Start on the riverbank underneath the castle and head upstream, ignore the first bridge, but after that cross the small bridges connecting the islands. On the other side you could look for the **Bught Floral Hall**, a greenhouse containing a wide range of sub-tropical plants in Bught Park. The design and lay-out, although small, is very pretty with the walkway passing a waterfall, ponds and palm trees. Fish lovers will find the school of overweight carp friendly enough to stroke - even tickle under the chin (count your fingers afterwards). Free entry. Afterwards

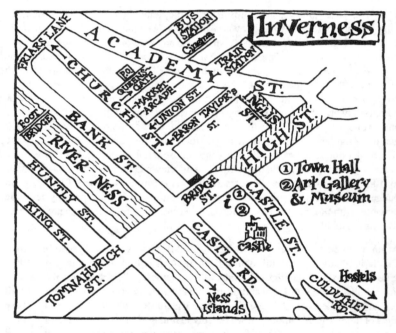

have a cup of coffee and watch the nature videos in the visitor centre. You can also carry on up to the oak-covered hill in **Tomnahurich cemetery**. There's a terrific view from the top amongst the gravestones. Another sweeping view of the town is from the site of the Pictish fort on **Craig Phadraig** hill. To get there you have to cross the **Caledonian Canal**, along which there is also a pleasant walk (the birdsong can be quite deafening here at dusk in springtime). You can follow the canal to the sea at Clachnaharry and there's a good pub there too. Dolphins can sometimes be seen should you take a wander over the **Kessock** bridge, as a large number live in the Moray Firth (see **Dolphins**).

i **Tourist Information**, tel:(01463) 234353, is above Bridge Street on Castle Wynd. Open daily, closed Sundays in winter, it usually shuts at 5pm or 6pm but in the very height of summer stays open till 8.30pm.

Inverness Student (and Backpackers) Hotel, 8 Culduthel Rd, tel: (01463) 236556, £8.50/£9.90, friendly and intimate atmosphere with a fire and an unsurpassed view over the river. Curfew 2.30am, 5 minutes' walk from the town centre. Linen supplied. Open all year.

Bazpackers, 4 Culduthel Road, tel:(01463) 717663, £8.50/£12. Small, quiet hostel with twin rooms. Open all year.

Inverness SYHA, 1 Old Edinburgh Rd, tel:(01463) 231771, Grade 1, £8.60/£11.10, functional but not welcoming. Curfew 1.45am. Located opposite the Student Hotel. Open all year.

Eastgate Hostel, 38 Eastgate, tel:(01463) 718756, £8.90, at the top of the High Street shopping mall. Twin rooms available. Open all year.

Ho Ho Hostel, 23a High St, tel:(01463) 221225, £8.50/£9.50. New comfortable hostel in the town centre.

Bught Campsite, tel:(01463) 236920, one mile from the town centre heading upriver and over the sports fields. Very cheap. Open April-October.

There are many **B&Bs** all over town, but the least expensive seem to be in the area behind the SYHA hostel.

TOURS FROM INVERNESS

There is a myriad of tour operators working in the Inverness area. Bookings can be made for all of those listed below at Tourist Information so this is the best place to go for up-to-date timetables and prices.

Loch Ness Tours

Remember that many of the full-day tours will take you to other places, not just Loch Ness, so ask for details. All tours pick up from outside Tourist Information.

Inverness Traction, tel:(01463) 239292. Full-day bus tour £9.50. Their half-day trip goes by boat to Urquhart Castle and then takes you back to Inverness by bus for £6. They also have a Loch Ness and distillery tour for £7. In winter a £7.75 coach tour is available only.

Peter Forbes Tours, tel:(01463) 236719. Full-day £8.50/£7.50, half-day £5.50/£5. Half-day trips only in winter. Friendly Peter Forbes runs flexible and informative tours at a good price.

Loch Ness Mini-Tours, tel:(01456) 450325. Tours run from Easter-October, 10am-2.15pm and 2.30pm-6.20pm, £5/£6.

Jacobite Coach and Cruise Tours, tel:(01463) 233999. Combined coach and cruise tours at 10am and 2pm everyday throughout the summer; £11.50/£9 (includes admission to castle and monster exhibition). Check their flexible timetables as it is

possible to spend a few hours at the castle and Drumnadrochit area. They also have a one-way ticket to Urquhart Castle which is good for anyone who is travelling on; £9/£7 (includes admission to Urquhart Castle).
Ken White's Tours, tel:(01463) 223168, operates all year. Full-day £9/£8, half-day £6/£5.

Other Tours

Guide Friday open-top buses, tel:(01463) 224000. Regular buses from mid-May to September with a jump-on, jump-off option taking you on a tour of Inverness and out to the battlefield at Culloden; £6/£4.50. Tourist Information pick-up.
Spa Coach Tours, tel:(01997) 421311. From June to September every day except Saturday, they have tours going to a different area of the Highlands each day so check their brochure. Prices are between £12 and £16 and leave as early as 8am from the Inverness bus station.
John O'Groats Ferries, tel:(01955) 611353. For a quick look at Orkney, their day trip tour costs £40, runs from June to 6 September and leaves Inverness bus station at 7.30am. (For a longer stay they also have the Orkney Bus leaving at 2.20pm daily, May-6 September, £37 return).

Dolphin Boat-trips

Before taking one of these tours ascertain what is the best time of day to see the dolphins as some boats sail regardless of the tide and likelihood of seeing any.

Moray Firth Cruises, tel:(01463) 232120, £10/£8, 5 tours a day in summer from March to end October. Departures from Inverness harbour on Shore St.
McAuley Charters, tel:(01463) 225398. Daily, every hour and a half from Easter to October. Leaves from Inverness harbour; £10/£8. Courtesy bus from town centre.
Dolphin Ecosse, tel:(01381) 600323. Their tours actually leave from Cromarty on the Black Isle; £15, all year.

Food and Drink

For cheap and hearty meals you won't find any better than at the **Castle Restaurant** on Castle St, last bastion of the crinkle-cut chip. Open daily from 8am-8.30pm. At lunchtime many pubs serve a pub lunch and for 'fast' type food at lunchtime, forget the multinationals and go to **Anne's Take Away** in the Market arcade off Church St - North Europeans, they serve chips with mayonnaise! The **Jade Garden** on the High St has Chinese take away meals at an excellent price, while **Nico's** on Haugh Rd serves filling but much more expensive meals in the evening.
For a drink, **Blackfriars** and **Lafferty's** on Academy St are both great pubs and sometimes have folk music playing, and good too are **Jock Tamsin's** and **The '45**, nearby on Rose St. **Johnny Fox's** on Bank St, has live music every night and is open until 1am. The pick for live music lovers, however, is the beautifully unpretentious **Market Bar**, which is at its best late in the evenings (in the Market Arcade off Church St, the upstairs bar). The **Gellions** on Bridge St occasionally has music, as does the **Glenalbyn** on the other side of the river.

If you feel like dancing try the nightclub **Blue** between the bus station and the Safeway supermarket (open until 1.30am). **Mr G's** nightclub on Castle Street is a poor second.

Inverness has two major supermarkets, **Safeway**, near the Bus Station and **Tesco,** across the river on King Street. There is also a small supermarket, **Barney's** on Castle Street which is open until 10.30pm daily.

Entertainment

Apart from Balnain House for live folk music, the other major venue for touring artists is the **Eden Court Theatre**, located on the riverbank. An events programme is available from Tourist Information as well as the venue itself. They also have a cinema screen with a changing programme of films. The **La Scala** Cinema on Strothers Lane near the bus station has mainstream releases.

Inverness' **Aquadome** in Bught Park has a wave lagoon, flumes and a swimming pool if you're looking for something different to do.

USEFUL ADDRESSES

TRAIN STATION
Academy St, tel:0345-484950 (24hr service). Left luggage facilities.
BUS STATION
Farraline Park off Academy St, tel:(01463) 233371. Open 8.30am-6pm, Mon-Sat,10am-6pm Sun. From 8am-8pm bus information is available on tel:0990 505050.
BANKS
Bank of Scotland, 9 High St. Open 9.15am-4.45pm Mon-Fri.
Royal Bank of Scotland, 38 Academy St. Open 9.15am-4.45pm Mon-Fri.
Clydesdale Bank, 15 Academy St. Open 9.15am-4pm M, T, W, F, and until 5.30pm Thursdays.
FOREIGN EXCHANGE
Usually more expensive than the banks is the foreign exchange service at Tourist Information on Castle Wynd (open daily but closed Sundays in winter). If they are closed a hotel might change money, but it will usually be even more expensive.
CAR RENTAL
Arnold Clark Car Hire, Harbour Road, tel:(01463) 713322. £18 daily/£101 weekly. Ask about any special deals they may have available. Minimum age 23 years.
Sharps Car Hire, 1st Floor, Highland Rail House, Station Square, Academy St, tel:(01463) 236684. £24 daily/£135 weekly. Outside the train station. Minimum age 23 years.
BICYCLE RENTAL
Great Glen Cycle Hire, Bught Caravan Park, tel: (01468) 627414. Summer months only.
CAMPING SHOPS
Graham Tiso's, 4 High St.

 Hitching from Inverness - see **Hitching**, Chapter 17.

Loch Ness

Lurking a few miles upstream from Inverness in the peaty waters of Loch Ness is that most famous of monsters, Nessie, a photograph of whom is essential for any holiday album. There was first talk of a monster in the loch's deep, dark waters in the 6thC. Since then Nessie has teased us by making only the occasional discreet appearance. What's more, the advent of photography seems to have blurred rather than clarified the monster debate. People travel from all over the world in search of her. The Italian air force claimed to have bombed her during the last war - an act that hasn't yet been forgiven by the locals (if you're Italian they can usually be placated by a glass of whisky). Monster-hunting is easy and open to anyone with a well-developed sense of patience. It is also an excellent excuse to spend some quality time on the pretty banks of this immense stretch of water - Loch Ness holds more H_2O than all the rivers and lakes of England put together. Travelling around the loch from Inverness on the North shore, the busy A82 passes more or less lochside for a few miles, culminating in a fabulous view of Urquhart Castle,

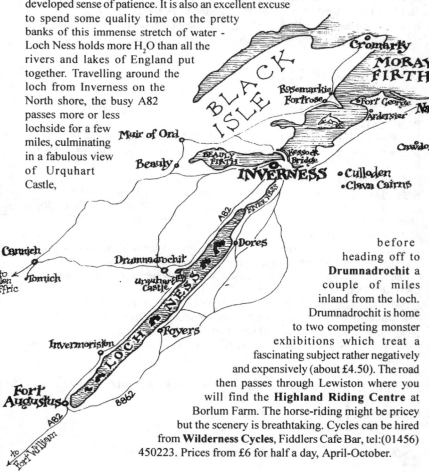

before heading off to **Drumnadrochit** a couple of miles inland from the loch. Drumnadrochit is home to two competing monster exhibitions which treat a fascinating subject rather negatively and expensively (about £4.50). The road then passes through Lewiston where you will find the **Highland Riding Centre** at Borlum Farm. The horse-riding might be pricey but the scenery is breathtaking. Cycles can be hired from **Wilderness Cycles**, Fiddlers Cafe Bar, tel:(01456) 450223. Prices from £6 for half a day, April-October.

Loch Ness Backpackers Lodge, East Lewiston by Drumnadrochit, tel:(01456) 450807, about one mile from the Loch, offers very comfortable hostel accommodation for £8.50/£9. Open all year.

The monster spotter's mecca of **Urquhart Castle** is one of Scotland's most popular ruins. Whether it's the best is debatable; £3.50/£2.80, HS. If you don't want to go in there are points on the road from where you can get a good view of the castle, and it is particularly beautiful when lit up at night. The castle seems to have been doomed to ruination almost since the day it was built, with its history reading more like a repair schedule. The repairs, started in 1398, weren't helped by the castle being blown up in 1689 and its owners finally gave up in 1912.

Heading on, the often busy, twisting road has only occasional views to the loch, and if you want to snap Nessie it's best to stop for a while at some of the many lay-bys. Ten miles from Urquhart Castle is the **Loch Ness SYHA**, tel:(01320) 351274, Grade 2, £6.10/£7.60, open 20/3-31/10. This is the place to stay for serious monster spotters as it is the only shore-side hostel. **Invermoriston**, three miles further on where the road to Skye branches west, is a great place to stop. If you stand on the bridge where the main road crosses the River Moriston and look upstream, you'll see another quaint ruined bridge over the rushing, cascading water; downstream, you'll see a stone hut perched on the rocky bank. Find the path and walk down past this hut, as it's a lovely stroll leading towards the loch.

At the bottom end of Loch Ness sits **Fort Augustus**, a pleasant cheerful place and the most interesting of all Loch Ness' towns. There is a historic abbey on the riverbank and cutting through the village are the locks of the Caledonian Canal. Built in the 19thC, the canal effectively sliced the mainland of Scotland in two by linking the east and west coasts nautically. In summer Fort Augustus is buzzing with many people, some watching the action as the boats go up and down the canal locks, others strolling to the lochside to see Nessie. There are boat trips, mountain bikes for hire and some great biking routes to take. There are also some good walks along the canal or up the River Oich. For the serious walker, take the Corrieyairack Pass to Laggan, while Nessie hunters should start out along the Foyers Road. After a few minutes you will see a way to the loch through a gate. Take this path, then wander along the shore for possibly the best views of Loch Ness.

You could see the **Fort Augustus Abbey** and its 'Exhibition of the Scottish Highlander' but it would set you back £5/£2.50, open all year. Headphones are issued for the tour and although informative, it's perhaps a little boring. The **Clansmen Centre**, beside the canal, is a bit more lively. Within a recreated turf-house they give a 20-minute talk on traditional Highland life. It costs £2.50/£2 to enter and afterwards for another £3.50/£3 you can dress up as a Highlander yourself and get a great photo to show off to your friends at home. Open April-October, daily until 5pm and from June to August they're open until 8pm.

Fort Augustus has quite a choice of cafes and pub meals for such a small town, and for a drink, the **Lock Inn** on the canal is usually a merry place.

Bike hire is available from the **Loch Ness Ferry Company**, tel:mobile 0802-232451 or (01320) 366579, £10 a day, £6 a half-day, £4 for 2 hours. They also run 50-minute cruises up Loch Ness, £4/£3.25, which depart from the pier in the abbey grounds. Another company called **Cruise Loch Ness**, tel:(01320) 366221/277, runs one-hour tours from near the canal bridge for £4.50.

i **Tourist Information** is open from April-October, tel:(01320) 366367. They have maps of the town and of walks in the area.

Fort Augustus Abbey Backpackers Lodge, tel:(01320) 366233, open April-October, £8-£9. Small, comfortable rooms and a bible by every bed. There is also the **Loch Ness Lodges Bunkhouse** attached to the good value 'Bothy Bite' restaurant, tel:(01320) 366710, open all year, £7.50 (no kitchen). There are several **B&Bs** or there's the **Fort Augustus Campsite**, tel: (01320) 366618/360, just south of the town on the A82, open May-September, £3.

After Fort Augustus if you take the B862 and B852 along the east side of Loch Ness, you'll notice that things are a lot quieter. You can sigh with relief knowing that you have escaped from the hordes of holidaymakers swarming around the well-laid tourist traps on the north-west shore. Here on the east side the occasional shops and pubs, primarily serving the local communities, have a little more time for their customers. At first, the quiet road sweeps away from the loch through hilly moorland to Whitebridge. Beyond Whitebridge all the way to Inverness there is a network of tiny roads twisting through charming countryside from which you can take your pick. If you choose to head back down to the loch at **Foyers**, stop at the village store and walk to the spectacular waterfall.

There is very comfortable accommodation in Foyers at the **Backpackers Bunkhouse**, Foyers House, tel:(01456) 486405. £8/£12, cooked breakfast at extra cost, bar and all-day menu, open all year.

As the loch-side road continues to Dores, more Nessie-spotting can be done at frequent lay-bys right on the shore. At **Dores** the road leaves Loch Ness behind, so why not pull in at the car park beside the Dores Inn, stroll down to the lochside amongst the ducks and wave goodbye to Nessie (it's not a bad pub either). Then it's time to race back to Inverness to get the snaps developed.

THE COAST AND HINTERLAND

There are some excellent day-trips from Inverness. Cycling to some of these is definitely an option but public transport is frequent enough, however check timetables for the last bus back.

Culloden Battlefield, five miles to the east of Inverness, is the site of one of Scotland's most famous battles. It's a boggish moor (much boggier in 1745 than now) and, most experts agree, a foolish place to hold a battle. However that's where Prince Charles Edward Stuart (or Bonnie Prince Charlie) wanted it and so it was. The battle was over in less than an hour, 1,200 of the Prince's followers were killed and Charlie spent the next five months on the run from the authorities. Not a great hero, Bonnie Prince Charlie said to his army words to the effect of 'every man for himself' as he headed off. The site is quite an eerie and sombre place to walk around and is free. There's also a well-presented display and audio-visual show inside the visitor centre,

(open February-December) which costs £3/£2, NTS, and there's a coffee shop.
Not well signposted, but less than a mile from the battlefield are the **Clava Cairns**, excellent stone circles and cairns dating back to around 2000 BC. If you haven't seen any stone circles while in Scotland, here's an easy opportunity to see an impressive three; free entry. To get to the cairns, as you leave the Culloden visitor centre car park turn right and you will soon see a signpost.

Cawdor Castle is one of Scotland's most popular castles mainly due to its connection with Shakespeare's play 'Macbeth'. The three witches correctly predicted that Macbeth would become Thane of Glamis, then Thane of Cawdor and finally King of Scotland. Shakespeare used his artistic licence in his retelling of Macbeth's life (Macbeth never lived here), but this is a splendid castle to visit, nevertheless. It is reached across a drawbridge and with beautiful gardens and nature trails, you could easily spend a few hours around the grounds. Open daily 1/5-11/10; £5.20/£4.20.

On the coast past Ardersier is **Fort George**, a post-Culloden fortification from a time when King George was determined never to be troubled by the Scots again. It's ideal as part of a cycle route for the area, but unless you're interested in things military, you may not want to pay the £3/£2.30 to enter; HS. The fully restored 17thC **Castle Stuart** should also be included on a cycle tour. There are informative guided tours for £4.50/£3.50 if you'd like a look inside; open daily May-September.

The Black Isle

The **Black Isle** is not actually as dark and mysterious as it sounds (it's not black and is not even an island), but don't be put off as it contains the lovely Cromarty. **Cromarty** is one of those rare towns where little seems to have changed in 200 years. You should head first for the **Cromarty Courthouse Museum** on Church Street. It has a good display on life in the area and of prison and courtroom history relating to the building. Chat with the late, shifty-eyed Sir Thomas Urquhart. Included in the museum's entry price is 'A Walkman Guide to Cromarty' - something different. In this, another late local, the geologist and author Hugh Miller (not as famous as he once was) takes you around the town imparting his knowledge of it. Make sure you stick with the tour and go up the hill to the old cemetery. The museum and walkman tour cost £3/£2 and should keep you well occupied for a couple of hours; open March-December.
Hugh Miller's Cottage is for those with an interest in geology, as there is a brilliant fossil collection inside; £2/£1.30, NTS, open May-September.
If you want to go for a country walk here, you can go to the South Sutor headland, where there's an excellent view and a 406ft drop. Carry on up the road past the old cemetery and at the Cromarty Mains Farm turn left. It's only a mile or so from the cemetery and is fairly easy. Take your museum walkman with you and pick up the tour on your return - check what time the museum closes though.
Dolphin Ecosse runs boat trips in search of dolphins from Cromarty, tel:(01381) 600323, £15. They have a high success rate and are informative and friendly. They also provide B&B accommodation or you can camp in their garden.
The **Cromarty Arms** has bar snacks and, of course, plenty to drink, while the **Royal**

Hotel at the harbour has bar meals at lunchtime. Buses to Cromarty leave Inverness about four times a day, £6.15 day return.

On the way to Cromarty you can stop at **Fortrose** (if you like dolphins or cathedrals) or **Rosemarkie** (if you like walking). Fortrose Cathedral is a fine ruin made of the local pinkish sandstone. Afterwards go through the town's coastal golf course to Chanonry Point for some dolphin-watching, often with results (see **Dolphins**).

From Rosemarkie there's a lovely, easy walk up into the Fairy Glen and another along the coast. If you're driving or cycling in this area, stop by the strange spring near Munlochy. It's a weird place - you have to see it to believe it. Garments are hung there by people who believe that as the fabric decomposes they themselves will recover from whatever ailments they are troubled with.

Dolphins

There are many dolphins in Scottish waters but by far the most visible and well-known are the Moray Firth dolphins. There are well over 100 bottle-nosed dolphins in this bay, and they are not only the world's most northerly, but they are also the largest at up to four metres long. They are completely wild, not in the least interested in or pampered by humans, and it is heartening to see them thriving so close to human technology. The easiest place to see them is under Inverness' Kessock Bridge - South Kessock is only 20 minutes' walk from the centre of Inverness or you could cycle or bus to North Kessock as here there is a cafe overlooking the firth. The best time is between three and one hours before high tide (find out when this is from Tourist Information) as they feed on the incoming fish-filled waters. The dolphins seem to spend as much time just playing around as hunting for fish, pairs often jumping clear of the water in unison. A few miles north-east near Fortrose, Chanonry Point offers perhaps the best place to watch wild dolphins on this planet. About five dolphins at a time can come quite close as they swim by the lighthouse. They usually swim by in pulses up to an hour apart from low tide onwards for about five hours (until near high tide). From here it is also possible to see many other rare or interesting species - harbour porpoises, arctic skuas, guillemots (similar to tiny penguins) and many seals. Even minke whales have been sighted. Although dolphins are present year-round, they are much more common in the summer months and in good weather, but you can never be certain of seeing them at any time of year.

Nairn & Findhorn

For those travelling by rail (you can take the bus too) who like the beach, head east to Nairn or Findhorn. **Nairn** is a quiet town with some nice sandy beaches. You can also take a walk up the river and check out the harbour. **Findhorn,** 4 miles from Forres station, is an interesting place. Geographically, it sits between the calm Findhorn Bay and the wilder Moray Firth; culturally, it sits between an air force base and the New Age Findhorn community. The village of Findhorn is a very picturesque place and the beach, a 10-mile band of silver, is really quite breathtaking as you watch it curve almost over the horizon to Burghead.

Living in perfect harmony with itself, the **Findhorn Foundation** is a popular pilgrimage for spiritual beings. Visitors can join in the community's activities - you pay £12 for a day, working for the community with meals provided. If you wish to stay overnight you can, but at an extra price. Phone ahead for details; tel:(01309) 690311.

Cannich & Glen Affric

Further from Inverness, located 12 miles east of Drumnadrochit, is the small village of **Cannich,** which is unremarkable really, except for the magnificent walking (and cycling) opportunities it presents, particularly into beautiful **Glen Affric,** one of Scotland's most picturesque glens, which contains large areas of Scotland's ancient pine woods. A worthwhile detour in this area is to the splendid **Plodda Falls,** 150m high and five miles away near Tomich.

Cannich is also a functional location with two establishments offering backpacker accommodation. Situated right nextdoor to each other are the **Glen Affric Backpackers Hostel,** tel:(01456) 415263, £5/£6.50 (with a games room and open January-November), and the **Cannich SYHA hostel,** tel:(01456) 415244, £6.10/£7.60, open 20/3-31/10. Bike hire is available at the caravan site near the hostels; tel:(01456) 415364, April-October, £10 a full day/£5 a half-day.

Buses to Cannich leave Inverness several times a day and a few of these go further inland to the hamlet of Tomich. This brings you closer to the Plodda Falls (3 miles away) as well as the remote independent hostel **Cougie Lodge,** located 6 miles from Tomich. The hostel's not fancy, it's homey, and you might just want to stay a few days; £7.50/£8.50, open April-October, no telephone, but you can leave messages or get information from tel:(01456) 414212. Bring supplies as the nearest shop is in Cannich and the nearest pub food in Tomich. (See **Walks in Glen Affric.**)

Strathpeffer

The discovery of spring waters at Strathpeffer (about 15 miles north-west of Inverness) turned this once quiet village into a hugely popular resort last century, during the reign of Queen Victoria. The grandiose Victorian architecture remains for the most part, and Strathpeffer makes an idyllic and charming base. Although the original Spa Pavilion and Pump Room are private property, you can still taste the mineral waters today. This can be done at the very centre of town at the **Water**

Tasting Pavilion, located where the spa baths once were, (open April-October). Afterwards, wander down the main street and on the right you will find the **Highland Museum of Childhood**, located in the delightful Victorian Railway Station which is sadly no longer in use. The museum depicts Highland conditions, traditions and superstitions relating to childhood; £1.50/£1, open mid-March-October. There is a cafe just next door, open from April-October, and some craft and gift shops. Back up the road and to the right, you'll see a sign to the **Eagle Stone**, an engraved Pictish stone dating from the 7thC. If the stone should fall while you're there, look out - the 17thC prophet, the Brahan Seer, predicted that if the stone should fall three times (it's apparently happened twice already) then ships will come sailing up the valley toward it.

The youth hostel at the top of the main road marks the beginning of walks through Blackmuir Wood and you can also walk to Loch Ussie to the south. Tourist Information sell a pamphlet, 'Walks around Strathpeffer', detailing them.

Another walk starts near the hostel. The footpath marked 'To Garve, 7 miles', will take you past Loch Kinellan to View Rock or on to the **Falls of Rogie** (about 4 miles from Strathpeffer).

Although Strathpeffer's quite a busy little centre with several hotels, there is no bank, so arrange your finances before you get here. Buses leave from Inverness - either the local Inverness Traction service or the Scottish Citylink bus to Ullapool (not all Ullapool buses stop here so check first).

i Strathpeffer's friendly **Tourist Information** is right in the centre of town, tel:(01997) 421415, open April-October.

Strathpeffer SYHA, tel:(01997) 421532, £6.10/£7.60, Grade 2, open 27/2-31/10. This hostel is up the hill from the bus stop.

WALKS IN GLEN AFFRIC

DIFFICULT

Affric is one of the most popular glens in Scotland for walkers and sightseers and it's hardly any wonder, considering that it's the site of one of the largest and most ancient Caledonian pine forests remaining in the country. At one time this great forest extended as far east as Braemar and south to Rannoch Moor. The mountain scenery is also superb, and there are many magnificent waterfalls and much wildlife.

Most people travel to Glen Affric from the east via Cannich and many drive almost as far as Loch Affric itself. Fortunately for walkers who want to get away from the traffic, there is an alternative route - coming into the glen from the south and staying over at the remote independent hostel at Cougie. From here it is possible to walk through Glen Affric to the youth hostel at Allt Beithe and then on to Shiel Bridge, thus avoiding having to carry a tent. There is another youth hostel near Shiel Bridge at Ratagan. The route is very isolated and during wet weather some of the river crossings will be difficult and sometimes dangerous. You will need to carry all of your food with you on the trip as there are no shops en route, although at Cougie Lodge you may be able to get dairy products.

Getting to Ceannacroc Bridge

Ceannacroc Bridge (O.S. Sheet 34; 225106) is 1.5km east of Bun Loyne Junction where the Inverness and Fort William roads to Skye merge (the A87 and A887). If you travel by bus, get off at Bun Loyne junction if you're on the Fort William/Glasgow route to Skye, or at the Ceannacroc bridge itself if you're on the Inverness route (but ask the driver nicely as it's not a normal stop).

Day 1 - Ceannacroc Bridge to Cougie

Distance : 15km (approx. 4-5 hours)
Map : O.S. Landranger 34 and 25

Start on the west side of the road bridge and follow the track on the left side of the river. There is a sign for the Ceannacroc Estate, a power station and B&B. The beginning of this walk is quite interesting - there is a charming old stone bridge across the river and a peculiar tunnel from which the river appears. Continue through to the B&B and follow the track, which rises slightly, along the left side of the River Doe. The scenery here is disturbed somewhat by the pipes and dams which are a part of the power station, but this is soon left behind and is compensated for by the waterfalls and patches of Caledonian Pine encountered along the route.

After 5km the track leads to a grassy flood plain where there is a river crossing and the path heads north along the western flank of Meall Damh, a gently sloping and heathery hill. The river crossing is where a length of wire is tied to trees on either bank. You can cross using the wire if you like, but unless you are an expert gymnast you will probably get your feet wet. The alternative is to hop across on the rocks slightly upstream. The path climbs gradually beneath the crags of Creag nan Gobhar and across wild and boggy moorland. Although this is a wild place it is far from being desolate. There is a rich variety of plants and mosses, some of which are coloured a deep scarlet. After about 5km you will be at the top of the moor and will have a view down the valley towards the Guisachan Forest. Follow the path to the edge of the forest, go through the gate and continue another 3km to Cougie. The forest in this area is a mixture of modern Forestry Commission plantation and the remains of the older Caledonian pine forest. The river which the path follows cuts deep into the forest floor and in many places leaves the path high above.

Cougie is a small hamlet of just a few houses. The first of these is Cougie Lodge which is a small and friendly independent hostel which makes an ideal stopping place for backpackers (see **Cannich**). The forest around is vast, there is a nature reserve nearby and the pretty Plodda Falls are within easy walking distance.

Day 2 - Cougie to Allt Beithe Youth Hostel via Loch Affric
Distance : 18km (approx. 5-6 hours)
Map : O.S. Landranger 25

Turn right out of the Cougie Lodge hostel, taking the track heading due west. After 3km you will leave the forest where there is a small loch. The track descends to cross a river over a makeshift bridge before climbing gently and undulating along the side of the valley. After another 3km a stunning view of Glen Affric, the loch, mountains and forest opens out.

At this point an old oil drum marks where a path cuts off right (north), down towards the glen (this can be a bit confusing as there are two oil drums around here). Follow this path down a short way on the right-hand side of a wire fence. When you get down to the tree line turn right, follow the narrow path along the river for about 30 metres to a gap in the fence and an easy one-step crossing of the Allt Garbh burn. Continue with this path down stream on the left (west) bank of the river. This part of the Caledonian pine forest is particularly spacious and gracious and provides a natural habitat for many creatures - otters live in the rivers here.

After 1km the path comes to a single track road. Turn left here and walk along the south shore of Loch Affric. The mountains surrounding this area are very imposing. They are rounded in shape and have long ridges and spurs stretching in many directions. At the end of the loch follow the track towards the white house with a red roof, cross the bridge and continue west out along the wide glen for another 5½km to the Allt Beithe Youth Hostel.

The Glen Affric SYHA hostel, **Allt Beithe** (£5.65, no telephone), is one of the most remote youth hostels in Scotland and is only properly open in the summer from 20/3-31/10. It is, however, kept unlocked and so can be used by walkers during the winter, although recent vandalism threatens this winter opening policy. As there is little other accommodation nearby you may wish

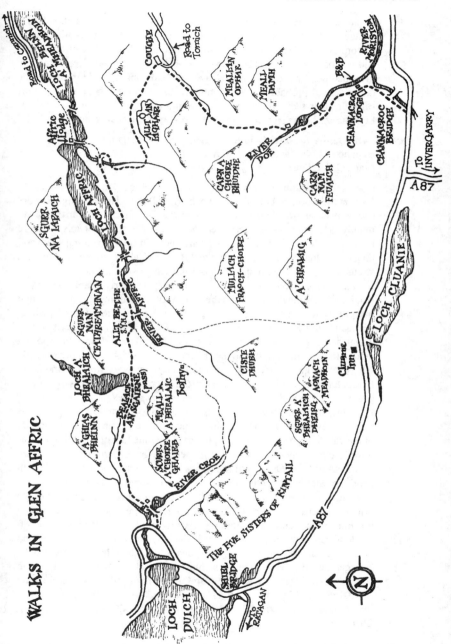

WALKS IN GLEN AFFRIC

to check that the hostel can still be used outside the summer months by contacting the SYHA in advance. The hostel is in a superb location at the bottom of Glen Affric and locked in by mountains from all sides. It's small and compact but does have an extra out-house and so can sleep fifteen or more people. A good tip is not to leave any food lying around for too long or the mice will probably eat it - definitely don't let them get anything with sugar in it or they will be running around all night keeping you awake. Lighting and heating is made possible by windmills and gas cooking is available.

Day 3 - Allt Beithe to Shiel Bridge via Bealach an Sgairne

Distance : 17km (approx. 5-6 hours)
Map : O.S. Landranger 33

Continue west along the track by the youth hostel for 1km to where the path forks at the wooden footbridge. Take the right fork and head along the more northerly of the two glens. (For 5km to Loch a' Bhealaich this is an extremely muddy path/track and in very wet conditions it would probably be more pleasant to follow the more distinct path from Allt Beithe heading south and then north along the River Croe to Shiel Bridge.) Halfway along this northern stretch is the ruined remains of an old settlement which used to be a small croft and which would have had cattle to graze on the riverbank. When you reach Loch a' Bhealaich, follow the path around its southern shore, through the grassy moraines towards the gap between the mountains Meall a' Bhealaich and A'Ghlas bheinn. This is the Bealach an Sgairne pass, which despite looking quite steep only takes 10 minutes to climb. This is an imposing mountain pass - narrow, surrounded by rocky crags and, it seems, permanently windy. From here it is virtually downhill all the way to Morvich and Shiel Bridge and the views are dominated by the steep and jagged cliffs of Sgurr a' Choire Ghairbh and the deep valley from which it rises.

From the top of the pass the path zigzags down to a waterfall where there is a narrow river-crossing on stepping stones. It then continues along the side of the valley, high above the river, towards the pine forest. A few kilometres down the path opens out onto more open and grassy land where there are views out to Loch Duich and the ridges of the mountains behind. The path continues along the south bank of the river to some white houses where it goes through a gap in the dry-stone wall towards a bridge. Cross over the bridge and turn right along the single track road. The road goes past bed and breakfast places and the Kintail Outdoor Centre to a T-junction. Turn left and left again at the main road and walk the last 2km past a cafe on the left and later a hotel and bar on the right to the bus stop in Shiel Bridge. This is at the cafe/garage which is open in the summer for a well-deserved cup of tea and slice of cake. There is a **SYHA hostel** a couple of miles away at Ratagan (tel:(01599) 511243, £7.75/£9.25, open all year except 4/1-28/1) if you're intending to stay overnight. The nearest town with all amenities is Kyle of Lochalsh.

5.The Far North

The route north to Orkney follows the eastern coastline of Sutherland and Caithness which few people take the time to stop and explore. While not as magnificent as the mountainous and awe-inspiring landscape of the west coast, there are several places of interest to break up your journey before arriving at the northerly towns of Wick and Thurso.

The north coast has many gems; Tongue, a small village in delightful surroundings, for example, and the remarkable Smoo Cave, as well as some of Scotland's most attractive and isolated sandy beaches.

Away from the coastline, Sutherland is a landscape of lonely, undulating moorland with distant mountains and lazy rivers. It is also home to the very popular SYHA hostel, Carbisdale Castle, and is quite possibly the most remote part of mainland Scotland.

Carbisdale Castle

After watching your holiday money carefully, it can come as a total relief to know that for less than £14 you can stay in a castle. Although built earlier this century and more resembling a mansion than a castle, it is still impressive, with statues and paintings decorating the interior and lending it a grand air. All typical SYHA rules and regulations apply, however, which quickly brings you back down to earth. The hostel is located quarter of a mile from Culrain train station. Tel:(01549) 421232, Grade 1, late access, £11.50/£14 (includes continental breakfast), open 27/2-3/5 and 14/5-31/10. The nearest shop is 4½ miles away so stock up.

Alternatively, there is an independent hostel south of Bonar Bridge at Ardgay, tel:(01863) 766766, open all year, £8. A few miles west of Lairg at Rosehall is the good value **Invercassley Cottage**, tel:(01549) 441288. A very comfortable place in a beautiful situation; from £10. If you do stay in Rosehall be sure to walk along the river to the Invercassley Falls.

TAIN TO THURSO

The **Glenmorangie Distillery**, a 20-minute walk from Tain town centre, operates one-hour tours for £2 (dram included and a discount voucher). Their friendly staff will explain the making of this delicious, smooth malt. Open all year.

Of all the towns along the south east stretch of the Sutherland coast, **Dornoch**, just off the busy A9, is probably the most appealing and complete. Its sturdy centre is full of character, and on either side of the town there are long stretches of sand ideal for beachcombing and enjoying the view. Dornoch's cathedral dates from the 13thC and the castle opposite is now a hotel.

The **Craft Centre and Town Jail**, has various items of interest. Afterwards head out to the golf course (you might be interested to know it's one of the top twelve courses in the world) and the beaches.

Dornoch's **Tourist Information**, is in the Square, tel:(01862) 810400, and is open all year.

There is no youth hostel in Dornoch but plenty of **B&Bs** and the **Dornoch Links Campsite**, just 3 minutes' walk from the town centre, tel:(01862) 810423, open April-October; £3.50-£5.50 a tent.

Overlooking the town of **Golspie** is a statue of the 1st Duke of Sutherland, a much-hated figure in these parts as he cleared the land of people to make way for sheep during the Highland Clearances of the early 19thC. Just north of Golspie is **Dunrobin Castle and Gardens**, home of the Sutherlands, a grandiose 19thC building, open Easter to mid-October, £5, but £4 with this book.

Hostel accommodation is available at Rogart, about 5 miles inland from Golspie. The **Rogart Railway Company** has converted a former First Class Railway Carriage into a 'camping coach' with showers, kitchen and a living room, tel:(01408) 641343, open Easter-October, £8.50 a night (10% discount for bicycle and train users). Trains on the Inverness to Thurso route stop at Rogart three times daily.

The town of **Brora** is situated where the River Brora meets the sea. You can walk out to the harbour and the fine beaches with roaring waves. The road inland along the river to Loch Brora also offers a pleasant walk. South of Brora is **Carn Liath**, a

2,000-year-old broch (fortification). You can imagine a frightened community in times of trouble clinging together within its secure walls. You could head to the **Clynelish Distillery,** one mile north of the village, for a tour and a wee dram. This costs £2 and you receive a £3 discount if you buy a bottle of their whisky, open all year, Tuesday-Thursday only in winter.

Further north of Brora at a spot alongside the A9 road is where the last wolf in Scotland was killed in 1700, so spare a thought for him (or her).

 There's no youth hostel in Brora but plenty of **B&Bs** and **Dalchalm Campsite,** open April-September, £6.50/£7.50, 1½ miles north along the A9.

Helmsdale, also at the rivermouth can make a good touring base as there is a **SYHA** **hostel,** though not a terribly inspiring one; tel:(01431) 821577, Grade 3, £4.65/£6.15, open 15/5-3/10. There is an excellent audio-visual display at the **Timespan Heritage Centre** - the long and interesting story of people in this area; £3/£2.40, open Easter-October.

Before Wick there are some ancient monuments you can seek out - the **Camster Cairns** (one of the best cairns on the mainland), the **Hill O'Many Stanes** (about 200 stones in 22 rows the original purpose of which can only be guessed at) and the **Cairn of Get**. Opposite the Cairn of Get sign on the A9 are the **Whaligoe Steps**. 365 of them lead you down the cliff to a small harbour, not in use today.

· **Red Deer** ·

Wick, John O'Groats and Thurso

These three places serve mainly as stepping stones to Orkney and Shetland. Thurso is the major town and it is from near here that the **P&O** ferries leave for Stromness. The alternative, **John O'Groats Ferries,** leave from John O'Groats to Burwick. Both have buses connecting you with the Thurso train and bus stations (see **Orkney** for ferry details).

The town of **Wick** is a fishing port with a long history. Though it's not a major tourist destination there are several walks to take in the surrounding area. It's 3 miles along the coast to **Noss Head** from where you can reach the dramatic ruins of **Sinclair** and **Girnigoe Castles**. To the south on the coast is **Old Wick Castle** - not as outstanding as the others, but getting there is a fine walk.

In the town itself you can visit the **Wick Heritage Centre** near the harbour for a record of the history of the area (summer only). You could visit the **Caithness Glass Factory** and see the glassmakers at work (just north of the town on the A9 - walking distance). Distinctive, handmade and stylish, there might be a present here for your mum; open Easter-October. Glassmaking factory visits are free but Monday-Friday only.

i Wick's **Tourist Information** on Whitechapel Rd, tel:(01955) 602596, is open all year. There's no youth hostel but many **B&Bs**.

The hamlet of **John O'Groats** stands at the end of the earth - the odd hotel and very few houses make it a pretty lonely place to visit. The naming of John O'Groats resulted from a Dutchman, Jan de Groot who settled here in the late 1400s. The Groot family's (Jan and seven sons) squabbles of precedence at important banquets led to Jan building an octagonal table within an octagonal room with eight doors, one for each person so that no one could claim precedence. The building has gone, but the shape of the John O'Groats Hotel loosely imitates it.

If you've posed under the cross-signposts at Land's End in the south-west of Britain, you can also smugly pose here at its north-east equivalent.

Two miles to the east lies **Duncansby Head** and one mile south from this promontory are the unusual rock formations of the **Duncansby Stacks**. It's a fine walk to take before you catch the ferry to Orkney, or take a boat-trip from John O'Groats to see a different view of the dramatic cliffs as well as the local wildlife. **John O'Groats Ferries**, tel:(01955) 611353, run these 90-minute 'Wildlife Cruises' at 2.30pm daily from 20 June-31 August; £12 per person.

The **John O'Groats SYHA** is in fact situated four miles away at Canisbay which is a very quiet and unassuming village; tel:(01955) 611424, Grade 2, £6.10/£7.60, open 20/3-30/10.

The **John O'Groats Caravan Site** is open April to mid-October, tel:(01955) 611329, £4/£5 a tent.

Thurso is probably the most functional place to choose for a stopover when heading to Orkney. There are two backpackers hostels, a campsite, and many B&Bs. It's a busy but friendly place with many shops and a couple of tourist attractions. Thurso provides fine river walks and its beach is lovely. If you take the walk out to Scrabster, the ferry port, two miles away, there's a good cliff walk heading west to **Holborn Head** - watch out for the blow holes. Another walk is to the north-east, about a mile along the coast to Harald's Tower.

The **Thurso Heritage Museum** on High Street has exhibits related to the area, including the intricately carved Pictish 'Ulbster Stone'; £1, open June-September. You can wander into the ruins of Old St Peter's Kirk near the harbour, dating from the 12thC.

i **Tourist Information** on Riverside, is open April-October, tel:(01847) 892371. Hire a bike at the **Bike & Camping Shop**, 35 High St, tel:(01847) 896124, and head east past Harald's Tower to beautiful Dunnet Bay for a paddle and on to **Dunnet Head**.

Ormlie House Hostel is a fairly new independent hostel on Castlegreen Road, just near the train station; tel:(01847) 896888, £8. The hostel at the **Thurso Youth Club**, Old Mill, Millbank, tel:(01847) 892964, £8 (including breakfast) is unfortunately only open to individual travellers in July and August, with group bookings only at other times.

Thurso Campsite, Scrabster Rd, tel:(01847) 894545, £3.60/£4.10 a tent plus 50p per person, open May-September. Overlooks Thurso Bay.

THURSO TO DURNESS

The stretch of coastline heading west of Thurso toward Bettyhill, although relatively flat, has some of Scotland's most beautiful and peaceful white sandy bays and beaches. Perfect for a summer's day picnic, these beaches are scattered along the coast, mostly not to be seen from the main road but never far away.

There is budget accommodation in the small village of Strathy at **The Focstle**, tel:(01641) 521205, open Easter-November, £8.50. It's next door to the **Strathy Inn** where you can get good food and a drink.

The village of **Bettyhill** makes a good stop, sitting right beside one of those magnificent beaches, Farr Beach, and close to another, Torisdale Beach. At the time of the Highland Clearances, Elizabeth, Countess of Sutherland, donated the land at Bettyhill to evicted tenants. The **Strathnaver Museum** within an old converted church has a fascinating display on the Clearances which you really should stop for if you're travelling through here; £1.50/50p, open April-October.

The village has a couple of shops, a **Tourist Information**, tel:(01641) 521342, open April-September, and several **B&Bs**.

The pick of the villages along the north coast simply has to be **Tongue**. It's very small and quiet but sitting beneath the grand (and most photogenic) Ben Loyal and being close to lovely beaches, it's in a great location. You can take a walk to the ruin of 14thC **Castle Varrich** for a superb view of the surrounding area. Alternatively, walk across the Kyle of Tongue's causeway which will give you a terrific view of Ben Loyal. After the causeway, turn right at the road to Melness. This road provides views to the Rabbit Islands and there's a pleasant sandy beach too. Coldbackie Beach 1½ miles to the north-east of Tongue is another, closer option. (Sorry to go on about beaches so much, but these are what this coastline's famous for!)

Cyclists might want to take the quiet road around the south of the Kyle of Tongue or perhaps head south along the A836 down to Loch Loyal.

Tongue's advantage as a backpacker's destination is that it has a hostel - **Tongue SYHA**, tel:(01847) 611301, Grade 2, £6.10/£7.60, open 20/3-31/10, located one mile down the road near the shore. Tongue also has a bank, a post office, a couple of hotels and pony-trekking.

Durness

Smoo Cave is an impressive triple-chambered cavern located at the east end of Durness. If the tide is low you can walk in as far as the second chamber but the third waterfall chamber can only be reached by fifteen-minute boat-trips (a dinghy actually). These trips are expensive at £2.50 and operate every day from April to October.

Durness (basically a string of hamlets) has a couple of shops, a restaurant, a bar and except for crumbling, dry-stone dykes, there's not much else. However it makes a good base for this corner of the world, as there are quite a few things to see. There's yet another lovely beach at Balnakeil and on the way to this beach you could drop in at the quirky **Balnakeil Craft Village**. These former military buildings have been taken over by a loose collective of artists and crafts people. It's very laid-back, there's a coffee shop and they make some rather unique items if you're searching for a souvenir - from pottery and woodcraft to life-size fibreglass killer whales!

If you haven't seen a puffin yet, you might catch a glimpse in early summer at Faraid Head, just a couple of miles further along the road from the craft village.

Cape Wrath (the most north-westerly, and possibly most remote, point of mainland Scotland) can only be reached by ferry from nearby Keoldale for £2.25, and then a linking minibus for £6 (May-September). From the lighthouse the dramatic high cliffs of Clo Mor to the east can be seen and, weather permitting, so can Orkney and the Isle of Lewis.

i Durness' **Tourist Information** and Visitor Centre, tel:(01971) 511259, is open April-October. Free guided walking tours depart from Tourist Information, 4-5 times a week to different places.

To get to Durness by public transport catch the bus from Inverness - one a day from Monday-Saturday. There may also be a bus from Thurso to Durness in July and August, however, you should check with Tourist Information.

Durness SYHA is beside Smoo Cave, tel:(01971) 511244, Grade 3, £4.65/£6.15, open 20/3-3/10, a simple, timber building. The **Sango Sands Campsite**, near Tourist Information and overlooking Sango Bay, is open Easter-October, tel:(01971) 511262, £3.20 per person.

If you are looking for an extremely remote place to stay, ask to get off the Cape Wrath mini-bus at Kearvaig Bothy, and then be picked up the next day. The bothy is located right on the coast and has no facilities - it's basically just a roof over your head - but it is free.

6. The North-West

On the Scottish mainland north of Skye the tide of tourism recedes dramatically, yet the landscape remains deeply impressive. If you make it up here you'll find quiet villages and roads, almost empty hostels and the most magnificent mountain wilderness.

WESTER ROSS

The route of the **Inverness to Kyle of Lochalsh railway line**, famed as one of the most beautiful in Europe, makes for an excellent journey (whether you travel by rail or road). As the route descends from the comparatively wild and bleak Achnasheen towards the west coast into Strathcarron, the vegetation becomes more lush, the air warmer and more moist. Lichens and ferns fill any gaps left by the pine plantations and pastures.

Achnashellach train station, almost overrun by rhododendrons and other shrubs, is the starting point for three mountain walks to Torridon, Kinlochewe and Strathconon.

Near here (about two miles away) you can stay at **Achnashellach Hostel**, Strathcarron, tel:(01520) 766232, £7.20/£8, open all year. Note - this is a non-smoking hostel.

Kylesku
Achmelvich
Lochinver
Summer Isles
Achiltibuie
LOCH BROOM
Ullapool
LITTLE Loch Broom
Dundonnell
Poolewe
LOCH MAREE
Gairloch
Craig Diabeg
Kinlochewe
Torridon
Achnasheen
Shieldaig
APPLECROSS
Achnashellach
Lochcarron
Plockton
Stromeferry
Kyle of Lochalsh
Kyleakin
Ratagan
Shiel Bridge
SKYE
A87

Just past Strathcarron station the route reaches the sea at Loch Carron. To discover the north side of the loch you must take the road which soon reaches **Lochcarron**, a quiet village of dainty cottages lying on the seafront. Here there is **Tourist Information**, tel:(01520) 722357, open Easter-October. The village has a bank, shop, pub, bike and boat hire as well as Brambles Restaurant, a good place to stop for coffee or a meal.

From this point, either carry on along the shore to the ruin of Strome Castle, which once guarded the entrance to this sheltered sea-loch, or over the hill to Kishorn from where you can head north to Sheildaig or west to Applecross over the daunting Bealach Na Bo Pass.

The train route, however, continues on the south side of Loch Carron which, on a good day, is like a mirror with the reflected hills resembling a string of beads. Fishing boats potter about between their creels and nets. Look out for the occasional seal. The ruin of Strome Castle sits across the water from the train's next stop at **Stromeferry**. By now the accompanying road has taken off half-way up the hillside to give some astonishing views, but the train, hugging the shore, gives the more tranquil, candid views until the end of the line at the Kyle of Lochalsh.

Plockton is the next train-stop and you really should get off here, at least until the next train comes, as this village is an absolute treasure. It seems like no other village could be so peaceful, with the silence only sometimes broken by a cow mooing or a cat miaowing. This spot is so sheltered that often there's not even a rustle of leaves from the waterfront palm trees, growing courtesy of the Gulf Stream. Plockton offers shops, at least one pub and a cafe at the station. If you have seen the television programme 'Hamish Macbeth', you might recognise Plockton as the fictional town of Lochdubh.

 You can stay here at the **Plockton Station Bunkhouse**, Nessun Dorma, Burnside, tel:(01599) 544235, £10 a night, open all year.

A mile or two east of Plockton you can visit the somewhat eccentric **Craig Highland Farm** where the animals seem to be running the show, with no humans to be seen. You'll never meet a more vociferous bunch of animals. Charlie the pot-bellied pig lives there, Sid the llama too. A fee of £1.50 is suggested and probably enforced by the malevolent-looking goats. The farm looks out to sea - great view.

On the way to the Highland Farm there is a fantastic 360° viewpoint just a mile or so east of Plockton, at the brow of the hill before the Duncraig College turning. If you see a passing place with a bench you're in the right spot to climb the adjacent hillock. It takes about ten minutes to the top from where you can see the mountains of Skye, Applecross, Strathcarron and Kintail with Plockton and the sea hundreds of feet below (it must be one of the best 'undiscovered' viewpoints in Scotland). In this corner of Wester Ross between Stromeferry and Kyle there is a delightful network of tiny roads - ideal for cycling (using plenty of gears).

Kyle of Lochalsh and Kintail

Kyle of Lochalsh is a small but busy town at the end of the rail line and at the start of the Skye Bridge. It's a place to stop for all those necessities, with banks, a post office, shops and a chip shop. There is a hostel, **The Islander**, Station Rd, tel:(01599) 534492, £8/£9.50, open all year - or you can stay nearby at one of the hostels across the bridge at Kyleakin (see **Skye**). If you free camp anywhere near here, remember that Kyle's public toilets have showers available for £1.20.

East of Kyle, along the A87, there is a pleasant woodland walk at Balmacarra and another five miles on from there is the fabulously picturesque **Eilean Donan Castle**. One of Scotland's most photographed castles and understandably so, it sits on a rock on **Loch Duich**. Originally built in 1220 to keep out the Danes, it now opens its doors to visitors, Danes included, for just £3/£2. You might recognise it from the film 'Highlander'. Open 24/3-end October.

The nearby village of Dornie has a good pub and a friendly tea-shop. On from the castle the road continues south-east along the lochside with the peaks of the 'Five Sisters' overlooking and often reflected in Loch Duich. In this area, as well as red deer, you can sometimes see wild goats - usually dark brown, they look like crazed unkempt sheep, but with horns almost the length of their backs.

Bunkhouse and B&B accommodation is available at Dornie, tel:(01599) 555264, £7.50/£9.50, open all year. A campsite is at **Shiel Bridge**. Turning off the main road here leads to Ratagan where there is a youth hostel in a lovely lochside setting. **Ratagan SYHA**, tel:(01599) 511243, Grade 2, £7.75/£9.25, open all year except 4/1-28/1.

Over the challenging Mam Ratagan pass is **Glenelg**, a peaceful, almost forgotten corner of the Highlands. Here you can visit the Iron Age brochs **Dun Telve** and **Dun Troddan** or take the very small ferry (summer only) to Kylerhea on Skye and visit the otter hide. Glenelg has a shop and **B&Bs**.

SHIELDAIG TO ULLAPOOL

North of Loch Carron and through the remote Glen Shieldaig, the tiny village of **Shieldaig** lies charmingly by the water's edge under the craggy slopes of the Ben. The bright and breezy street consists of the bare essentials (houses, hotel, shop). A lovely natural pine wood leads away southwards along the hillside to a small loch. There are also boat-trips and boat hire.

To the west of Shieldaig lies the wild and windswept Applecross - a place to really get away from it all. Eastwards Loch Torridon reaches inland, beside which the road leads. After just a mile or so you can take a walk towards Loch Damph to find the Balgy Falls.

The vast desolate heights of Liathach look down on the minute hamlet called **Torridon** (although this name also refers to the whole area). It's just a string of houses with a shop and is situated half a mile off the main road. Between Torridon and the turning you'll find the NTS **Deer Museum** (£1.50/£1 to enter), a cheap campsite and the fairly ugly but spacious **Torridon SYHA**, tel:(01445) 791284, Grade 1, £7.75/£9.25, open 30/1-31/10. For a beer, a coffee or a meal you'll have to go back to the main road to the **Ben Damph Lodge**. A couple of miles east of Torridon on the A896 is a bunkhouse (£4, stove and fridge available but no showers). 13 miles from Torridon and via the Lower Diabeg road is the rather interesting **Craig SYHA** (no telephone), Grade 3, £4.65, open 15/5-3/10, bring a sleeping bag. Being five miles from the nearest road, this hostel is perhaps the most remote in Scotland. It has no electricity and everything is extremely basic. For the washrooms you take your chances with Mother Nature, who has generously supplied a pool up the river, and vast expanses of moorland. It's a fabulous place, but there are a few things to mention - it's a tiring 5-mile, two-hour walk from the road-end, the nearest shop is in Torridon and you'll need a German phrase book in summer. Outside summer check with Torridon SYHA whether it's open.

A couple of miles east of Torridon village along the A896 is a plaque explaining the phenomena of the Corrie of the Hundred Hills. This is the start of the Corrie Dubh Mor to Corrie Mhic Nobuil walk through the nature reserve around Ben Liathach - 8 miles, 3 hours. Further along the road to the south starts the 8-mile walk to Achnashellach (the nearest train station) through the Coulin Estate, past lochs and pine woods.

The village **Kinlochewe** is built around the T-junction of the A832 and A896 roads, and is a pleasant place set amongst the marvellous mountain and moorland scenery of the Beinn Eighe Nature Reserve.

A mile or two north starts the splendid **Loch Maree**, with surrounding hillsides that boast many rare mammals and birds in its ancient pine and oak woods. The nature trail which starts on its banks, a couple of miles from Kinlochewe, is fascinating as well as scenic. Scottish Natural Heritage, which runs the Reserve, also provides free camping at Taagan, near the Aultroy Visitor Centre, one mile from Kinlochewe at the head of the loch. Otherwise there is the **Loch Maree Log Cabin** at Talladale, tel:(01445) 760288, £10-£15, open March-December.

Gairloch

The coastal town of **Gairloch** has quite an interesting variety of sights. It has a cramped, busy harbour, separated from the town centre by a long, sandy beach.
Gairloch has a year round **Tourist Information** (tel:(01445) 712130, closed weekends in winter) and the award-winning **Gairloch Heritage Museum** (free), as well as a bank, shops and pubs.

For accommodation there are several choices. In the town itself is the **Achtercairn Hostel**, Gairloch Sands Apartments, tel:(01445) 712131, £7.50, open March-November, while 3 miles from the town is the **Carn Dearg SYHA hostel**, tel:(01445) 712219, Grade 2, £6.10/£7.60, open 16/5-3/10 - there are splendid views along the road to the hostel. Half a mile further along this road is a campsite and even further at Melvaig, the **Rua Reidh Lighthouse** (and tea-room) makes a rather unique place to stay; tel:(01445) 771263, £7.50, open all year. South of Gairloch at Badachro is the **Badachro Bunkhouse**, tel:(01445) 741291, open all year, £8.50 a night. Getting to Gairloch by public transport is not easy. Only one bus a day, Monday-Saturday, leaves Inverness - it is run by Westerbus, tel:(01445) 712255.

On the shores of the next bay north, where the waters of Loch Maree empty into the sea, sits **Poolewe**. In past centuries it was a major port to the Hebrides and had an iron works. It's hard to imagine now as it's extremely small and quiet - perhaps Friday night in the 'local' is different. As well as the pub, the village has a shop and a coffee shop, a campsite and a swimming pool. Poolewe's big attraction these days is **Inverewe Garden**. Due to the mild climate they have many exotic plants including small palm trees; at £4.80/£3.20 it's pricey, NTS.

Heading north, the road, the A832, jumps over the weather-beaten headlands from one sandy cove to the next, towards Gruinard Bay, which has a sandy beach, a couple of caves to explore and an old watermill. Take the turning to the beach at magical Mellon Udrigle.

Under the 1062 metres of An Teallach lies Little Loch Broom, a dark blue finger of sea jutting eastwards. A boat from Badluarach can take you across to the tip of the Scoraig Peninsula, a delightfully remote corner.

Near the head of Little Loch Broom, situated on the roadside by Dundonnell, is the **Sail Mhor Croft Hostel**, tel:(01854) 633224, £7-£10, open all year except Christmas and New Year, (a bus going from Inverness to Gairloch stops at Dundonnell every Monday, Wednesday and Saturday only). Otherwise, to the north of the loch, the **Badrallach Bothy** is an interesting place to stay, but you must bring your own sleeping bag and mat. It is basic accommodation but they do have showers, a peat stove and you can camp here too; tel:(01854) 633281, £2-£4, same price for campers, open all year. To get there take the dead-end single track road to Badrallach which starts 1 mile east of the Dundonnell Hotel on the A832. The bothy's at the end of the road. Alternatively, take the Altnaharrie Hotel's ferry (tel:01854-633230, £2.50, dependent on tide and weather, takes bikes) from Ullapool across Loch Broom, and the 4-mile walk.

Twelve miles south of Ullapool, stop and see the **Falls of Measach** at the Corrieshalloch Gorge.

Ullapool

Sitting on the north shore of Loch Broom, **Ullapool** is the ferry port to Stornoway on the Outer Hebrides. Its harbour is also used by many fishing boats, often from abroad, and this gives the town a strangely cosmopolitan atmosphere at times.

Most of the town centre is located on the seafront by the harbour. Being by far the largest town around (though still not very big) it has all the amenities including **Tourist Information**, tel:(01854) 612135, open April-November.

The **SYHA Hostel** is on the main street overlooking the harbour, tel:(01854) 612254, Grade 1, £7.75/£9.25, open all year except 4/1-28/1. The **Ceilidh Place Bunkhouse**, 14 West Argyle St, tel:(01854) 612103, has bunk-beds and some double beds for £10 (but no common room), open April-October, or go to the

West House Hostel, also in West Argyle St, tel:(01854) 613126, £8-£10, open all year. The **Broomfield campsite**, tel:(01854) 612020, is ridiculously central and costs £5 for two. If you have a car, park it outside and save a few quid.

All in all everything is rather conveniently arranged. In summer boat tours ply their trade with promises of seals and dolphins. Take a stroll into the lovely wee museum full of local bits and pieces at the bookshop; free/donation. For a bit of slightly highbrow culture, the **Ceilidh Place** puts on the occasional concert - quite frequently in summer. It's also a good place for a coffee. Periodically there are other folk/culture events in the town, and failing that there's always the pub, the pick of which is probably the **Ferryboat Inn** or, for the more sophisticated amongst you, back to the **Ceilidh Place**.

The Stornoway ferry leaves at least twice a day - £12 single/£20.55 five-day return.

North of Ullapool

Beyond Ullapool the west coast scenery remains, as ever, spectacular. To the north-west is the inspiring Coigach Peninsula with the ragged, jagged ridge of Stac Pollaidh punching into the sky. Beneath it the small road heading to Achiltibuie winds above Loch Lurgainn offering fabulous views (with some enticing beaches to cool down in after climbing Stac Pollaidh). There is a lovely beach with white sand at Achnahaird. Beyond here, on the peninsula's western shores, lies a string of hamlets in a land of thistles, crumbling dykes, broken fences and rusting tractors. Off-shore lie the Summer Islands, a delightful outcrop of wild, windswept rocks and, beyond those, the mountains of Wester Ross. **Achiltibuie** is the main village here with a shop, post office, bar, art gallery and, in complete contrast to the surroundings, the **Hydroponicum** - a high-tech, enthusiastically-run 'garden of the future'; £4/£3 for a tour. There is an adjoining cafe serving great food, open daily 6/4-30/9. Achiltibuie incidentally has the finest field of thistles ever seen.

 A mile or two further on near the end of the road is the **Achininver SYHA**, tel:(01854) 622254, Grade 3, £4.65/£6.15, open 15/5-3/10.

Despite the mountains and rolling terrain the roads are relatively flat and very quiet - excellent for cycling.

Heading north towards Lochinver from the western end of Loch Lurgainn is a lovely road through the **Inverpolly Nature Reserve** which squiggles through glens, up and down hillsides, around lochs, past scruffy sheep, barren moorlands, stunted birch trees and heather and bracken, sometimes bumping into the coast at sheltered bays. A few miles before Lochinver you can take the walk to the falls of Kirkaig. The moorland scenery, with the peak of Suilven waiting around the corner, makes it a very pleasant trek. Surrounded by this magnificent coast and countryside is the town of **Lochinver**, which is a serious fishing port, as well as a peaceful town set between the mouths of two small gushing, rocky burns. The town has the usual signs of civilisation including shops, a pub, a bank and the nice, new **Assynt Visitor Centre** (free/donation) which shares the same building as **Tourist Information**, tel:(01571) 844330, is open March-October.

The nearest budget accommodation is 3 miles north at the **Achmelvich SYHA**, tel:(01571) 844480, Grade 3, £4.65/£6.15, open 20/3-3/10, and adjacent campsite. Achmelvich's small sandy beach sits perfectly amongst the barren rocky coast, a cockleshell's throw from the youth hostel. Much further inland in a lovely, peaceful situation at Inchnadamph is the **Assynt Field Centre** hostel, tel:(01571) 822218, £8.50/£14.50, open all year but phone ahead from November to March.

The coastal road from Achmelvich carries on twisting its way from bay to bay through crofting communities, past sandy beaches, over rocky moorland in the shadow of Quinag.

The hamlet of Kylesku is in a peaceful corner just out of sight of the bridge and makes a pleasant stop for a refreshment at the hotel. Boat trips leave from here to Eas Coul Aulin, at 658ft Scotland's highest waterfall. Note - someone's garden shed is the post office.

On the other side of the A894 road is the independent hostel **Kylesku Lodges**, tel:(01971) 502003, open Easter-October, £9-£10.

North of Kylesku there is more spectacular scenery and you can visit the coastal village of Scourie (which has a campsite, petrol, shop and pub) and detour to the busy fishing port of Kinlochbervie.

Public transport is scarce in this area so it would be wise to invest in the bus and ferry transport guide to 'North Highland and Orkney' for £1, available at Tourist Information centres or write to the Public Transport Section, Highland Regional Council, Glenurquhart Rd, Inverness, IV3 5NX.

7. Skye

The overpowering brutal grandeur of this island can leave even the most happy-go-lucky tourist speechless. It's not pretty, it's magnificent and a bit frightening - the bleak loneliness in parts can chill your soul. Immerse yourself in it (don't just look at it through the bus or car window). Forget the weather, the midges, your own bed at home, your leaking shoes - you'll suffer. It's seldom a kind place, but you'll be in no doubt that you're alive.

At the island's centre are the **Cuillin Mountains**, the Black Cuillins to the west, jagged and inspiring, the Red Cuillins to the east, rounded and brooding. The name 'Isle of Skye' comes from the native Gaelic 'An t-Eilean Sgitheanach', which means 'winged island'. These 'wings' of **Trotternish** and **Waternish** along with **Duirinish**, **Minginish** and **Sleat**, stretch out into the sea to give a gentler but still mysterious and haunting landscape. The Gaelic nickname is Eilean a' Cheo (Island of Mist) and as the clouds sit or curl slowly over the hills and fjords this is when Skye's truest beauty can be admired.

A Brief History

Prior to this millennium, Skye's history is as misty as its landscape with just the occasional landmark to hint at its unknown contours. Ptolemy, the 2ndC Egyptian astronomer, included it in a map, and Saint Columba visited in 585, at which time it is believed the people were followers of an Irish monk, Baedun. In these times it is uncertain who the locals were, perhaps Goths or Goidelic Celts or Picts; vague evidence points in different directions.

Things get clearer by the end of the 8thC when the Norse started to arrive, at first pillaging, etc., but soon settling on Skye as well as on other islands and mixing with the population. This era of Scandinavian rule and influence continued until 1263 when the Viking King Haakon of Norway, after stopping at Kyleakin with his 120 ships, sailed on to defeat at the Battle of Largs (near Glasgow), leaving the Hebrides under Scottish control.

In the ensuing centuries, as with most of the Highlands and Islands, the clans and their chiefs wielded the power, and in Skye bitter feuds often broke out between the MacLeods and the MacDonalds.

In 1746 the defeat of Bonnie Prince Charlie and his Highland Army caused a great change. By the 19thC the clan chiefs, influenced by the now dominant English system, turned their backs on their people in preference for sheep and the Highland Clearances began. Nowadays the remaining people live mainly from crofting (crofts are small farms), some fishing and tourism.

In keeping with most of the Highlands, the towns and villages are of little visual interest and do not merit visiting for their own sake. They do, however, offer some of the comforts and necessities of life here on the edge of civilisation. In the summer they are often bursting with visitors, while in the off-season (sometimes the best time to visit) they are half asleep, though there's always a glimmer of life emanating from the pubs and especially from the occasional ceilidh.

Southern Skye

Kyleakin, just over the bridge, is Skye's prettiest village, with its peaceful rocky harbour overlooked by the ancient crumbling Castle Moil. It's really quite a happening place with some wild nights available at the King Haakon Bar or at Saucy Mary's. What's more, having three hostels, cheap daily car hire, bike hire and guided mini-bus tours, Kyleakin makes a good base for seeing the island.

The village has fine views eastwards along Loch Duich and, at the bridge, westwards to the Cuillin Mountains. At the village green gaze out over the narrows as seals, otters, dolphins and even whales can sometimes be spotted here. The pebble beach below is where King Haakon's 120 Viking longships pulled in 700 years ago on their way to battle. Incidentally, Kyleakin's name derives from the 'straits of Haakon'. Excellent meals are served all day at **Saucy Mary's**, just next to the post office, or you can eat at the **King Haakon** restaurant or the cosy **Pier Coffee House**.

The village also provides a wee grocery, a post office and a late night shop at the Skye Bridge petrol station.

Kyleakin Car Rental offers great value with prices starting at £2.50 an hour - very cheap when shared; tel:(01599) 534431. Otherwise go to the Dun Caan Hostel which hires out cars for £35 a day, minimum age 21 years. **Skye Bikes** offer a cheap deal on cycle hire at the pier for £5-£10 a day. Places to explore include the otter hide at Kylerhea and, on the mainland, Plockton or Eilean Donan Castle. In summer boat-trips leave from the pier. For the two **minibus tours** ask at the hostels - Ted's is more informed (£15), Nick's more flexible (£12). The normal buses to the rest of the island all stop in the village. A shuttle bus runs between Kyleakin and Kyle of Lochalsh on the mainland every half hour and costs 55p one way.

Skye Backpackers, Kyleakin, tel:(01599) 534510, £8.90/£10.90, open all year, 2am curfew. Very comfy and good fun, with a real fire on those long winter nights. Advance bookings can be made by credit card, by post with an £8.90 deposit, or you can book through the High Street Hostel, Edinburgh; Backpackers-Royal Mile, Edinburgh; Inverness Student Hotel, Fort William or Oban Backpackers. **Kyleakin SYHA**, tel:(01599) 534585, Grade 1, £8.60/£11.10, open all year, 2am curfew. A well-run official hostel with good facilities. Their annexe has twin rooms at £10.60/£13.10 per person.
Dun Caan Hostel, tel:(01599) 534087, £8.50, open all year. New hostel not far from the King Haakon bar.
Camping: no campsite, but nobody minds if it's out of sight - try behind the football field. Note - showers for £1.20 at Kyle toilets beside Tourist Information.

Broadford sits at the foot of Beinn Na Caillich, the first of the Cuillins. Although the town has quite a large population, it is more a strung-out four-mile hamlet. At the north end, where the architecture thickens up a bit, you can find shops, banks, 24-hr petrol and some hotels with bars. Broadford's **Tourist Information**, tel:(01471) 822361, is open from April to October.
Broadford houses Skye's **Environmental Centre** at Harrapool. They have a small free museum, a nature walk along the adjacent beach with a rough map showing things of interest and, circumstances permitting, you can see the occasional destitute seal pup being cared for (usually late summer). Better still, go on their minibus-walking trip which focuses on the wildlife and the environment; £10/£12. Phone a day or two beforehand to arrange, tel:(01471) 822487. Nearby, the **Serpentarium** at the Old Mill offers some rather different creatures - snakes, frogs, lizards and tortoises; £1.50. You can hire a bike from **Broadford Cycle Hire** just up the Elgol road, tel:(01471) 822270 for £7 and perhaps head off towards Torrin, the museum at Luib, or for a pint at the Isle Oronsay Hotel (make sure you tell the hotel owner what you think of the bridge tolls).
Broadford SYHA, tel:(01471) 822442, Grade 2, £7.75/£9.25, curfew 11.45pm, open all year except 4/1-28/1. 800 yards from the main road.
Fossil Bothy, Lower Breakish, tel:(01471) 822644/822297, £7, April-November. The friendly owners at **3 Waterloo**, tel:(01471) 822869, provide accommodation for bikers - motor-bikers - only; £9/£10 includes breakfast.

From Broadford, a small road leads west through Torrin where white Skye marble is extracted, and under the shadow of the Cuillins to **Elgol**, a tiny village perched on the edge of a fabulous natural arena. From here you can see unbelievable sunsets (weather and time of day permitting, of course). There is some spectacular cliff scenery just to the south of the village. It's possible (at low tide only) to seek out and explore the cave where Bonnie Prince Charlie spent his last night on Skye whilst hiding from the English Redcoats in 1746. The boat to **Loch Coruisk** leaves from Elgol, and is an experience not to be missed. This 2½ hour boat-trip costs £12.50 and runs from April to September about four times daily. You should book in advance on tel: freephone 0800-7313089 or for enquiries only tel:(01471) 866244 (phone 7.30-10pm the night before or 7.30-10am on the day of departure). Elgol has only a small shop and no accommodation except **B&Bs**. Public transport out to Elgol consists of the occasional bus and the post-bus from Broadford with no service on Sundays.

Bonnie Prince Charlie

Overwhelming sentimental affection is held for Prince Charles Edward Stuart, the man who led a Highland army in the final attempt to restore the Stuart (and Catholic) line to the British throne. His grandfather, James VII and II, had been deposed and forced into exile by the Protestant William of Orange, giving life to the Jacobite cause. Prince Charlie, having been brought up in Italy in exile, came to Scotland in 1745 to claim the thrones of Scotland and England for his father. Arriving in the north-west of Scotland the Highlanders' support was strong and moving south they conquered successfully as far as Derby in England, but retreated believing they had insufficient men to tackle London. Government forces pursued them northwards with the decisive battle held at Culloden near Inverness. Charles' tired and outnumbered army lost badly in a bloody battle which was all over within an hour. Charlie himself fled from the battlefield and spent the next five months on the run from the authorities and at one time was even disguised in a dress as Flora MacDonald's maid. He eventually left for the continent. He never returned to Scotland and he died a sad and pathetic drunk at the age of 68.

Sleat, the southernmost part of the island, has the calmest landscape but the views across the Sound of Sleat (if you listen carefully you can just hear it) are quite something. The main road to and from the Mallaig-Armadale ferry passes this way through a series of hamlets. Between Teangue and Ardvasar is the **Gaelic College** - Sabhal Mor Ostaig - go on, sign up for a course (beginners welcome). Accommodation is also available here from £14-£18 **B&B**, tel:(01471) 844373. If you take the lovely winding Tarskavaig Road you'll find a magnificent view of the Cuillins - try to find the ruin of Dun Scaith Castle. Just north of Ardvasar is the bright and breezy **Clan Donald Centre**, aimed solely at tourists, but the coffee's okay. There is a museum and gardens nearby, but at £3.40 it's over-priced unless perhaps you're a MacDonald clan member; open March-October. Ardvasar itself has a certain charm, so don't be in too much of a hurry to pass on by. It has two pubs, and nearby the Armadale SYHA overlooks the pier. It also has a shop, takeaway food, a cafe and bike hire at the petrol station. While in this area try to make it out to the Point of Sleat where hopefully a storm will brew up to add dramatic effect to the view of the islands of Rhum and Eigg.

Armadale SYHA, tel:(01471) 844260, Grade 2, £6.10/£7.60, open 20/3-31/10.

Hairy Coo Backpackers Hostel, Toravaig House, tel:(01471) 833231, open all year, £8.50. They have a bar, with live music occasionally. It is located four miles north of the Armadale ferry point and they will provide transport to and from the ferry if required.

Sleat Independent Hostel, Kilmore, 3 miles north of Armadale, tel:(01471) 844440, £7. This bunkhouse will also provide transport to and from the ferry point.

Camping: behind the nearest bush.

Leaving Broadford, heading towards the north of the island, the road winds its way around the Cuillins for the next 15 miles. If driving, try to keep your eyes on the road and watch out for sheep. You could also stop at the **Luib Museum** and find out about Bonnie Prince Charlie's travels on Skye; £1, open April-October. After passing the Sconser Hotel and Raasay Ferry, you will eventually come to **Sligachan** which offers just a hotel and campsite. This is the start of some hill walks (see **Walks in the Cuillins**) and a base for mountaineers and it's plain to see why with such majestic mountains rising all around. Here the road forks to Dunvegan or Portree.

Northern Skye

Portree is Skye's only real attempt at a town (you know, with streets, banks and traffic lights). It has a variety of shops and hotel bars and a year-round **Tourist Information**, Meall House, is above the harbour; tel:(01478) 612137, open all year, closed Sundays, Saturdays, too, in winter.

Unlike most Skye villages, the sea views from Portree are a bit obscured. The best view is south towards the clustered peaks of the Black Cuillins. By day the harbour is of course worth taking in and you can stroll around **The Lump**, which lies behind Tourist Information, or to the **Black Rock**. The two nearby hills, **Ben Tianavaig** and **Ben Na Greine**, are a relatively straightforward day's walk (but you'll want somewhere to dry your feet afterwards).

Several pubs offer good value lunches. The **Aros Skye Heritage Centre** a mile south serves a well-filled plate of food till 8pm for £5-£6 (the heritage centre's tour, however, is ponderous and pricey). On Wentworth St is **Jansport**, a camping store.

 Portree has quite a selection of independent hostels.
Portree Independent Hostel, Old Post Office, The Green, tel:(01478) 613737, £7.50/£9, open all year.
Portree Backpackers Hostel, 6 Woodpark, Dunvegan Road, tel:(01478) 613641, £7.50/£9, open all year.
On the pier is **Portree Backpackers**, 2 Douglas Row, tel:(01478) 613332, a small place which offers basic backpackers' accommodation, £7.50/£8.50, open all year.
Camping - Torvaig, 1½ miles north of Portree, tel:(01478) 612209, open April-October, £6 for two. There is a choice of two fields, one sharing, one without (sheep that is). No shop at campsite.

Trotternish

Travelling north from Portree towards Staffin, the scenery is breathtaking. At first the **Old Man Of Storr**, a vast finger of rock standing below some ragged cliffs, dominates the view, but this is soon matched by the vista across to the isle of Rona and the mainland. A minor distraction from this is the **Lealt Gorge**, which is worth carefully peering into (the road zips by it so don't blink).

 You can stay here at **The Lealt Falls Hostel**, tel:(01470) 562363, £7.50, open March-January.

A mile or two south of Staffin there are the impressive **Kilt Rock** and **Mealt Falls**. There is also a very good set of information plaques showing how the strange rocks were formed and the local wildlife that you might encounter.

Staffin is a strung-out crofting community (a couple of shops, **B&Bs**, no pub). At this point the road divides - you can turn west up the formidable **Quirang** (excellent views from the top of the climb), or carry on to the northern tip of Skye. Here the ruin of **Duntulm Castle**, seemingly about to crumble into the sea, is a reminder of more troubled times. The backdrop across the sea is now, of course, the Western Isles. Two miles south at Peingown, Kilmuir, is the rather good **Skye Museum of Island Life** near Flora MacDonald's grave; £1.50, open April-October.

Dun Flodigarry Hostel, by Staffin, tel:(01470) 552212, £7.50/£8.50. Open all year. Very comfortable hostel with great beds and great sea views. A wonderful place to go and relax for a few days.

Uig is the ferry port to the Western Isles, and offers a few hotels (and bars), shops, petrol, but no bank. You can go canoeing, windsurfing or pony-trekking (**Uig Hotel**, tel:(01470) 542205), or hire a bike for £8 a day (ask at the SYHA for directions) - but by far the most curious attraction near here is the **Fairy Glen**. To get to the Fairy Glen head south out of town, then take the two-mile trek up the Balnaknock Road.

Once there you'll find yourself walking through an enchanted miniature landscape (where did that stream disappear to?). Just behind the next hill fairies abound.

 Uig SYHA, tel:(01470) 542211, Grade 2, £6.10/£7.60, open 20/3-31/10. A mile from the ferry. Overlooks Uig Bay and a chunk of Loch Snizort.

Uig Camping and Caravan Site, tel:(01470) 542360, 15/3-September, £3.50-£5.50, 200 yards from the ferry.

South from Uig

If passing through Skeabost towards Waternish, take the turning towards Tote, where you can see a carved Iron Age standing stone commemorating a wedding (perhaps two of your ancestors). At **Edinbane** (a shop, two hotels, good craft shop, petrol) there are sometimes free ceilidhs at the **Lodge Hotel** in summer.

 Glenhinnisdal Bunkhouse, tel:(01470) 542293, £7, open all year. 4 miles south of Uig then 1½ miles up the Glenhinnisdal road.

Waternish

The **Fairy Bridge** marks the turning north to Waternish. This bridge is where the local MacLeod Clan Chief received the Fairy Flag which can be seen in Dunvegan Castle.

Stein, a small collection of houses, offers a pub and a restaurant down at the water, while further on a good place for a picnic is the ruins of Trumpan Church. Here the MacDonalds sought to avenge a previous massacre of their own people on the Isle of Eigg by arriving while the local MacLeods were in church. They set fire to its thatched roof and killed any who tried to escape the inferno - something to think about as you munch your Cheesy Wotsits.

The views to the west in this area are wonderful and for equally impressive eastward views go over the hill to **Geary**.

At the head of the seal-infested Dunvegan Loch is the very small town of **Dunvegan**, which has shops, hotels, cycle hire, petrol and, best of all, an excellent bakery-cum-coffee house. While in the village check out the **Giant Angus MacAskill Museum**, open April-October, £1, with its very friendly owner. You can also walk up to **MacLeod's Tables**, the strange-topped hills overlooking Dunvegan. This is the land which inspired the Pibroch, a sombre, melancholy style of playing the bagpipes.

Dunvegan Castle, just a 20-minute stroll out of town, is the seat of the MacLeods of Skye, one of the most powerful clans in Scotland in days gone by. The castle (cleverly hidden by trees and shrubbery, so you have to pay to even get a glimpse of it) is looking a bit shabby on the outside these days, but prim and proper inside. By far the most interesting (but least pretty and least well presented) artefact is the ancient **Fairy Flag** which rather importantly has magic powers and has seen the MacLeods through some troubled times. It is said to have been given as a farewell gift to the MacLeod Chief by his fairy wife when she left him. The castle is overpriced at £4.80/£4.20; gardens only, £3.50; open daily 23/3-31/10. The best deal is 200 yards before the castle entrance - go down to the pier to check out the seal cruises (while deciding you can get a good look at the castle). Afterwards, try hand-feeding the chaffinches in the car park.

Four miles beyond the castle there's a place you should go to - the **Coral beaches.**
At Claigan take the footpath (starting at the car park) down to the beach. After a
while you'll reach a patch of white sand. If you pick up a handful you can see it's
made of coral, but don't stop here. Carry on for another ten minutes to the next bay
where the white coral stretches out beside lush green pasture, perhaps tempting you
to have a swim with the usually present seals.

 Locals don't really like people free camping along here so you should stay
at one of the two **campsites**. There are also several **B&Bs**.

Duirinish

This land to the west of Dunvegan, dominated by MacLeod's Tables, is well populated
(for Skye) in the north but completely deserted in the south. The road leads through
scattered communities with the occasional cafe, shop, post office and museum. The
Colbost Folk Museum gives a very good idea of a peasant crofter's life in the
19thC, open April-October. The entrance fee of £1 is a bit pricey for such a small

museum - and it's a shame the
whisky-still isn't in production.
Near the end of the road to Galtrigil
is the **Piping Centre**, where you
could learn to play the bagpipes if
that takes your fancy. Beyond the
village of Glendale is one of the most
dramatic headlands you'll ever be
careful not to fall off of - **Neist
Point**. The precarious path leads out
to the lighthouse. If it weren't for
the Western Isles beyond, you might
think you were on the edge of
the world.

· Neist Point light house ·

Minginish

In the shadow of the Black Cuillins, this area with its moors and small hills has only
a couple of villages, a few hamlets and a lot of sheep. At Carbost, have a look around
the **Talisker Distillery** - not a bad malt. It's £3 to enter, but you get a discount if
you buy a bottle of their whisky. Open all year, Monday to Friday (Saturdays, too,
from July-September), but afternoons only in winter. Through Portnalong and past
Fiskavaig you can walk out to the headland for an excellent view.
Glen Brittle, with the fiercesome Cuillin Mountains rising on the east, is a must.
Being a deservedly popular location for mountaineers it has a youth hostel and a
campsite a mile further at the beach. On the gentler side of the glen there is a circular
walking or mountain-biking route along forestry tracks taking in Loch and Glen
Eynort. For those of you who wish to walk in the mountains, there is a path to
Sligachan (see **Walks in the Cuillins**). Along the south shore a path leads three
miles to some archaeological sites. Anything else to the east - forget it unless you're
a properly experienced mountaineer.

Croft Bunkhouse and Bothies, near Portnalong at the northern end of Minginish, tel:(01478) 640254, £6/£7.50, open all year. Bikes for hire. Comfortable accommodation with fine views overlooking the sea and mountains. The owner, Pete Thomas, can give sound advice on walking in Skye if you need it.
Skyewalker Hostel, also near Portnalong, tel:(01478) 640250, £7, open all year.
Glen Brittle SYHA, along the road heading south through Glen Brittle, tel:(01478) 640278, Grade 2, £6.10/£7.60, open 20/3-31/10.
A **campsite** is at the shore at the end of the Glen Brittle road, tel:(01478) 640404, open April-September.

Raasay

If Skye's too hectic for you, get away from it all by taking the boat at Sconser (£3.50 return) to Raasay, a quiet and surprisingly large island. Bicycle is perhaps the best way to explore, Brochel Castle in the north being what you should aim for. Near the ferry, Inverarish has a shop and nearby hotel (pub).

Raasay SYHA, tel:(01478) 660240, Grade 3, £4.65/£6.15, open 20/3-31/10. No showers.
Camping - just about anywhere.

Getting to Skye

This is an experience to be enjoyed in itself. Probably the best way is by **train** from Inverness to Kyle of Lochalsh and then the 55p bus trip across the bridge to Kyleakin. Skye can also be approached by train from Fort William arriving in Mallaig and from there by the ferry to Armadale (see Mallaig) - both these rail routes are very beautiful. The cheapest public transport to Skye is of course the **bus**, leaving Inverness or Glasgow three or four times daily. These journeys, though taking a different route from the train, are well worth staying awake for.

By **car** (and hitching) the main road is the A87 and you cross the toll bridge at Kyle; £4.40/£5.40 per car. Taking the Armadale to Mallaig ferry (although much more expensive at £14.45 one-way plus £2.50 per passenger) also makes a very worthwhile circuit including the Silver Sands of Morar. An alternative driving route is with the ferry at Kylerhea - a lovely twisting and climbing road - which runs in summer only. Skye is also on the **Go Blue Banana** and **Haggis Backpackers** minibus routes (see **Getting Around Scotland**). You might of course be travelling by ferry from the Western Isles, where you will arrive at Uig in the north (£7.85).

If **cycling** from Inverness, consider the more northerly route, the A832 and A890 via Achnasheen. The views are great and the road is much quieter than the main route via Loch Ness. From Fort William it's a choice between the quietish A830 to Mallaig and the expense of the ferry, or the very quiet and flat Great Glen Cycle Route to Invergarry followed by the busy A87 (free bridge at Kyle).

WALKS IN THE CUILLINS

DIFFICULT

These should only be attempted by people who know what they are doing as inexperience or naivety often leads to danger. If you are inexperienced contact Pete Thomas, tel:(01478) 640254 for advice or G. Akroyd, tel:(01478) 640289, who may take you (with a group). There are also various leaflets and books dealing with hill walking on Skye available at Tourist Information offices and some shops. Their guidance should be followed carefully.

For these walks buy O.S. Map Landranger 32, South Skye, 1:50,000. You should take a compass, though it is sometimes of doubtful use due to the mountains' magnetic qualities.

Glen Brittle to Sligachan via Bealach A' Mhaim

14km (approx. 4-5 hours) starting from the Glen Brittle campsite.

The first few kilometres of this walk are along the only road out of Glen Brittle. There is little traffic, however, to disturb the peace - the views towards the Cuillins are excellent and the full-flowing river tranquil. There are many waterfalls in this area and these can easily be found by following almost any stream up towards the mountains for a kilometre or so.

After 6km there is a forestry commission gate just where the conifer plantation begins on the right-hand side of the road. The path follows a north-easterly direction up towards the Bealach a' Mhaim pass. However, if at the gate you follow the river upstream and not the path, you will soon discover a series of waterfalls and plunge pools which on a fine day will make an excellent spot for lunch. Sometimes, when the light is right, it is possible to see the colours of the rainbow in the spray from the waterfalls.

From the top of the pass it is only another 5km downhill into Sligachan. The path is straightforward; keep to the north of the stream. The rounded and distinctive top of Glamaig acts like a guiding beacon and, before you know it, you will be at the Sligachan Hotel with a warming dram of whisky in your hand and ordering a plate of hot food.

The views from Sligachan are dominated by Sgurr nan Gillean and the northern peaks of the Cuillin mountains to the south-west and by the round-topped, scree-sloped Glamaig to the east. In 1899 the Gurka Karkabir Thapa set an amazing record by climbing or running to the top of Glamaig and then descending, or more likely falling, in a mere 55 minutes. An annual hill race up Glamaig takes place in July with the current record under 45 minutes! It takes a normal climber hours to trudge up the 775 metres of scree.

Buses to Sligachan - Sligachan is on the Skye to Glasgow and Inverness bus routes and is well served, several times daily.

105

Sligachan to Kilmarie via Camasunary Bay

17 km (approx. 6 hours)

This walk goes south through Glen Sligachan and is flat, but a little wet in places. The terrain is varied, consisting of heathery moors, boggy flood plains, luscious pasture and craggy cliffs. The views are also spectacular, with the Black Cuillins' daunting, razor-sharp spikes rising from huge walls of bare rock to the west and the isolated Red Cuillin peaks of Glamaig, Marsco and Blabheinn to the east, rising straight out from the valley floor. The path begins after crossing the old bridge at the Sligachan Hotel and is signposted to Loch Coruisk. Follow the path, which is cairned, for about 1½ hours (6km), to the two small lochs (Lochan Dubha) at which point there is a fork - the path to the right heads south-west over Druim Hain to Loch Coruisk and the other to the left heads south towards Camasunary. Take this left fork, and continue through the V-shaped valley Strath na Creitheach where the massive and cracked rock face of Blabheinn towers above Loch an Athain. On a bright day this scene offers a sight of rare beauty. The path continues at the base of the mountain and alongside Loch na Creitheach and then to a slight hillock, beyond which is Camasunary Bay. At Camasunary Bay there is a kilometre stretch of beach and fine views across Loch Scavaig towards the islands of Soay and Rhum. There is an expanse of grassy meadow behind the bay which would be excellent for camping in fine weather, with the opportunity to pick up drift-wood from the beach for a camp fire. There is also a bothy here on the western side of the bay by the river mouth.

A path heads back to civilisation to Kilmarie on the Elgol-Broadford road. This south-easterly route is well-used and reaches the road after 4km. The only public transport which goes through Kilmarie is the postbus from Broadford to Elgol that leaves Kilmarie at approximately 11am Monday-Saturday.

Camasunary Bay to Loch Coruisk

5km (approx. 2 hours)

This route, which follows the coast, is a challenging walk which entails a difficult river crossing at the west end of Camasunary Bay, then a cliff walk which culminates in an obstacle known as the 'Bad Step'. The river crossing is not too bad given fair weather and the ability to hop across stepping stones. However, if the water is high or the rocks are wet you will have to look upstream for a suitable crossing point and even then you are likely to end up with wet feet. The Bad Step, 1km from Loch Coruisk, involves having to climb around an overhanging slab of rock with a very nasty 10m drop into the sea and rocks below. However, it can be negotiated by moving out along a crack using handholds. After about 6 metres, and having gone around the corner of the slab, look for the route leftwards onto lower, easier

SLIGACHAN HOTEL
A863
A850
GLAMAIG
boggy
BEALACH À MHÀIM
GLEN BRITTLE
RIVER SLIGACHAN
stepping stones
N
SGURR NAN GILLEAN
SGURR NA BHAIRNICH
MARSCO
RED CUILLINS
SGURR THUILM
LOCHAN DUBHA
RUADH STAC
GARBH BHEINN
S.Y.H.A.
BLACK CUILLINS
SGURR A GHREADAIDH
DRUIM NAN RAMBH
DRUIM HAIN
LOCH AN AFFHAIN
STRATH NA CREITHEACH
SGURR NA BANACHDICH
SGURR DEARG
LOCH CORUISK
LOCH NA CREITHEACH
BLA BHEINN
SGURR ALASDAIR
SGURR DUBH MOR
LOCH BRITTLE
SGURR NAN EAG
SGURR NA STRI
CAMASUNARY
Bothy
The Bad Step
KILMARIE
BOAT
SOAY SOUND
LOCH SCAVAIG
A881
SOAY
ELGOL

ground and continue to Loch Coruisk. Provided you have a head for exposed positions and a sense of balance, the Bad Step will be more exhilarating than frightening, given that all the footholds and handholds are secure and reachable. (The only way to get to Loch Coruisk avoiding the Bad Step is by taking the Elgol-Loch Coruisk boat or by taking the Druim Hain route.)

About Loch Coruisk

Being in the shadow of the Cuillin mountains, Loch Coruisk has a sense of shady darkness which provided a myth-like status in the Victorian age when the popular notion was that the sun never shone on Loch Coruisk. The area around the loch is an exceptionally wild and cut-off place - the slabs and spurs of the Cuillin ridge encircle the north and western shores and the Druin nan Ramh rock wall cuts off any escape to the east. There is a mountain hut here on the western bank of the river leading into Loch Scavaig but this is kept locked.

Loch Coruisk to Sligachan

10km (approx. 4 hours).

This walk over Druim Hain begins at the south-east corner of Loch Coruisk, just after the Bad Step (see above). The path climbs up the hill in a north-westerly direction through the pass between Sgurr na Stri and Druim nan Ramh. At an altitude of 150 metres there is a small loch and after another 150m the ridge of Druim Hain, which is marked by a series of large cairns, is reached. From here it is an easy descent into Glen Sligachan picking up the path mentioned in the Sligachan to Elgol Walk at Lochan Dubha and then another 6km along the valley floor to the Sligachan Hotel.

· Black-faced Sheep ·

8.Fort William Area

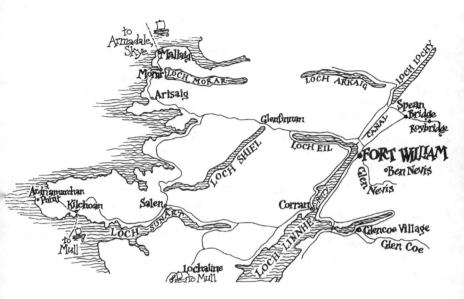

Fort William

Sitting in the shadow of Ben Nevis amidst magnificent mountainous scenery, Fort William is a big destination for holidaymakers. Its close proximity to the beauty of Glen Nevis, the daunting crags of Glencoe, and many other mountain slopes makes it a popular base for climbers, walkers, skiers and other adventurers.

Although Fort William sits on the shores of Loch Linnhe, a long arm of the sea which reaches in amongst the mountains, the town has sadly turned its back on the loch. The centre consists of a long pedestrian precinct, the High Street with the train and bus stations at the north end, and the very well set out **Tourist Information** halfway along at Cameron Square; tel:(01397) 703781 (always open until 4pm Monday-Saturday, and up until 8pm in July and August; Sunday - open in the summer). They sell cheap information sheets on walks and drives in the area which can be invaluable.

Cameron Square also houses the cinema and the curious **West Highland Museum**. It's an old-fashioned museum that doesn't, like so many others these days, explain everything simply and chronologically - instead it is filled to the brim with a little bit of everything to do with the Highlands. Also inside is photographic evidence of Henry Alexander's monumental drive up Ben Nevis in 1911. It's only £2/£1.50 to enter and worth a look, open all year. From the town centre you can go on a seal cruise (4-5 times daily from Easter-October) for £5/£4.50 from the quaint old pier, home to the red and white Crannog Restaurant (good food but not cheap), or take the ferry across the loch (80p) for either a peaceful walk, or take a bike and cycle back the long way around Loch Eil. Land-lubbers could take the short but steep hike up Cow Hill behind Fort William for a fantastic view down the Great Glen towards Mull. A mile or so out of town towards Spean Bridge is the 13thC **Old Inverlochy Castle** which has a certain gloomy presence. Unfortunately part of its fortifications these days is barbed wire and a locked gate.

In the summer there should be a steam train running between Fort William and Mallaig. It's expensive but it is a novel way to spend a day. Ask at Tourist Information or the train station for details.

Fort William Backpackers, Alma Rd, tel:(01397) 700711, £8.90/£10.90 (free tea and coffee). This homey and comfortable hostel has an open fire and is five minutes' walk from the centre. Good view. Curfew 2am. Open all year.
Calluna, Connochie Rd; tel:(01397) 700451, from £8 a night. Offers self-catering accommodation and is up the hill at the back of the town.
Glen Nevis SYHA, Glen Nevis, tel:(01397) 702336, Grade 1, £8.60/£11.10, open all year. Often very busy with climbers in winter as well as summer. 2½ mile walk from town; few buses. Curfew 2am.
Ben Nevis Bunkhouse, Achintee Farm, Glen Nevis Rd, tel:(01397) 702240, £7.50. Very basic accommodation, 1½ mile walk from town, cross the stream at Ionad Nibheis Visitor Centre. Open all year.
The Smiddy, Station Rd, Corpach, tel:(01397) 772467, £8.50. Open all year. Catering mainly for climbing groups, at Corpach, 3 miles from Fort William. Frequent buses.
Camping: At the beginning of Glen Nevis on the right side is a small field that offers camping for a low price. If this is full, another couple of miles up the glen is the Glen Nevis Camping Park, tel:(01397) 702191.

In the town of Fort William there are quite a few amusing ways to spend some time. The **Lochaber Leisure Centre** offers about a dozen sports from squash to wall-climbing to swimming at affordable prices. The new **Marco's Leisure Centre** has the likes of ten-pin bowling and an auditorium with the occasional event/concert.
Food-wise the town has plenty of reasonably-priced cafeterias, pub and hotel food, a kebab/pizza/fish and chip shop and a Chinese takeaway. For drinks the many bars are pleasant but much the same with the interesting exceptions of the **Maryburgh**, suitably tucked away up a close, and on a good night the **Station Bar** (nowhere near the station) with some occasional wild local music.

USEFUL ADDRESSES

TRAIN STATION

Fort William's train station is separated from the rest of the town by the busy A82 road. You can dodge the traffic, but there is a subway which brings you out at the beginning of the High Street. Tel:0345-484950 (24-hour service).

BUS STATION

In the car park behind the train station. In fact there is no bus station as such; you buy the tickets from the driver. For information, tel:0990-505050, 8am-8pm daily.

BANKS

Bank of Scotland, Royal Bank of Scotland and the Clydesdale banks are all located on the High St.

FOREIGN EXCHANGE

As well as the banks, Tourist Information (open daily until at least 5pm, 8pm in summer, but closed Sundays in winter) and Nevisport at the top of the High St in the upstairs craft shop (open daily until 5.30pm) have foreign exchange services.

CAR RENTAL

Nevis Car Hire, Nevis Garage, Ardgour Road, Caol, tel:(01397) 702432. £35 daily/ £210 weekly. Minimum age 21 years.

Budget Car Hire, North Road, tel:(01397) 702500. £34 daily/£210 weekly. Minimum age 23 years.

BICYCLE RENTAL

Off Beat Bikes, 117 High St, tel:(01397) 704008. £12.50 full day/£8.50 half day, mountain and touring bikes.

 Hitching from Fort William - see **Hitching**, Chapter 17.

Around Fort William,

Climbing Ben Nevis

The more intrepid of you will doubtless be setting your sights on a conquest of the dizzy heights of Ben Nevis which, at 4406ft, is Britain's highest mountain. There is a well-worn path to the summit starting in Glen Nevis from either the Ionad Nibheis Visitor Centre about a mile from the town, or more usually a mile further along the road at the SYHA hostel. Be careful and sensible as every year people are killed on this mountain, although in most cases these are people on different, more difficult routes. Take winter clothing (even in summer there is usually ice on the top - and though you might see people climbing in shorts and T-shirts they seldom reach the summit), waterproof clothing, plenty of food, a map and compass and sturdy boots. You can buy a pocket-sized, plastic-coated map locally; make sure you know exactly where you are on the map at all times in case the mist comes down suddenly. Don't go alone and tell your hostel/hotel/B&B when you expect to return. Don't underestimate the time it will take (allow 3-4 hours up and 2-3 down) and make sure that you have enough daylight. Don't hesitate to turn back if you're getting cold, tired or worried. Again, be careful - even just a twisted ankle can become a real problem if other conditions become bad. As long as you're sensible you should be all right, and you can enjoy a very satisfying experience, the details of which you can bore your friends senseless with for days.

Glen Nevis

Of all Scotland's glens this is perhaps the most beautiful. The scenery may look familiar to you if you've seen the films 'Braveheart' or 'Rob Roy' which starred Glen Nevis. Grand and magnificent at its beginning under the slopes of Ben Nevis it leads, after many miles, deep into the mountain wilderness. The valley floor is lush in most places, with Highland cows grazing in unfenced meadows beside the tree-lined banks of the Water of Nevis.

In the lower part of the glen this wide burn has a gentle, lazy feel to it and makes a relaxing companion on a walk. Further upstream, as it crashes through narrow gorges, it should be treated with caution. Across the burn on the hillside above, the colours are intense as birch, heather and bracken all compete for attention, each winning in different seasons. Opposite, the western slopes, dark with pine plantations below steep rocky outcrops, provides a moody contrast. On those slopes is the route of the West Highland Way as it rises up the glen, starting out on its 95-mile journey to Glasgow. Take this opportunity to walk along the start of this path. The views become spectacular as the path rises and then, before it leads you over the ridge into the next glen, drop back down to the forestry track heading south. This track, which is peaceful even at the height of summer, offers lovely elevated views of the glen. It rejoins the road two or three miles further on at Achriabhach, marked by some farm buildings and a waterfall under the road bridge. Here the glen turns eastward and becomes much wilder.

The road twists and turns upwards, past huge boulders, under old craggy trees and is overshadowed by giant rock slabs. The end of the road is marked by an awesome

· Golden Eagle ·

waterslide where the water cascades many hundreds of feet down the mountain slope in a mad frenzy, quite frightening when in spate. Beyond this point lies a fabulous walk through the narrow tree-lined Nevis gorge with fierce waters rumbling below. Admire the grand old Scots pines on the opposite slopes and curse the sheep amongst them preventing these remnants of the once vast forest from regenerating. After a half-hour hike along this rocky trail, you come to the stunning Steall Waterfall.

The **Ionad Nibheis Visitor Centre**, at the start of the glen about a mile from Fort William, provides bright and interesting displays. A mile further on, beside the youth hostel, is the friendly and good value Glen Nevis Cafe, where bikes and boots can be rented, open April-October.

Glencoe

The majestic extremes of Scotland's landscape are nowhere more evident than in the infamous Glencoe, with its severe, towering mountains. Steeped in the darker side of Scottish history, Glencoe is of particular significance to the clans of MacDonald and Campbell. The chief of the MacDonalds of Glencoe had unintentionally missed the deadline, by a few days, to swear an oath of allegiance to William III in 1692. This gave the government an excuse to rid themselves of this troublesome clan. A few weeks later the Campbells were billeted on the MacDonalds and, having been welcomed as guests by the MacDonalds for 12 days, the Campbells turned on their hosts in the middle of the night, slaying 38 and forcing the rest to flee. It was not the number of people murdered, but the act of betrayal that marks the atrocity of the massacre and anyone with the surname of Campbell has had to answer for it ever since.

Glencoe Visitor Centre (run by the National Trust) at the foot of the glen provides information and advice on walking in Glencoe. It's disappointing that you have to pay 50/30p simply to enter, but included in the price is a video programme on the Glencoe massacre, showing regularly. Anyone travelling by road between Fort William and Glasgow will pass through the 11-mile long glen, and if you have your own transport make sure you stop and go for a wander to soak up the atmosphere. If you're here on a day-trip by bus from Fort William, ask to get out at the top/last car park. From here there is a demanding walk (requiring decent shoes and a map) up to the Hidden Valley, or if you want to keep your feet dry, from the car park walk back down to the visitor centre, and then along the quiet old road past the youth hostels to Glencoe village where you can catch the bus back. The **Clachaig Inn** on the old Glencoe road is an oasis for walkers and mountaineers all meeting at the end of a hard day to swap stories and get absolutely steaming. They have bike rental too - £12 a day, £8.50 a half day, tel:(01855) 811252.

 Glencoe SYHA, tel:(01855) 811219, Grade 1, £7.75/£9.25, open all year. Perfectly adequate accommodation in a pleasant setting.
Glencoe Bunkhouse, Leacantuim Farm, tel:(01855) 811256, £6.50/£7.50, open all year. The 'alpine' accommodation is expensive for what you get (bring own bed linen) but it's the cheapest around. **Red Squirrel Campsite** is next to the bunkhouse and has the same phone number, £3.

Roy Bridge

The very small village of Roy Bridge, 11 miles north-east of Fort William, makes an enjoyable step aside from the major tourist centres of this area. There's a hostel in the town and another one 2 miles outside it, and a shop and hotel bar means that all essentials are provided. This is a hugely popular area with mountaineers (because of the Grey Corries nearby), but there are also many easy walks, along the quiet road that leads into Glen Roy in particular. Here on the hills can be seen the remarkable 'parallel roads' - lines marking the level of lochs during the last Ice Age. The other side of Roy Bridge, along the railway line and the River Spean, is also worth exploring. Easy to get to, Roy Bridge has a train station on the Glasgow to Fort William line, and a regular bus service from Fort William.

The Grey Corrie Lodge, behind the Roy Bridge Hotel, tel:(01397) 712236, £9/£10.50. Check in at the hotel, where there is a bar and games room with pool, darts, a small ten-pin bowling lane and perhaps the last bar billiards table in existence. A good place to procrastinate if the weather's bad. Open all year.

Aite Cruinnichidh, 1 Achluachrach, by Roy Bridge, tel:(01397) 712315, £7. This unpronounceable independent hostel is 2 miles from Roy Bridge east along the A86. This is a really cosy hostel but to get here you'll have to drive, cycle or walk. Make sure you head up the road near the hostel to the church and graveyard. Open all year. There are two **campsites** in Roy Bridge.

South-West of Fort William to Ardnamurchan

In a part of the world that sees many tourists, it is pleasantly surprising that this beautiful area remains largely unvisited even in the height of summer. If you want to get away from it all, this could be the place for you. The villages here are small and functional rather than picturesque, but it is the overall character that captivates. The main road from the Corran ferry takes you through the areas of Ardgour and Sunart to Ardnamurchan. It passes alongside the picturesque oak-covered north shores of Loch Sunart and through Salen, a lazy, leafy hamlet with a hotel, B&Bs, a shop and a tiny harbour.

The **Ardnamurchan Natural History and Visitor Centre** near Glenborrodale is interesting and free and also has a coffee shop. To the west of the Ardnamurchan peninsula is the small village of Kilchoan and a ferry pier (to Mull). A few miles past this is **Ardnamurchan Point**, the most westerly point of the Scottish mainland. A lighthouse stands at this wild, secluded and dramatic spot.

Taking the road that heads north out of Salen you can get to the impressive **Castle Tioram**, which sits on an island in Loch Moidart (this 14thC ruin can be reached and explored at low tide). The road later meets up with the scenic Mallaig to Fort William route, the 'Road to the Isles'.

To get to the Ardnamurchan Peninsula, take either the **Skyeways** or **Citylink** bus south-west from Fort William getting off at the Corran ferry at the bottom of Loch Linnhe. The ferry crosses frequently and is free for foot passengers. (Before you go across, however, check out the great wee bar at the back of the hotel - unspoilt and very plain it's basically a tin hut.) Public transport from Corran is scarce, with usually only one bus a day, so unless you're hitching you'd be best to have a car or bicycle to tour the region. It is possible to reach the island of Mull from either Kilchoan (summer only) or Lochaline.

Accommodation in the region is difficult as there are few B&Bs and no hostels. Campers, however, will have no problem. There are lots of places for free camping and at least two campsites. The Kilchoan House Hotel will let you camp for a small amount (though there are no showers). Two miles east of Salen is the **Resipole Caravan Park**, open Easter-October, tel:(01967) 431235, £8.50/£9.50 for two people.

Glenfinnan

Magnificently set at the head of Loch Shiel on the 'Road to the Isles' is the historic village of **Glenfinnan**. It was here - well, just up the hill a bit - that Bonnie Prince Charlie raised the standard at the outset of his Jacobite campaign in 1745. The monument at the lochside commemorates the Highlanders who died for the cause and can be climbed for £1.50/£1; NTS. The visitor centre nearby has a display on the Prince's campaign for the throne as well as a small shop.

The small church up the hill, which is usually unlocked, provides a peaceful sanctuary and the tiny old-fashioned train station is worth a visit, too. It has a small museum and a cafe inside old railway carriages - and what a view.

The **Glenfinnan Sleeping Car** at Glenfinnan station, tel:(01397) 722295/400, costs £7 a night and is open all year (but telephone ahead from November-March).

MALLAIG, MORAR AND ARISAIG

The few miles of coastline south of Mallaig hold a rich variety of attractions, including the Silver Sands of Morar.

Arisaig is a lazy village with fishing boats in the bay. On the main street down at the shore you can find the usual Scottish village shop, hotel etc., and after a few minutes' walk along the foreshore is the small pier. There are pricey boat trips to Eigg, Rhum and Muck, with the possibility of seeing whales, eagles, otters and red deer.

Heading towards Morar between the rocks and in the bays and inlets you will see the **Silver Sands** - in places golden (as featured in the film 'Local Hero'). This is excellent paddling country - swimming, though tempting, is only for the brave or the seals.

By **Morar** village the sands have amassed into long stretches and fill the whole of the rocky walled bay where Loch Morar, just out of sight but only a stroll away, flows into the sea. Loch Morar is a vast expanse of water stretching eastwards into the wilderness - it's the deepest freshwater loch in Europe. Take your camera in case you see its very well-kept secret - Morag the Monster (and you thought Nessie was unique).

The village train station is an excellent spot to view the Fort William to Mallaig steam train (should be running daily in summer). Being on the platform beside it is an intimidating but exhilarating experience. Otherwise you can watch it puffing towards you from the brilliant panoramic viewpoint above the village. Watch out for Morag as you wait for the train.

This whole area is ideal for cycling with quiet, winding roads that aren't too hilly.

Mallaig

Definitely a fishing and ferry port, Mallaig is not a beautiful place (more like somewhere to find a beautiful plaice). It has an enjoyably busy, fishy atmosphere, giving a welcome contrast to the nearby tranquillity. (Perversely the fish and chip outlets in Mallaig are very poor, so if you can't afford a restaurant get your camping stove out and try our very own fish recipe.) Around the town you can find various shops, pubs and banks as well as the **Mallaig Heritage Centre**; £1.80, open all year but from November-Easter open one or two days a week only. If you go to Mallaig's **Marine World** you can see Cromwell the Lobster who met the Queen; £2.75/£2, open all year.

i • There is a **Tourist Information**, tel:(01687) 462170, open April-September, and a railway station with three or four trains daily to Fort William.

Sheena's Backpackers, Harbour View, Mallaig, tel:(01687) 462764, £6/£11, open all year. Very handy for ferries and trains, busy central location. **Camping**: the coast is cluttered with camping and caravan sites of various prices and virtue. There's the odd spot for free camping too.
The area abounds with **B&Bs** and some hotels.

From Mallaig you can catch ferries to many islands and even other parts of the mainland, but the most usual destination is Armadale on Skye - passengers £2.50, cars £14.45. If you are going to the island of **Muck** there is a bunkhouse at Port Mor which has accommodation for £7.50/£8.50, tel:(01687) 462042, open all year.

EASY RECIPE

Ingredients: One piece of haddock/plaice/herring etc. (fresh from the fishmonger)
1 egg
cup of rolled oats (raw porridge)
one lemon
bag of savoury rice
some oil or butter
1 bottle of Moniack Castle Silver Birch Wine

Utensils: Frying pan, saucepan, one or two gas cooking rings

Ready? Put the rice on to boil. Dip the fish in the raw egg and cover in the oats (like breadcrumbs), fry the fish for about ten minutes, squeeze the lemon over it and serve up with savoury rice and the bottle of wine.

West Highland Way

This 95-mile trail through many varied types of Scottish scenery makes a fine challenge for the motivated backpacker. The path runs from Milngavie (pronounced mul-guy) on the outskirts of urban Glasgow, past lochs, over mountain passes, through bleak moors, under daunting mountain peaks, past pine woods, rivers and farmland, ending under the slopes of Ben Nevis at Fort William.

The recommended direction of travel is from south to north for three reasons. Firstly, this keeps the sun out of your eyes and warms your back (what sun? you're asking), secondly, the southern stretches are easier and make for a gentle build-up to the more arduous northern parts, and, thirdly, travelling from the relatively flat and domesticated south to the untamed mountainous north makes the journey all the more dramatic.

There are many hostels, bunkhouses and B&Bs on the route but it's a good idea to take a tent - although it adds weight to your pack, camping gives you freedom; the length of your day's walking is flexible and you won't experience the disappointment of arriving at a hostel which is full, and it's obviously a lot cheaper too. Just use the many hostels during bad weather or when you need some of life's comforts. It is advisable to camp out of sight as although few landowners object to the occasional camper on uncultivated land, it stops any problems arising. Needless to say, when you move on you should leave no trace of your presence behind.

Don't take too much with you but do take waterproof gear, worn-in boots, a hat, midge repellent in summer (or you'll be eaten alive!), suntan lotion, food for the next stage of your journey (remember there is a 28-mile stretch with no shops between Tyndrum and Kinlochleven), camping stove and matches, the map, a bottle of whisky, pack of cards, War and Peace, etc.

The majority of walkers plan on walking about 15 miles a day and taking 6-7 days to complete it. Due to British public holidays, May is a particularly busy time, so perhaps the best months of the year to go are June and July - before the midges get really bad in August. It's also a good idea to start mid-week because most people start at the weekend and this means there are a lot of people looking for accommodation at the same time.

If you want to save yourself the hassle of carrying your luggage, **Travel-Lite**, tel: (0141) 9567890, will take it to your destination along the Way each day for a fee of £28. This service is available from 18/4-25/9.

Although the Way is marked by small signposts, it is important to have a good map with you. Either buy the relevant Ordnance Survey Maps or a map specifically about the Way which will give all the information you need. Look for Footprints Map for £3.50 or Walker's Routes waterproof map for £6.95. The West Highland Way's Official Guide by Richard Aitken (published by HMSO), includes a detailed book and map of the path and costs £14.95.

West Highland Way

Starting at the Milngavie railway station, the beginning of the West Highland Way is very easy to find as there is a huge sign outside the front door of the station. Follow the directions and look out for the WHW symbol which marks the route. Go through the underpass, turn left up the main pedestrianised street, follow that for two minutes then turn right just before the bridge over the Allander Water. Almost immediately the path enters woodland. It is a very wide, gentle track that travels through Mugdock Wood, across a minor road, along a cart-track, through forestry plantations, past Craigallian Loch and up to the B821. Turn left here and follow the road for five minutes, before turning right into farmland. Here, we get the first major change in the countryside. The view opens up and you can see for several miles. Some ancient standing stones are along here to the right of the path.

The Way continues through farmland, and comes to an old railway line which it then follows for the next 4 miles. This is very easy to walk, but can get muddy in wet weather. Just before Dumgoyne you could visit the Glengoyne Distillery, a few hundred yards off the Way. At Dumgoyne, there is a pub that has a big sign welcoming walkers if you're in need of refreshment. From Gartness (where there is a walker-friendly tea-room) the Way follows a minor road for two miles and skirts past the outside of Drymen. Drymen is the last decent-sized town until Kinlochleven.

The Way then briefly follows the road before heading into a forestry commission plantation. A few miles later, the path leaves the forest, climbs over Conic Hill and then descends to the very small village of Balmaha, on the edge of Loch Lomond.

From Balmaha to Rowardennan the Way follows close to the edge of Loch Lomond, usually through forest and occasionally along the road, passing several small hills. In Rowardennan there are no shops but there is a hotel and the youth hostel sells basic food. The path to Ben Lomond also starts here.

Past the youth hostel there is easy walking with good views of the loch, but, after about 4 miles, and all the way to Ardleish, the Way is at its hardest. The track is still obvious, but narrow and rough, and after rain it gets very muddy. At Inversnaid there is a hotel, public toilets and an impressive waterfall. In summer a ferry runs across the there. Afterwards, the Way plunges back onto its narrow loch-side track. (Across the top end of the loch at Ardlui is another ferry which can be summoned to the east bank by raising a buoy up a flag pole. The railway station at Ardlui is on the Glasgow-Fort William/Oban line.)

The Way now leaves Loch Lomond and passes through Beinglas Farm. An essential rest-stop near here is Inverarnan where you can drink at the famous Drover's Inn.

Loch Lomond is now left behind and the Way passes through farmland, the hills become larger and the countryside truly begins to look like the Highlands.

It is 7 miles from Inverarnan to Crianlarich mostly following the River Falloch. The A82, however, is never far away and sadly the sound of vehicles is fairly constant. The Way slowly climbs all along this stage.

One mile from Crianlarich the Way enters a forest and turns left. Those wishing to visit or stay at Crianlarich must walk for a mile downhill to the town, otherwise, the path meanders down through the forest, across the main road and past the ruins of St Fillan's Chapel.

The Way is now easy and opens into the village of Tyndrum where there are restaurants, hotels, shops, two train stations and the Green Wellie Shop (which sells camping equipment).

From here the Way follows the old military road. This is initially a gentle climb and then a long, slow, downhill stretch to Auch.

The remaining 3 miles to Bridge of Orchy climbs slightly and finally drops down to the railway station of this very small village, where there is a hotel.

From Bridge of Orchy to Inveroran the path has great views of Loch Tulla and the Black Mount Lodge. Remember that free camping is not officially permitted on Rannoch Moor but is allowed alongside the burn further on from the Inveroran Hotel. The hotel has a small, local public bar that serves a limited selection of meals. Herds of deer come down in the evenings to graze the valley floor here.

From Inveroran there is a 10-mile walk across the bleak, barren Rannoch Moor. The Way mostly follows the old military road which is very easy to follow. Rannoch Moor is one of the most exposed sections of the Way and walkers should be appropriately attired as the wind can be bitterly cold. There are old stone bridges every mile or two which can provide some shelter.

The Way slowly climbs for 6 miles then drops the last 2 miles to the White Corries ski tow. From here it's another mile to Kingshouse, crossing the main A82 road as you go. From Kingshouse consists of a hotel only, and the Citylink bus stops at the road-end. From Kingshouse the path runs close to the A82. To the west the spectacular peaks of Glencoe soon become visible.

From the farm at Altnafeadh the Way parts company with the road and climbs over the Devil's Staircase - at 800 feet, the biggest climb along the entire route. It's quite steep but is soon over. The route then slowly descends towards Kinlochleven where there are hotels, B&Bs, campsites, bunkhouses, shops - but no banks.

From Kinlochleven the Way is well-signposted, climbing quite steeply out of the town and up to the old military road, which goes through a treeless barren glen. Two ruined buildings about a mile apart offer the only (basic, roofless) shelter in the glen. You'll start to pass through patches of forest and some very beautiful forest-walking is to be had along here. The Way goes up and down a bit, goes around a corner - until Ben Nevis impressively dominates the skyline to the east.

The Way steeply drops into Glen Nevis following the forestry road. Once you hit the public road it's less than 2 miles to Fort William.

Budget accommodation available, listed from south to north -

Glasgow Backpackers, 8 Park Circus, summer only, tel:(0141) 332 9099; Glasgow SYHA, 8 Park Terrace, tel:(0141) 332 3004; Berkeley Globetrotters, 65 Berkeley Street, tel:(0141) 2217880; Easter Drumquhassle Farm, Drymen, tel:(01360) 660893; Rowardennan SYHA, near Drymen, tel:(01360) 870259; Rowchoish and Doune bothies, Loch Lomondside (both free, no facilities); Beinglas Farm (bunkhouse, campsite), Inverarnan, tel:(01301) 704281; Crianlarich SYHA, tel:(01838) 300260; Auchtertyre Farm, Tyndrum, tel:(01838) 400251; Pine Trees Bunkhouse, Tyndrum, tel:(01838) 400243; The 'Way-In' Bunkhouse, Bridge of Orchy Hotel, tel:(01838) 400208; West Highland Lodge, Kinlochleven, tel:(01855) 831471; Grant's Garage, Kinlochleven, tel:(01855) 831666 or 831478; Glen Nevis SYHA, tel:(01397) 702336; Ben Nevis Bunkhouse, Achintee Farm, tel:(01397) 702240; Fort William Backpackers, Alma Rd, tel:(01397) 700711.

Note that Milngavie to Rowardennan, and Bridge of Orchy to Kinlochleven are long stretches with little or no budget accommodation.

Walking Across the Central Highlands

 DIFFICULT

Dalwhinnie to Fort William via Loch Ericht, Loch Ossian and Glen Nevis

This 70km-route traverses the Central Highlands from east to west and reveals its many different aspects, from the rounded and rolling Grampian Mountains in the east to the impressive heights of Ben Nevis in the west. The walk begins at the A9 at Dalwhinnie and follows the north bank of Loch Ericht. It then stretches across the northern parts of Rannoch Moor and heads towards Fort William through the spectacular scenery of Glen Nevis. The route described here is divided into four sections, unequal in distance, for the convenience of those travelling without a tent who will need to use the various bothies and hostels which are along the way. There are plenty of fine camping places for those who do have the extra independence which a tent affords.

The route passes through both deer and sheep-grazing estates and areas of both the older Scots pine and more recently imported conifers. Most of the paths are well defined and rivers can be crossed by permanent bridges or stepping stones provided that weather conditions are not too atrocious. During the stalking season (between mid-August and the end of October) it is important not to stray far from the paths, but at other times the opportunities for exploring the area more fully may prove too tempting to resist.

Getting to Dalwhinnie

Dalwhinnie (O.S. sheet 42; 635849), at the northern end of Loch Ericht, is the starting place for this route. It can be reached either by coach or rail services. Choosing the train will save you the 2km walk from the bus stop into Dalwhinnie village.

The village has an impressive whisky distillery, and the Toll House Store for stocking up in. The excellent Ben Alder Cafe, which serves good value meals all day, has a pool table, a bar and friendly staff - the best in Scottish hospitality in fact! For these reasons the cafe is the recommended starting point for this journey.

Dalwhinnie to Benalder Cottage Bothy

Map: O.S. Landranger 42

Distance: 23km (approx. 6 hours)

From the cafe turn left (south) and down to the petrol station 5 minutes along the road. Turn right after it by a short row of houses. Follow the track under the railway line to the top of Loch Ericht and cross over to the northern shore where you pick up the track coming from the railway station and follow this along the side of the loch. Loch Ericht is a long finger-shaped loch which stretches for over 30km and is seldom more than 1km wide. The first

10 km of the track is through conifer forest with open views of the Grampian Mountains on the south side of the loch and the corries of the Ben Alder plateau directly in front.

After 8km the track reaches the Ben Alder Lodge, where another track leads off to the right and provides an alternative route around the north of Ben Alder via the Culra bothy. However, stay on the lower track and pass through the lodge grounds to the left of the main house, following the loch edge. Keep to the loch shore all the way to the Benalder Cottage Bothy, taking care where the path crosses a short rocky section just before the end.

The bothy, owned by the Ben Alder Estate, is in good repair and left open for the use of walkers in the area. From mid-August to the end of October is the deer shooting season, during which you should stay on the paths and not go wandering over the hill-sides. There is firewood nearby, but you will have to explore the woods on the other side of the Alder Burn to find the best logs. There is another of Bonnie Prince Charlie's many hiding places in a cave just near here - try and find it if you can and be glad that you do not have to spend the night in such a miserable hole!

Benalder Cottage to Loch Ossian Youth Hostel

Map: O.S. Landranger 42

15km (approx 4-5 hours)

Follow the path from the back of the bothy beside the metal posted fence, away from the shores of Loch Ericht this time. The path climbs gently for 4km following the Alder Burn to the top of the Bealach Cumhann pass. At the top of the pass the path levels out, the slopes of Ben Alder are behind you and the peaks of Aonach Beag and Glas Choire are across the valley before you. Hopefully you will see many of the deer that roam the mountain slopes in this area. At this point the path turns and heads north-east up the glen and along the broad flanks of Ben Alder. This is where you will have to leave the path temporarily and carry straight on across the open heather and down to the floor of the glen. Cross over to the north bank of the Uisge Labhair river to where the path starts again.

Follow the path through the open glen down towards Loch Ossian and then take the sturdy bridge which crosses the river. The path now heads through the woods to the Corrour Shooting Lodge and then turns to follow the loch around the southern shore. Follow the track through the forest to the Youth Hostel at the far end of the loch. Hopefully you will arrive in time and still have the energy to participate in the traditional 'run around Loch Ossian in an hour' competition and then have a refreshing swim in the loch.

Loch Ossian SYHA, tel:(01397) 732207, Grade 3, £4.65, open 20/3-31/10. The youth hostel is very well equipped for such a relatively isolated location, with a coal-heated stove and wind-generated electricity. The former warden had an unusual empathy with some of the local stags which would sometimes come down to the hostel when he called - hopefully the deer will still turn up. If the hostel is full, about 1½ km further on lies Corrour Station where Morgan's Den bunkhouse, tel:(01397) 732236, offers basic accommodation year round; £4.

Up until 70 years ago Corrour Station was privately owned by the Corrour Estate and the youth hostel used to be the reception centre/boat house for people arriving from the station to go on to the lodge. An amazing journey to have witnessed would have been the estate owners, deer stalkers, estate workers, their families and school teachers plus servants, a butler and various pets, travelling from the station to what was then the boat-house. They would have to unload from train to horse-drawn carriage and then to a steamboat before travelling down the loch to the old Corrour Lodge. It must have been chaotic as 60 or so people lived at Corrour in those days; now the population is down to 7. The steamboat has since been dismantled and removed from the loch and the original estate house burnt down.

Loch Ossian to Meanach Bothy

Map: O.S. Landranger 41

12km (approx. 3-4 hours)

From the youth hostel continue on the estate track for a short while around Loch Ossian. The first turning is the track to Corrour railway station; go past this and take the next left which is the footpath to Loch Treig and then the Meanach Bothy. The path heads off over open moorland and on towards the railway, passing underneath the line and following the direction of the railway for a short time.

Follow the track to Loch Treig and around the southern end of the loch towards the Creaguaineach Lodge. Cross the bridge just before the Lodge

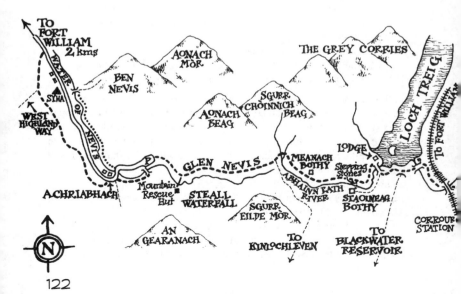

and follow the path on the northern side of the Abhainn Rath river. The signpost for Glen Nevis points along the southern side of the river, but crossing over to the northern side and following the path allows for much easier walking. The landscape changes at this point to a more sheltered glen. The river is wide and flows intermittently over bare rock and then past steep green, grassy banks.

Further up the Abhainn Rath there is a series of waterfalls in a small area of woodland.

The Staoineag bothy is only 3km along this path but is on the south bank of the river (stepping stones are available). The Meanach bothy is an hour's journey further from here at a point where the glen opens out into very exposed moorland. Unless you have plenty of daylight hours left or a tent, you would be well advised to spend the night at Meanach. This is an excellent place to stay. Being close to Ben Nevis and surrounded by numerous high mountains, it gives a very real sense of being in the wilderness.

Meanach Bothy to Fort William

Map: O.S. Landranger 41

22 km (approx. 7-8 hours)

The path continues from the bothy along the river over some scraggy moorland, to where the Abhainn Rath river tails off and the Water of Nevis begins its journey to Fort William and Loch Linnhe. The path continues through Glen Nevis, now following the Water of Nevis into narrower sections of the glen.

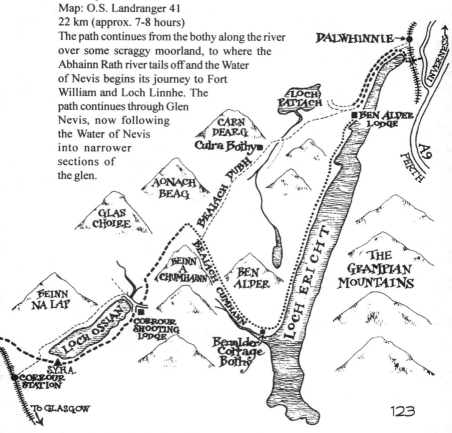

The lower slopes of the surrounding mountains come low down into the glen to make a magnificent journey through some of the most popular mountains of the Highlands. You will occasionally be able to catch glimpses of Ben Nevis, the highest mountain in Scotland.

In the shadow of the spectacular Steall waterfall, the path follows the river past the Mountain Rescue hut and its perilous-looking suspended wire-access bridge. Resist the temptation to impersonate Indiana Jones and stay on the right hand bank of the river. Follow this frequently-used path through the gorge with fiercesome rumbling waters below and daunting mountains above. You will shortly be rejoining civilisation as this path soon brings you to the car park at the top of the Glen Nevis road. You are now 11 km from Fort William. Set out along this narrow and relatively busy tarred road, but take the opportunity to regain the tranquillity by crossing the river just 1km down the road at a small wooden bridge beside a shed on the opposite bank (this is not signposted, so keep an eye out for this bridge). Once across the bridge you can proceed downstream on the quiet south side of the river. A further 1½ kms will bring you back down to the road at the very small hamlet of Achriabhach. At this point the glen takes an almost 90° turn, heading north to Fort William. The road crosses the River Nevis and you now have two pleasant alternatives to the tarmac road. One is either to cross the road bridge to the north-east bank of the river for a very gentle walk along the grassy banks, though there is no specific path. After less than an hour you will cross the ever-popular Ben Nevis path leading from the SYHA hostel. You can cross the foot-bridge here for a delightful cafe, a campsite and a pub as well as the youth hostel. The other is to remain on the east bank until you reach the foot-bridge between the Ionad Nibheis Visitor Centre and the Achintee Bunkhouse. It is now a 2km roadside walk into Fort William.

The alternative at Achriabhach is to complete the journey along the Forestry Road which offers some lovely elevated views of the glen and the ben as it makes its way through avenues of dark pine plantations and clearings. This route is especially recommended if the weather is wet - it is also lovely in fine weather. Pick the route up at Achriabhach where you see the sign 'Forest Walks'. Take the forestry road through the gate (as opposed to the footpath) - it's an easy route to follow, just carry straight on, and don't turn left at any point unless you want to enjoy a diversion up the hillside. Should you wish to get to the Glen Nevis youth hostel/cafe/campsite/start of the Ben Nevis walk, take the only turning to the right (after about 4km) leading through a gate, past some houses, then turn right at the main road. If not, the route continues for a further 2km or so where it finally meets the main road a short walk from Fort William at the - don't laugh - 'Braveheart' car park. During this stretch it merges briefly with the West Highland Way, which comes in from the west. Well done!

9.Argyll

This south-westerly scattering of islands and peninsulas, with over 2,000 miles of coastline, offers a lovely assortment of scenery.

It was here that the Scots first arrived from Ireland around AD600 and their kingdom grew eventually to dominate the Celtic and Pictish populations. Much later the region became a constant problem for the Crown with belligerent clan chiefs and Lords taking advantage of the sea and mountain barriers.

These days the natives depend mainly on fishing, farming and some gorgeous whisky distilling. Tourism, of course, plays its part but there are many areas so out of the way that it is hardly noticeable.

Oban

The hillsides around Oban bay form a natural amphitheatre with the action-filled harbour of this vibrant port centre-stage and the islands of Kerrera and Mull providing a fabulous backdrop.

Down at the quayside, ferries from half of the Hebrides disgorge their goods and passengers, fishing boats tie up and unload, yachts and pleasure boats slink about, trains and buses arrive and leave. It's a busy, buzzing place and, should the action cease briefly, there's usually a seal and a couple of swans mixing with the fishing boats to take your attention.

The waterfront is packed full of hotels, pubs, guesthouses, cafes, souvenir shops and more, with everybody wanting a good view of the comings and goings and everybody getting one. From Oban you can reach an assortment of Hebridean islands by ferry including the hugely popular Mull, the religious centre of beautiful Iona and the geological spectacle of Fingal's Cave on Staffa. Accessible too are the quieter islands of Kerrera and Lismore, and the more remote Coll and Tiree. If you have time to spare while you wait for your ferry, Oban itself will easily keep you occupied with things to do and see, and for the backpacker there are three hostels to choose from.

McCaig's Tower stands high above the town looking out to the islands and truly is a glorious place to watch the sun set. McCaig, a wealthy banker, had the tower built in 1897 as a memorial to his family but more significantly it was a scheme to provide work for the local unemployed. It's free and always open. The **Oban Distillery** in Stafford Street is one of Scotland's oldest, established in 1794. They run guided tours and also have a visitor centre detailing the history of the town, including an audio-visual display. The visitor centre is free, the tour £3, and you are given a £3 voucher for any whisky you buy in their shop; open all year.

The intriguing museum, **A World In Miniature**, near the Columba Hotel, depicts numerous miniature scenes. It may not sound like much but the longer you stay the more fascinating it becomes and you simply have to admire the people who put the time and effort into it; £1.80, open daily April-October.

i **Tourist Information** is located at Argyll Square, tel:(01631) 563122, open all year. (Open up to 5pm but 9pm in the height of summer, shorter hours at weekends, and not Sundays in winter.)

Bikes can be rented from **Oban Cycles**, Craigard Road, tel:(01631) 566996; £10 a day or £2.50 an hour.

The **Oban Inn** on Stafford St is a very popular pub with a terrific atmosphere while **O'Donnell's** on Breadalbane St has live music at the weekend and is open until 1am.

Walks

Apart from the essential walk up to **McCaig's Tower**, you can stroll north along the esplanade enjoying the sea view toward **Dunollie Castle**, and it's a short scramble up the hill to this appealing ruin. The road continues to the bay of Ganavan, and if you walk even further along the coast you will eventually reach **Dunstaffnage Castle** (£1.80/£1.30 to enter), a formidable 13thC stronghold, and Dunstaffnage

Bay, about four miles away. Walking south of Oban you can go up **Pulpit Hill** for another fine view of the town, the islands and even as far as Ben Nevis. There are pleasant views from along the two-mile road to Gallanach and from Gallanach you can catch a boat to Kerrera (see boat-trips from Oban).

Oban Backpackers, Breadalbane St, tel:(01631) 562107, £8.90/£9.90, open all year, 2.30am curfew. Central location, impressive beds and a laid-back atmosphere.

Oban SYHA, Esplanade, tel:(01631) 562025, Grade 1, £8.60/ £11.10, open all year except 4/1-28/1, 2am curfew. The only hostel with views across the water, it's a very pleasant 10-minute walk from town along the waterfront.

Jeremy Inglis, 21 Airds Crescent, tel:(01631) 565065, £7.50, open all year. Just near Tourist Info, good price but small kitchen. Twin rooms available.

Hitching from Oban - see Hitching, Chapter 17.

Boat-trips from Oban

To take all the hassle out of organising ferry and local bus times you might be interested in taking one of the many organised boat-trips available. Along the esplanade, just past the Columba Hotel, a selection of small boats depart for day trips to **Mull**. They take you to either Duart Castle or Torosay Castle near Craignure, and can be a very good idea if you're short on time. Tour companies **Gordon Grant Marine** and **Bowman's** both have a range of tours. Their full-day tours incorporating the large Caledonian MacBrayne ferry, taking you to **Mull** and **Iona** as well as the amazing island of **Staffa** for £26 are very good value. Tours to Mull and Iona only are £16. Gordon Grant tickets are available from the Railway Pier, tel:562842, while Bowman's tickets can be bought from their office in Stafford Street.

Of course you can always catch the **Caledonian MacBrayne** ferry to Craignure on Mull yourself and explore at your leisure. Meeting most ferries in Craignure are local bus services going either to the north and the island's main town of Tobermory, or to Fionnphort, the ferry port for Iona and Staffa. For more information on **Mull**, **Iona** and **Staffa** see later in this chapter.

Much closer to Oban are the small, scarcely populated and untouristy islands of **Kerrera** and **Lismore**. The ferry to **Kerrera** leaves from Gallanach, two miles south of Oban, and costs about £2.50 return, with crossings every hour or so, but less often in winter. A small island (four by two miles) it's just perfect for a few hours' exploration. Head for the south of the island to the ruined 16thC Castle Gylen or climb the island's highest point of 600 feet called Carn Breagach for terrific views. There are several paths you can take. You could stay overnight at the **Gylen Bothy**, Lower Gylen, tel:(01631)570223, £7, open all year. They offer a lift to and from the ferry by arrangement.

The larger island of **Lismore** (about 10 miles in length) can be explored on foot or by bicycle (if you hire your bike in Oban). Ferries leave from Oban a few times each day at the main ferry terminal; £3.60 return. Once ashore seek out the ruined castles of

Achadun to the south-west and Coeffin to the north-west; to the north-east there is the ruined broch of Tirefour. Take food and supplies with you to either of these islands.

Other islands you might consider for a day trip are **Seil** and the much smaller **Easdale** island south-west of Oban. The severely humped bridge you'll come to is the crossing to Seil and it's attractive village, Ellanbeich, has a **Highland Arts Centre** with local art and craft exhibitions and items for sale. The ferry to Easdale runs on demand, from April-September, until 9pm but only until 5pm on a Sunday. Easdale Island is tiny and it doesn't take long to walk around, so you may wish to visit the **Folk Museum** (open April-September) for details on the island's slating history; £2.50. Local buses operate from Oban to Easdale. Cycling is possible but the road heading out of Oban is initially quite busy.

Mull

The hectic pace of life slows down refreshingly as you cross the Firth of Lorn to the isle of Mull. While many of Mull's visitors are in a rush to see it all in a day, you are well advised to slow down to the relaxed pace of the islanders and discover the island's delights at your leisure.

The capital in the north, Tobermory, bustles with activity as fishing boats and tourists head in and out of the pretty town, while the west of Mull has a coastline of exquisite tranquillity including the white sandy bay of Calgary. The highest peak of Ben More overlooks all from the centre of the island, and from Fionnphort boats leave for Iona and Staffa.

Pensioners love Mull so there's always someone over 60 to have a chat with. There's only one hostel on the island at Tobermory but there are campsites and many B&Bs.

On arriving at Craignure most visitors rush out of town on their way to the north or towards Iona, but Craignure has its own attractions. For something different you can take Mull's miniature railway for a scenic 1½ miles to Torosay for £2.20 single/£3.30 return. At its end you can visit **Torosay Castle and Gardens**, a 19thC mansion open Easter to mid-October (gardens open all year); £4.50/£3.50.

Another mile and a half along from Torosay is the more dramatically positioned **Duart Castle** that dates from the 13thC. You can see the castle dungeons and there are fine views from the wall walk; £3.50/£2.85, open May to mid-October.

Accommodation in Craignure is restricted to a few **B&Bs** and the well-equipped **Sheiling Campsite**, tel:(01680) 812496; £4-£5.50 per person, open April-October. They also have hostel accommodation in structures called 'shielings' which are carpeted, cottage-like tents with beds inside; £6.50-£7.50 per person, open early May-September.

North Mull

Heading north-west from Craignure the first dot on the map is **Fishnish** where the ferry arrives from Lochaline. Fishnish merely consists of a pier and a nearby campsite. A few miles further on lies the small quiet village of **Salen**, where you can walk down to the pier for a look over Salen Bay. It's a sleepy place (perhaps that's just what you're looking for) with a couple of shops, a hotel serving bar meals and a few **B&Bs**.

It's then about 10 miles north to one of Scotland's most irresistible seaside villages - **Tobermory**, with its many-coloured seafront houses, is enough to brighten any gloomy day. Cheerful and busy, the fishing port has a few indoor attractions, but just wandering through the village soaking up the atmosphere and taking the easy coastal walks makes it a valuable stop. The **Mull Museum** on the seafront is a modest museum which features local history on all sorts of subjects and many old photographs; 70p. **Tobermory Distillery** costs £2.50 to have the process of whisky distillation explained to you with a dram of their produce included in the price. Open daily Easter to mid-October (Tuesdays and Thursdays only in November and December).

Past the ferry terminal to the north of the town is a coastal walk leading to a lighthouse 1½ miles away. Alternatively the path to the south of the village (the path starts at the back of MacGochan's pub) is good too. The start of this walk will give you Tobermory's best angle and it then continues along the coast and into Aros Park, with its waterfalls and an ornamental loch. Return to Tobermory the way you came or along the A848 road.

Tobermory SYHA, tel:(01688) 302481, Grade 3, £6.10/£7.60, open 27/2-31/10. Basic facilities, closed during the day. Bike hire. **Newdale Campsite**, tel:(01688) 302306, 1½ miles out of town on the road to Dervaig, £3 per person and £1 for a shower, open April-November. For **B&Bs** try **Tourist Information** at the ferry terminal, tel:(01688) 302182, open March-October.

For food there are a couple of cheap places along the main street and anyone with a sweet tooth should make a beeline for the **Tobermory Chocolate Factory**. Tobermory has Mull's one and only bank (although there is a mobile bank that goes around the island every Wednesday), so check your finances before you leave town. Destinations of ferries leaving Tobermory are Kilchoan and Oban on the mainland .

Five miles south-west of Tobermory is **Dervaig**, a pretty and quiet conservation village with a coffee shop and a couple of hotels serving bar meals. The town is home to Scotland's smallest professional theatre, the **Mull Little Theatre**, located in a converted cowshed. Check at the ticket office in the centre of the village or phone (01688) 400245 to see what's playing. Three-quarters of a mile out of town is **The Old Byre**, a well presented audio-visual museum and heritage centre depicting life on Mull through the ages; £2/£1.50, open 5/4-23/10.

Fine white sand lines the shore of **Calgary Bay**, a sheltered beauty spot that might tempt you in for a swim. Swimming in Scottish waters could be an experience you'll never forget.

The island of **Ulva** can be reached from the ferry departure point near Lagganulva. Ulva has some of the remarkable basaltic rock formations that are found on Staffa and at the Giant's Causeway in Northern Ireland and you can visit the **Boathouse Visitor Centre** to find out about it. The island has signposted walks you can take. Ferries also leave for Staffa and the Treshnish Isles from this ferry terminal. The road as you approach the Ulva ferry point has some of Mull's most beautiful vistas, looking across to Ulva and up to the picturesque Ben More. Australians might be interested to know that at Gruline there is a mausoleum for MacQuarrie, the Governor General of New South Wales in the early 1800s.

South Mull

Splendid views again can be seen on the west coast on the road south of Gruline and anyone looking for a challenging and rewarding walk could take the turn-off to **The Burg** to see a 50-million-year-old fossilised tree. It's a 5½ mile walk from the road-end alongside high cliffs and can only be attempted at low tide and with some difficulty.

The A849 road that cuts across the south of the island from Craignure through Glen More and onto the Ross of Mull is well used by visitors as they streamline their way to the magical island of Iona. There are a few worthwhile detours to take from this route, one being the road to **Loch Buie** and the ruin of **Castle Moy**. The other is the road to Carsaig from where you can walk for 3 miles to the **Carsaig Arches** - formed by the sea in the basaltic rock - and see the Nun's Cave on the way. They can only be reached at low tide, though.

Getting to Mull

Ferries arrive at three points on the island - Fishnish from Lochaline, Tobermory from Kilchoan, and Craignure from Oban, which is the most frequent and popular crossing. Ferries always leave Oban at 10am, 12 noon, 2pm and 4pm, with some extra crossings (check Caledonian MacBrayne timetables). The price for one foot passenger is £3.25 single/£5.60 return and taking a bicycle costs £2 extra. Taking a car will set you back £22.70 single/£39 return plus £3.25/£5.60 per passenger - quite an expense, but you will be able to explore the island thoroughly. All return prices quoted are for a five-day return ticket; there is no cheap day-return ticket. The ferries from Oban get very busy and the sooner you book your ticket the better.

Iona

Bringing the message of Christianity to Britain, Saint Columba arrived on the remote isle of Iona in AD563. He founded a monastery, and from this unlikely base managed to convert the mainland. Understandably it is a place of pilgrimage for Christians but it is an island of such enchanting beauty that it delights all visitors. This small island with its crystal-blue water, white sandy beaches and ragged coastline is a treasure to explore.

Visitors descend on the historic **Iona Abbey** in hordes and the Iona Community, which is responsible for its upkeep request, or rather demand, a £2 donation before you enter. The abbey which stands today was founded in the 13thC but is understood to be built on the site of Columba's much earlier monastery. The abbey cloister is most attractive and hung upon its walls is the story of the abbey and the Iona Community. Within the abbey grounds is Iona's oldest standing building, **Saint Oran's Chapel**. Built in the 11thC, it stands in the centre of Scotland's ancient burial ground, **Reilig Odhrian**, reputed to be the burial site of 48 Scottish kings including Macbeth. To this holy site a king's body would be carried from the mainland and interred. At the front of the abbey is **St Michael's Cross**, a Christian cross standing where it has done since the 8thC. In the museum at the back of the abbey the remaining fragments of the similarly dated **St John's Cross** are reassembled. This museum also contains numerous Christian stones and medieval effigies moved from the graveyard for protection from the elements.

On your way to the abbey you will pass the ruins of the 13thC Nunnery as well as the **Iona Heritage Centre** which gives you a very detailed introduction to the island, and there's a coffee shop at the back. The island certainly has a special atmosphere but you may well be put off by the camera-happy tourist brigade - if so, don't worry as most of these visitors go no further than the abbey and yet there is so much more to the island.

Take the road past the abbey to the north shore for beautiful white sands and lovely views. To the west of the village is the long beach known as the Bay at the Back of the Ocean, while to the south is the sheltered Port na Curaich. For a climb, head up Dun 1 (such a strange name for a hill) only 101m high.

A tour of the island is given on Wednesdays at 10am, from March to November, assembling at the Abbey. It is a lightly religious pilgrimage all around the island which lasts for a few hours and can be enjoyed by all.

Accommodation on the island is limited with only a few **B&Bs** but you can camp if you ask permission first. There's no Tourist Information but the Finlay Ross general store might be able to help you with advice on accommodation. They hire out bikes for a low price (the island's small enough to walk so only rent them if you're really short of time) and have a laundry service. If you do stay overnight you'll see Iona as it should be seen - quiet and without the tourists.

Ferries run regularly from Fionnphort on Mull to Iona costing £3 return. If you're not staying overnight check when the last ferry goes back; it's usually around 6pm. Boat-trips to Staffa leave from Iona (see Staffa).

STAFFA

Slow-cooling volcanic lava about 50 million years ago resulted in one of Scotland's most incredible natural features. Tall hexagonal columns of basalt rock constitute this small, unpopulated island and within the high cliffs is the magnificent **Fingal's Cave**. The cave inspired Mendelssohn to write his overture of the same name after a visit to Staffa in 1829, already a popular tourist destination. It was even visited by Queen Victoria. Puffins can be seen at close quarters on the island from about May until the end of July. Excellent three-hour boat-trips depart from Iona at 9.45am and 1.45pm (and leave Fionnphort on Mull at 10am and 2pm); £10, April to mid-October. You can also get to Staffa from Ulva on Mull with **Turus Mara**, tel:(01688) 400242, or arrange an all-inclusive tour from Oban (see **Oban**, boat-trips).

Tiree

Tiree, the most outer of the Inner Hebrides, derives its name from the Gaelic, meaning 'land of corn'. Though the island is quite flat (except for a couple of modest hills and seaside cliffs) it has some of the most beautiful beaches in Scotland, just perfect for walking, cycling, windsurfing, bathing (perhaps) and just generally exploring. You might not believe this, but in the months of May and June, Tiree tops the sunshine records of Scotland. There are also many ancient ruins of archaeological significance, making Tiree the more diverse and interesting choice between it and Coll.

The ferry arrives at **Scarinish**, a harbour town that contains the island's bank and post office. From near here it is possible to hire a bike, or take the island's postbus for your tour of the island. If you're walking, there are places to enjoy close at hand. North of the town is the long and sandy beach of Gott Bay, two miles in length and very nice for a stroll. On the northern shore is Vaul, and nearby the remarkable Dun Mor Vaul, a well-preserved broch. If you continue west along the coast you'll reach the Ringing Stone, a stone with mysterious prehistoric marks which makes a metallic sound when struck.

Although the coastal scenery all around is worth seeing, the south of the island is where you should make the effort to reach. The south-west headland of Kenavara has great cliffs and is a paradise for birdwatchers. It is possibly the most dramatic part of Tiree and a lovely and lonely place to retreat to. Happy Valley to the west of Hynish is also a wild place, again of ragged cliffs and popular with birds.

At Hynish is the **signal tower museum** which tells the story of the building of the Skerryvore lighthouse, alone in the sea 10 miles south-west of the island. Until 1954 a lonely lighthousekeeper was stationed here.

For accommodation there are few cheap options. If you are staying overnight Tourist Information in Oban or Tobermory can give you an accommodation list - it's best to plan ahead, unless of course you're camping. There's no campsite on the island but you can camp anywhere provided you get permission from the landowner.

Bike hire is available all year from the **Lodge Hotel** along Gott Bay, tel:(01879) 220353; £8 a day for mountain bikes.

Coll

Fewer people live on the island of Coll, and there is less to see than on Tiree, but it still possesses those beautiful remote sandy beaches worth travelling a long way for. For those looking to get away from civilisation, Coll is largely unspoilt and has many corners to explore.

The majority of the population live in the village of **Arinagour** where the ferry arrives. The bays of the west coast are truly remarkable and Feall Bay even has an Iron Age fort. At Totronald there are two standing stones and further north at Killunaig, along the road to Sorisdale, are the ruins of a medieval church.

4½ miles from the ferry at the southern end of the island is Breachachadh Castle. You can camp in the grounds of this castle, tel:(01879) 230374; from £5, open April-October. It's a lovely base from which to explore the island and the friendly owners also provide B&B accommodation all year. There are a limited number of B&Bs on the island and if you're planning to stay you should definitely phone ahead.

Getting to Coll and Tiree

Travellers to these islands might get frustrated with the ferry timetables. Ferries depart once a day from Oban but not on Thursdays or Sundays. Departure times differ but they usually leave Oban at 6.30am! Check timetables carefully or phone **Caledonian MacBrayne**, Oban, tel:(01631) 566688. Prices: Oban to Coll or Tiree - £17.80, 5-day return; Coll to Tiree - £4.45, 5-day return. Bicycles £2 extra per trip.

Islay

The gentle rolling hills, rich farmland and gorgeous long sandy beaches all around the coast make up the remote island of Islay. It has many places of historical interest and lots of activities such as horse-riding, diving, fishing and of course, drinking - the island is, after all, most famous for its whisky. Each distillery on Islay produces a malt whisky with a flavour and character all of its own. All but one of these distilleries offer tours, showing and explaining the stages of malt whisky production - malting, mashing, fermentation, distillation, then finishing with the final stage, drinking. A great time to visit Islay is when the music festival is on (23-31 May in 1998), with plenty of bands and ceilidhs running until the early hours.

Most of the ferries coming from Kennacraig on the mainland arrive at **Port Ellen**, a small village clustered around a harbour with a post office, a bank and a couple of bars. Bicycles can be hired from the grocer's shop **Macaulay & Torrie**, tel:(01496) 302053, full day £10, half day £5. There are about six buses a day heading up the island but not on Sundays.

Along the coastal road east of Port Ellen are a few of those distilleries. The first, not far from Port Ellen, is the **Laphroaig Distillery**, tel:(01496) 302418. Free tours with a free dram of whisky are at 10.30am and 2.30pm on weekdays from Easter to September, but outside these months tours are by appointment only. Further along the Ardbeg Distillery is not open to visitors, but the **Lagavulin Distillery** not far from it is, tel:(01496) 302400. Tours of the distillery cost £2 (but you get a £3 discount if you buy a bottle of their whisky) and are at 10.30am and 2.30pm, Monday-Friday, Easter-October, dram included - you need to phone ahead to book a place on the tour.

Near this distillery are the ruins of the 16thC **Dunvaig Castle**, which was built on the site of an earlier stronghold of the Lord of the Isles, while several miles further on is the **Kildalton High Cross**. Standing in a churchyard, it is the only surviving complete Celtic High Cross in Scotland.

Kildalton Cross

It was carved about AD800 and you can still make out the Biblical carvings on the front.

To the west of Port Ellen is a road that takes you into a piece of land called the Oa. There are some excellent walks in the hills here where you can see ruins of deserted villages, empty since the Highland Clearances. You might be lucky and see one of Islay's golden eagles as one pair roost in this area.

A brilliant place to stay here is at the **Kintra Farm Bunk Barns**, on the north part of the Oa, at the start of Laggan Bay, a 7-mile sandy beach, tel:(01496) 302051, open all year, £5.50/£7.50. This working farm with a bunkhouse also offers B&B for £16, camping from £4 and a restaurant open April-September. They have organised walks and birdwatching trips in summer. The 4-mile taxi ride from Port Ellen to Kintra (tel: 302155) is only about £3.

Bowmore, the largest village on the island, has many shops and Islay's only **Tourist Information**, tel:(01496) 810254, open all year, closed at weekends in winter. The main street is on a hill, and at the top there is one of only two remaining round churches in Scotland. It is said that they were built this way so that there was no corner for the devil to hide in. The bottom of the street ends at the harbour, with the excellent Harbour Bar which serves food during the day. The **Bowmore Distillery** is just round the corner, tel:(01496) 810671. Tours cost £2 (with a £2 voucher) and are at 10.30am and 2pm Monday-Friday (extra tours during summer plus10.30am Saturday). Included in the price is a dram of whisky and a 20-minute video about the place and the process.

In Bowmore you can hire bikes at the post office for £10 a day, tel:(01496) 810366, Easter-September. Cars are for hire for £30 a day, tel:(01496) 810206 (day), 810207 (evening).

On the road from Bridgend heading west to Port Charlotte, there is a turning right to the RSPB Reserve at **Gruinart**. They conduct guided walks showing you some of the 200 different bird species on Islay. There is a viewing platform with binoculars, or alternatively, if the weather is bad, you can watch the birds from inside through the large panoramic window.

There are some excellent walks from here. If you go up the east side of Loch Gruinart, you will find Killinallan Beach with its extensive sand dunes and further on up the coast you will see Islay's raised beaches, formed when the sea receded. There are several good reasons for visiting the quiet village of **Port Charlotte**. Apart from there being a SYHA youth hostel, there is an excellent **Museum of Islay Life**; £1.60/£1.10, open daily from Easter-October. A small museum which shows life in Islay from the early Bronze Age until recent times, it has information on how distilling began on the island, agricultural methods, and lots of amazing old photographs. Next door to the SYHA is a field centre with an informative exhibition of bird skeletons, plant life and photographs of Islay's birds. Just out of Port Charlotte is the **Rockside Farm Trekking Centre** where you can go pony-trekking.

Port Charlotte SYHA, tel:(01496) 850385, Grade 2, £6.10/£7.60, daytime lockout, open 20/3-31/10.

The coastal village of **Portnahaven** is simply stunning with small traditional old houses gathered prettily around the harbour. There is a tiny pub in one of them where you will come into very close contact with the locals.

There is one small shop here but no B&Bs; however, you can camp anywhere along the superb shoreline. North of Portnahaven, along the road to Kilchiaran, you can visit **Lossit Bay**, the best sandy beach on the island where you are unlikely to meet anyone. To get there you must leave the road and walk for a mile down a footpath (there are no signposts, so a map would be helpful). All of the beaches on this stretch of west coast are dangerous for swimming as there is a strong undercurrent, so do not be tempted.

The road east from Bridgend to Port Askaig goes past Ballygrant with its pub offering dinner of local beef, lamb, game, fish and shellfish. Just past Ballygrant is a left turn to **Finlaggan**, which was the home of the MacDonald chiefs from the 12thC to the 16thC. These 'Lords of the Isles' ruled over land from Kintyre to Lewis and this was their centre of administration and an important meeting place - kings came here from Scotland, England and France. There is a **visitor centre** which has an exhibition explaining what the different buildings were used for and shows what the yearly excavations have found; £1, open May-October a few afternoons a week.

From Finlaggan the road goes to Port Askaig, from where ferries go to Kennacraig, over to Jura and to Colonsay. Port Askaig has only a hotel and a small shop.

Just north of Port Askaig are two distilleries - **Caol Ila**, tel:(01496) 840207 (£2 tour with a dram included and a £3 voucher, open all year by appointment only) and **Bunnahabhain**, tel:(01496) 840646 (free tour with a dram included, by appointment only, any time of year).

Jura

The unspoilt wilderness of the mountainous Isle of Jura is a unique place to escape to. The name Jura comes from the Norse meaning 'deer island', and today the deer population outnumbers the human inhabitants by 20 to 1. The only road on Jura runs from the south up the east coast.

Jura's tallest standing stones can be seen about a mile and a half before you reach Ardfin (just near the road), while **Ardfin House** is worth a visit mainly for its excellent walled garden and walks along the clifftop and shore; £1. Seven miles from the ferry point at Feolin is the village of **Craighouse**, the main centre of the island's population. The **Craighouse Distillery**, which produces a good 10-year-old malt, gives tours if you phone ahead, tel:(01496) 820240, Monday-Friday, all year, free. The hotel here, the only one on the island, does bar lunches which you can enjoy in the beautiful, grassy beer garden overlooking the quiet harbour.

From Craighouse the road goes to **Ardlussa**, where it becomes a track suitable only for Land Rovers, mountain bikes and walkers, but it is one of the best parts of the island. You can visit **Barnhill**, the house where George Orwell lived while writing his book '1984', and right at the northerly point of Jura is the **Corryvreckan Whirlpool**, which is awesome on a wild day when there's a strong wind from the west and a rising tide. (On the day ask the locals when is the best time and if it's worth the walk out there, or you could phone the Coastguard.) Jura's uninhabited west coast has some of the finest raised beaches in the world.

The **Paps of Jura**, the island's hills, make an amazing day out. Remember to go prepared with the correct hiking gear - the top slopes are rough with scree and large lumps of quartzite (and also the weather changes so quickly). There are many different routes you can take so be sure to get detailed information. Islay's Tourist Information sells a guide to Jura for walkers by G. Wright. Remember there are restrictions to walking in the hills in the stalking season, August to September.

In Craighouse there is very little accommodation apart from the hotel but there is a free bothy in Glengarrisdale - a very basic shelter where anyone can stay. You must take all your food with you and a sleeping bag (it is about 5 miles over rough and wet land from Ardlussa). You can camp almost anywhere on Jura. The ferry to Feolin travels from Port Askaig, Islay (frequent sailings Monday-Saturday, less frequently on Sundays, price 80p one-way, cars £5.75 one-way, bicycles free, for details tel:(0141) 3329766). The journey takes under 5 minutes.

Getting to Islay and Jura

Ferries to Islay must make their way to Kennacraig on the mainland where ferries depart one to three times a day. A single ticket costs £6.45 and a 5-day return costs £10.90. Cars cost £34.50 extra for a single ticket, £58 for a 5-day return.

MAINLAND ARGYLL

The peninsula of **Kintyre** is a seldom visited corner of Scotland, and yet its tip, known as the Mull of Kintyre, inspired one of Paul McCartney's most successful songs. It is a quiet and attractive part of the world and you certainly won't see many other backpackers down here. The west coast looks across to Ireland while the east shelters the mountainous island of Arran.

Public transport on Kintyre is rare so read your timetables carefully and don't be late. Hitching's a possibility but not to be relied upon, so having your own transport is obviously the best way to get around.

Pine Marten

At the north of the peninsula is the town of **Tarbert**, which sits at the isthmus connecting Kintyre to the mainland. Like all harbour towns it has a special atmosphere as the attention of the town focuses on the incoming and outgoing boats and fishermen.

Tourist Information is on Harbour Street and open from April-October, tel:(01880) 820429.

An impressive ruined castle in the area is **Skipness Castle and Chapel**, 10 miles south of Tarbert. Turn off at the B8001 road and then go north-east from Claonaig. Free entry and in a pretty area.

The west coast of Kintyre has an incredible 5-mile long beach at the bottom of which is the quiet holiday resort of **Machrihanish**. This is a magnificent stretch of sand designed for leisurely strolling and the contemplation of life. To the east of Machrihanish is the peninsula's busiest town, **Campbeltown**. The lyrics to an old song are 'O Campbeltown Loch I wish you were whisky, Campbeltown Loch och aye, Campbeltown Loch I wish you were whisky, then I would drink you dry'. It was once a major area for whisky too, with over thirty distilleries - now there are only two. It is not as pretty a place as Tarbert but if you're looking for a walk with a difference, you can get to Davaar Island from Campbeltown at low tide. Within the island's rock is a cave, and painted on its wall is a local artist's depiction of the crucifixion, painted last century. It's worth seeking out but don't get stuck over there

i - check for tidal times with **Tourist Information** at the Pier; tel:(01586) 552056, open all year.

There are no youth hostels in Kintyre but if you are camping you'll have a choice of places to stay. **Campsites** are at Tayinloan, Clachan, Muasdale and Machrihanish on the west coast, Peninver and Carradale on the east and Southend at the southern end. All sites are open from Easter to October. None of the **B&Bs** in Kintyre are remarkably cheap. Tourist Information in Tarbert and Campbeltown have accommodation lists.

Inveraray

Standing on the shore of Loch Fyne is the elegant and very attractive resort of **Inveraray**. On the site of a former fishing village, this town was built by the Duke of Argyll in 1743 coinciding with the construction of his nearby castle. There is a youth hostel here which makes Inveraray an ideal backpacker stop.

Inveraray has a good selection of places to visit. At the top of Main Street there is the **Inveraray Jail**, now a museum showing the building's history in a novel way with mannequins and courtroom dramas; £4.30/£2.65, open daily all year. At the other side of the town square from the jail is Inveraray's **Bell Tower**. You can climb to the top of the tower from where there is a splendid view over Loch Fyne and the surrounding area; however it costs £1.20. Down on the water is the **Arctic Penguin Maritime Experience**, a museum on board the first sea-going steamship the 'Arctic Penguin'; £3/£2.20, open all year.

Inveraray Castle is 2 miles from the town centre. Dating from just 1743, it is still home to the Duke of Argyll; £4.50/£3.50, open April to mid-October and closed on Fridays except in July and August.

You can see an old Highland village at **Auchendrain Township**, 5½ miles south-west of Inveraray. People have lived together as a community on the site for hundreds of years and many buildings have been restored, some with thatched roofs; £3, open April-September.

 Tourist Information is on Front Street, open all year, tel:(01499) 302063.

 Inveraray SYHA, tel:(01499) 302454, Grade 2, £6.10/£7.60, open 20/3-31/10.

LOCH LOMOND - THE WEST BANK

Loch Lomond is Scotland's biggest loch and one of its loveliest. Wedged between some gorgeous mountain scenery it is for most of its 24-mile length only a mile across until it widens out at the southern end providing room for its many islands.

The busy A82 runs the length of the loch's west bank and makes for a delightful (and very traditional) scenic drive. If you want to stop for a cuppa, a cruise or a tartan souvenir, the place to stop is at **Luss**, the Loch's most charming village (which features in a well-known - if you're Scottish - TV soap). If you pass **Inverbeg**, consider taking the pedestrian ferry (summer only) across to Rowardennan on the quiet eastern side of the loch from where there are many walks. If you're travelling by train, the few miles between **Ardlui** and **Tarbet** are short but wonderful - you could get out at Tarbet and go for a paddle (though it is a 15-minute walk from the station) or take a boat trip, departing several times a day in the summer. The other option for rail travellers is to arrive at Balloch at the southern end, but this is not the best part, and you should endeavour to bus or hitch northward on either bank, or take a cruise.

Apart from the scenery another attraction is the impressive **Loch Lomond SYHA Hostel**, Arden, Alexandria, tel:(01389) 850226, Grade 1, £8.60/£11.10, late access, open all year. The hostel is a large mansion house complete with ghost - though the many school groups may have chased her away - in a green rural setting 10 minutes from the water. It's easy to get to by bus (ask the driver to stop at the hostel) but a bit of a hike from Balloch railway station. Leaving the station go to the left. After a few hundred yards turn right at the Burmah petrol station and it's a couple of miles up this disused road. When you meet the main road you'll see the signposts to the hostel. If you need provisions buy them in Balloch.

Being out of town the hostel's surrounding nightlife is a bit sparse. The bright lights of the gaudy Duck Bay Marina may allure but they probably won't shine for you due to their strict dress code and indifferent attitude. Strangely the truly grand four star Cameron House Hotel nearby is much more welcoming (but polish your shoes first). A drink in their club bar is not cheap but is impressive. They also have a bar with a more casual atmosphere another five minutes along the loch at the golf and marina clubhouse. Otherwise it's a walk to Balloch for the thirsty.

Balloch itself has little to offer the visitor, however on the main street you'll see **Tourist Information**, tel:(01389) 753533, open April-October, where you can pick up leaflets on many things to do. They also have a free short video about Loch Lomond. A hundred yards to the right is a bridge over the boat-infested River Leven and you can take cruises up the loch from here.

Apart from many **B&Bs**, there is a **campsite** about ¾ of a mile west of Tourist Information, the **Tullichewan Holiday Park**, tel:(01389) 759475, £7.50-£9 for 2 people,£6.50-£8 for 1 person, open all year except November. They hire bikes for £10 a day, £7.50 a half day.

(For **East Loch Lomond**, see 'Central Scotland')

BRIDGE OF ORCHY TO TAYNUILT
BY GLEN KINGLASS AND LOCH ETIVE

DIFFICULT

If you like long distance walks with the added certainty that there is very little chance of making a navigational error and getting lost, then this is a good route for you. There is a well-trodden footpath on the first half of the walk and a landrover track on the second half. Despite such an obvious track you will meet very few people on this walk and being in the Highlands of Scotland the scenery is of course magnificent.

Other advantages to this route include proximity to public transport services at the start and finish points. Both are well served (compared to anywhere else in the Highlands) by train and coach services from Glasgow. As you would expect there is at least one pub at either end of the walk.

Distance: 31 miles, 50 km (14-16 hours) 2 days
Map: O.S. Landranger 50, 1:50,000

Starting from Bridge of Orchy railway station head down the hill towards the main road. Cross over and continue past the Bridge of Orchy Hotel, go over the bridge to where the road sweeps round to the right. At this point you will head up the muddy path which leads into the woods. This is signposted as the West Highland Way, which is a long distance track between Glasgow and Fort William.

You may not realise from the above description, but you will now have walked right through the heart of Bridge of Orchy within the space of 90 seconds. There are no shops here so do not go much further on this walk unless you have enough food to last a couple of days. If you want to spend the night in Bridge of Orchy you have a number of options, starting with the most expensive - you can stay in the hotel, the bunkhouse next to the hotel or you could camp by the river just along from the bridge, (although there are no facilities for campers). A better place to camp is by the Inveroran Hotel, a two mile walk from Bridge of Orchy, along the path marked West Highland Way. Again there are no facilities here (although there are tentative plans to provide some) but this area is recognised more as a bona fide camping spot.

The path between Bridge of Orchy and the Inveroran Hotel is about as steep as it gets on this route. The path climbs up through the woods then traverses the side of the hill before descending to the Inveroran Hotel. When you are at the top you will have a good view of the land you will soon be trekking through. You will get a good view of the beautiful old Scots Pine forest around Loch Tulla, Forest Lodge and the river which heads west towards Glen Kinglass.

From the Inveroran Hotel turn left (west) towards Victoria Bridge and Forest Lodge. At Forest Lodge you will take the footpath headed west which is signposted to Glen Kinglass. Follow the track along the Abhainn Shira river to the Glasgow University mountain hut where the path forks, you should stay on the path close to the river bank on the south side of the woods. This stretch of path can be boggy during the wet season and you might have to make a few side-steps to avoid larger than usual wet patches. After a couple of kms and before you have cleared the woods the path crosses to the south bank of the river over one of a series of rickety old bridges.

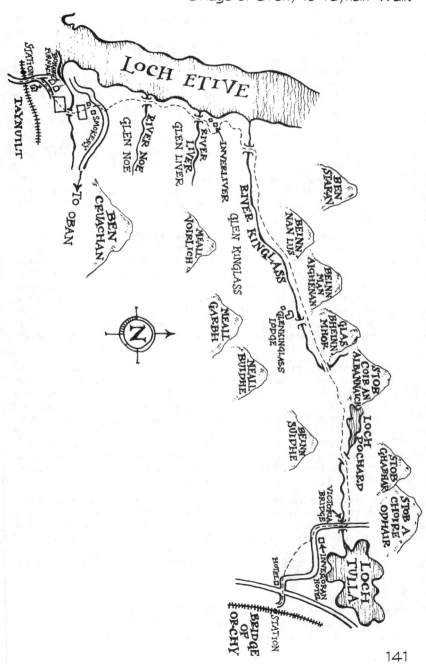

141

Now the path is quite dry and very straight forward to follow all the way to the head of Glen Kinglass and down to Glen Kinglass Lodge. On the way you will pass close by a series of bonnie waterfalls leading up to the shores of Loch Dochard then the path will lead you up a little higher revealing some spectacular mountain scenery to the north. At the top of the pass the path hits some large flat slabs of rock which you can walk over quite easily but refuses to wear into a normal path. Luckily the only routes down are into Glen Kinglass, which is the way you want to go, or back the way you came from. You should be able to see the bridge which takes you onto the north bank of the River Kinglass which you will now follow all the way to Loch Etive.

There are some beautiful waterfalls on this next stretch of path as the river descends quickly and often has to spread out over the large areas of rock it chances to meet. All too soon you will find you have reached Glen Kinglass Lodge with its wall of protective trees and here the path becomes a large track. Further on in the lower reaches of the glen you find patches of forest and there are sheltered places to camp on the river flood plain.

Continue along the track and eventually the wide expanse of Loch Etive will come into view just as you come to a junction where you will turn left, cross over a bridge and head south-west along the shore of the loch. It can be quite windy on this stretch as the path climbs up to positions ideally placed to catch the wind gusting across Loch Etive. This is a working loch and you will see bits of fisheries scattered along the shore as you follow the track into the hamlets of Inverliver and Glenoe. After Glenoe you climb up into a heavily forested area which starts off as mixed woods then turns into pine plantation. Keep following the track, past a sign to Port na Mine then at last onto the road. Turn right at the road to take the tourist route into Taynuilt, past the Smokery then Bonawe Furnace.

At the Smokery you should first treat yourself to some smoked fish as reward for your efforts so far before heading over the river into Taynuilt. From the Smokery you can see the pipeline bridge which crosses the river. To get there follow these instructions carefully: go past the Gift Shop then turn right just before the Exhibition Centre and walk down the faint path towards the field. Go through the gate and follow the track along the field fence and round the herd of cows to the bridge. Now cross the bridge then turn right through another gate into another field, walk diagonally across this field to a gate in the opposite corner. Go through this gate then continue along a track travelling in the same direction (NWW). When you get to some houses the track will fork - take the left fork past the Bonawe Furnace chimneys.

In summer you may visit the Bonawe Iron Furnace, said to be the most complete remaining charcoal fuelled iron works in Britain. If however you are in desperate need of a visit to the pub to refresh yourself after this challenging walk then continue along the road to the church, turn left down a hill then take the first right and follow the road into the village centre. The railway station is about halfway down the high street, some shops and a pub/hotel at the far end. Now you deserve a drink and an opportunity to rest your aching feet.

Accommodation:

Bunk House and B&B Hotel at Bridge of Orchy, B&B at Taynuilt.
There are rough camping places at Bridge of Orchy, Inveroran and in Glen Kinglass.

There's not a castle in sight, yet Glasgow is home to some of Scotland's most outstanding architecture. Architectural students from all over the world come here to see Glasgow's impressive buildings, which owe their splendour either to the wealthy tobacco lords of the 1800s or simply to the sheer talent of their designers. One in particular, Charles Rennie Mackintosh, has become Glasgow's pride and joy. Recent stone-cleaning and renovation of many of the older buildings has revealed a vibrant and cosmopolitan city, and with over 70 parks (the highlight being the superb park of Kelvingrove), a very green city too. More of a working, living and breathing city than a tourist mecca, it is possible to feel less like a tourist and more like a person, even at the height of the season. You are more likely to meet the locals here than other travellers, and since Glaswegians might well be the most friendly city-dwellers alive, meeting them is essential to any visit.

Artistically and culturally the city is thriving with activity. There is a multitude of galleries and museums to choose from and various events all year round. And for all kinds of music-lovers the Glasgow live music scene is alive and kicking.

Although at times it may seem like just another big city, it has a magnetic charm and strong sense of community that will draw you in. Glaswegians wouldn't live anywhere else.

A Brief History

Glasgow supposedly owes its existence to its patron saint, St Mungo, who established a church here in the 6thC and the town which grew up around it was named Glas Cau, Gaelic for 'dear green place'. As you look around the city today, you will see that Glasgow's coat of arms, which consists of a fish, a ring, a bird, a tree and a bell (all the symbols relate to the miracles of St Mungo), appears everywhere.

Over the centuries the town grew, with its university founded in 1451 and its merchant trade relatively prosperous, but it wasn't until the 18thC, when the trade between Glasgow, the Americas and Europe developed, that the city's history altered dramatically. The main import (which was mostly re-exported to the European continent) was tobacco, but sugar, spices and rum were also traded.

Close on the heels of the tobacco era came the Industrial Revolution. Glasgow developed into an important centre for heavy industry and was later world-renowned for its shipbuilding quality and expertise.

All this wealth and commerce brought astounding employment opportunities and people flocked to Glasgow, turning it into the highly-populated city it is today. Glasgow, following a period of relative decline during the 1960s and '70s, has recently been revitalised, taking its place as one of Europe's most dynamic cities. Selected to be the 'City of Architecture and Design, 1999', the city has been given an opportunity to promote and develop its rich heritage.

West End

A visit to the lovely **Kelvingrove Park** is essential. With what seems like a thousand paths in it, it's not too hard to get lost. If you find a river, it's the River Kelvin, and if you find a magnificent building made of red sandstone, you've found the **Kelvingrove Art Gallery and Museum**; open daily all year, free. Glasgow's main art gallery and museum is an exquisite piece of architecture and you should seek it out, even if you're not in the mood for going through it. The main hall is impressive, too, and every second Sunday there's an organ recital - this is great for about five minutes. It makes excellent background music, though, as you walk through the exhibits. There is too much to see on just one visit so if you're short on time go to the 'Scottish Room' which highlights many different aspects of Scottish life and culture. As you walk around, spare a thought for the architect - legend has it he was devastated to find that his building had been built back-to-front and committed suicide.

Overlooking the museum from the hill is the equally imposing **Glasgow University**. Built in a Gothic style, it was actually only completed in 1887. Walk up to it for both the view and to walk into the courtyard.

- GLASGOW SCHOOL ⚬ ART -

The **Hunterian Museum** is inside, so named because William Hunter left the university his extensive collection of treasures; open all year, free. The first room details the university's history and its most famous students and lecturers. The **Hunterian Art Gallery** across the road (in a fairly ghastly modern building) is of great interest; open all year, closed Sundays, free. Home to a large collection of beautiful work by Whistler, the gallery also has a splendid reconstruction of a flat that Charles Rennie Mackintosh decorated and lived in - a beautiful residence. It's closed on Sundays. The university has a Visitor Centre for any questions you might have, and inside this is a cafe.

Just opposite the Kelvingrove Art Gallery and Museum on Argyle Street is the **Museum of Transport** which contains a display on all kinds of transport from prams to oceanliners; open all year, free.

The area in which the youth hostels are located is an architectural conservation area called the **Park Area**, with Park Circus at its centre. Built in the mid-19thC, these prestigious houses once belonged to the wealthiest of Glasgow-dwellers. Today they're offices except for the occasional youth hostel or student residence. Only a minute from Kelvingrove Park, it is one of the most elegant areas in the city.

Glasgow's **Botanic Gardens** on Great Western Road are excellent for a pleasant walk especially if approached via the Kelvin Walkway which begins in Kelvingrove Park. Within the gardens is Kibble Palace, not a palace at all, but a 19thC conservatory.

East End

To the east of the city centre is the cathedral precinct. The **Cathedral** itself is a grand structure completed in the 1500s, although a cathedral has been sited here since the 12thC, and is pleasant to walk through. Make sure you head downstairs to the Blacader Aisle (open 9.30am-1pm, Monday-Saturday, 2-4pm, Sunday 2-5pm; free). Nearby the **St Mungo Museum of Religious Life and Art** is unique in that it provides an (almost introductory) exhibition about most of the world's religions along with a relevant collection of art, including Salvador Dali's 'Christ of St John of the Cross'. Opposite, the oldest house in Glasgow, the **Provand's Lordship** (built in 1471), now contains a museum. It and the Cathedral are the only remaining medieval buildings of the city. Both are free and open all year (however, Provand's Lordship may be closing).

On the hill behind the cathedral is the **Necropolis**. This cemetery contains some splendid tombs, making it a most intriguing graveyard. A statue of John Knox, the protestant reformer, overlooks the city from here (although he's actually buried under a car park in Edinburgh). To enter the Necropolis you need to find the bridge which crosses to it. This place is probably too spooky to enter outwith the hours of daylight. (For a coffee try the Cathedral House Hotel's bar.)

City Centre

If you want to get your bearings in Glasgow, stand in **George Square**. The very heart of the city, it is often a cultural, artistic or political venue, and if you're here around Christmas there are really gorgeous Christmas lights. Overlooking the Square is the **City Chambers**, a magnificent building with sumptuous interiors. To get past the front entrance hall you need to take the free, guided 45-minute tour (Monday-Friday, 10.30am and 2.30pm).

The area to the south-east of George Square is known as the **Merchant City**. Although there are several impressive buildings, the area has been neglected and only fairly recently has become the centre of a major campaign for renovation. Perhaps in 10 years, once all the work has been done, the Merchant City will be tremendous, but for now the tourist-aimed 'Merchant City Trail' may have been set up prematurely.

The **Gallery of Modern Art**, on Queen Street just south of George Square, is an exciting and very popular, recent addition to Glasgow's art galleries, with four floors of Scottish as well as many international artists' work; free, open all year.

The **People's Palace** is situated on parkland known as **Glasgow Green** and is a museum telling the story of the real people of Glasgow, covering the beginnings of the city until the present day. There's a cafe and a 'Winter Garden' filled with tropical wildlife; open all year and free. It is just a short walk south-east of the city centre. Once the site of public hangings, speeches, parades and celebrations, Glasgow Green's past has been eventful.

Southside

Sir William Burrell collected some 8000 objets d'art during his lifetime and, upon his death, bequeathed them to the City of Glasgow. **The Burrell Collection** is notable chiefly because it is a private collection. Most literature suggests that a visit to Glasgow without seeing the Burrell Collection is not complete. This sentiment is debatable - the Burrell Collection may be something to see on your third or fourth day in the city, but certainly not the only thing. As the collection is too large to display everything at once, the pieces are exhibited in rotation. It's a diverse collection which includes many paintings, tapestries and historic artefacts, with a large proportion from the Orient; open all year, and free.

To get to the Pollock Country Park where the collection is situated, you can catch a train from the Central Station to Pollokshaws West Station (watch out for foxes) and then follow the signs. The Burrell Collection is in the modern building. A wander around the park is recommended as it is very pleasant and you can also visit **Pollock House** which contains, among other things, many Spanish paintings (El Greco, Goya).

Other Museums and Galleries

Thriving with activity, Glasgow has many museums and galleries. The CCA (Centre for Contemporary Arts) and the McLellan Galleries, both on Sauchiehall Street, are the most notable (though they might charge an entrance fee). (In 1998 the McLellan Galleries is hosting an exhibition 'Scrolls from the Dead Sea' from May-August.) Exhibitions are constantly changing, so check the magazine 'The List' or ask at Tourist Information for the Glasgow Galleries Guide.

Festivals

In early summer try to catch the acclaimed **International Jazz Festival,** from 26 June to 5 July, with impressive paying concert acts but also plenty of free jazz in the pubs and on the streets. There is also Glasgow's traditional fair, the **Glasgow Fair**, held at Glasgow Green on the 20 July. If it's to your liking, come for the **World Pipe Band Championships** on the 15th of August - hundreds of pipe bands competing in Bellahouston Park. (This is all very well, except the pipe bands seem to take up every single empty bed in the city, so at this time arrive early or phone ahead.) For those travelling in winter, Glasgow has an excellent **Celtic Connections** festival in January, celebrating Celtic music and culture.

CHARLES RENNIE MACKINTOSH

The refinement and beauty of Charles Rennie Mackintosh's work has to be seen to be believed. Mackintosh was an innovative architect and designer who lived from 1868 to 1928, and his style is so attractive even by today's standards that you have to marvel at his foresight. Any budding designers should take heed - if only all architecture could be like this. With great attention to detail, his was a complete vision, but unfortunately Glasgow mostly failed to recognise his talents until after his death. Now, of course, his design trademarks can be seen imitated all over the city.

For a free introduction to his work, go to the **Hunterian Art Gallery** (just opposite the main university building, in Hillhead Street, closed on Sundays) and see the Mackintosh House, a reconstruction of a nearby flat in which he and his artist wife, Margaret MacDonald, lived. If this whets your appetite, head for his most famous achievement, the **Glasgow School of Art** in Renfrew Street. Tours of the building start at 11am and 2pm Monday-Friday, 10.30am Saturday, with extra ones during the summer. It costs £3.50/£2 and is definitely worth it. The library is simply stunning.

In 1901, Mackintosh entered a competition to design a **'House for an Art Lover'** and the house has recently been built, inspired by his original drawings. This beautiful house, set in Bellahouston Park, to the south of the city centre, costs £3.50/£2.50 to enter and is open daily in summer. In the winter months telephone 353 4770 to check which days it is open (usually weekends only). To get there catch bus 9a from Jamaica St near Central Station.

There are other buildings in Glasgow designed by Mackintosh that are open to the public (most notably the Willow Tea Rooms on Sauchiehall Street), so if you're interested get a leaflet from Tourist Information. However, if you've got the time for a day-trip out of town, highly recommended is **The Hillhouse** in Helensburgh. Entrance costs are quite high at £5.80/£3.90, April-October, 1.30pm-5.30pm, NTS. Trains go regularly from Charing Cross and Queen Street Stations, get off at Helensburgh Upper (£3.30single/£4.10 off-peak day-return).

Tourist Information

i Glasgow **Tourist Information** is located centrally at 11 George Square, tel:(0141) 204 4400.

Opening hours are-

> April - Mon-Sat, 9am-6pm; Easter Sunday only, 10-6pm.
> May - Mon-Sat, 9am-6pm; Sun, 10-6pm.
> June and September - Mon-Sat, 9am-7pm; Sun, 10-6pm.
> July and August - Mon-Sat, 9am-8pm; Sun, 10-6pm.
> October-March - Mon-Sat, 9am-6pm

Glasgow Airport has a tourist information desk too, tel:(0141) 848 4440. They are open 7.30am-5pm Monday-Saturday, 8am-4pm Sunday.

Guided Tours of Glasgow

Discovering Glasgow Guided Coach Tours run a circular, jump-on jump-off service every 15-30 minutes, from April to November and 4-5 times a day in winter. Not only does this tour save you walking time, it is an invaluable introduction to the city. Tickets can be purchased on the bus. The one-hour tour officially starts at George Square, but you can jump on at, for example, the Park stop on Woodlands Road near the youth hostels if you wish; £6/£4.50. This company also runs day trips out of Glasgow, tel: (0141) 204 0444 for details.

Guide Friday offer a similar jump-on jump-off service every half an hour from May to October and weekends in April; £6/£4.50.

Glasgow City Walks operate from May to September, starting at Tourist Information, St Vincent Place. The Glasgow Walk is at 6pm, Mondays-Fridays and 10.30am on Sundays, while the Cathedral Walk is at 2.15pm on Wednesdays and Sundays; £4/£3, about 1½ hours.

Accommodation

Glasgow SYHA, 8 Park Terrace, tel:(0141) 332 3004, £11.50/£14 (includes continental breakfast), Grade 1, open all year. An impressive building but unfortunately with a fairly sterile atmosphere. Many group bookings year-round make availability unpredictable so call ahead. Bus 44 or 59 from Hope St, 11 from Cathedral St or Bath St - all will take you to Woodlands Rd. Turn left into Lynedoch St and follow hostel signs from there. The front door closes at 2am but if you let reception know in advance, the night porter will let you in after this time.

Glasgow Backpackers Hostel, 8 Park Circus, tel:(0141) 332 9099, £9.50/£10.90, open 4 July to 24 September only. This university residence converts into a youth hostel for the summer. Spacious and comfortable it has a more relaxed and fun atmosphere than the official hostel. Twin rooms available. 24-hr access. Same buses as above to Woodlands Rd, go up Lynedoch St and at the top turn right and then left into Park Circus Place which leads you to Park Circus - the hostel's on the right.

Berkeley Globetrotters Hostel, 65 Berkeley St, tel:(0141) 221 7880, £9.50/£12. An independent hostel open all year but the not the cleanest of establishments.

Alamo Guest House, 46 Gray St, tel:(0141) 339 2395, £18 single, £16 twin. Open all year except Christmas and New Year. A B&B in a good location looking onto Kelvingrove Park, near the Art Gallery and Museum.

Hazelcourt Hotel, 232 Renfrew St, tel:(0141) 332 7737, prices can vary from £12.50-£16 B&B. Open all year.

Glasgow University, tel:(0141) 339 8855, and **Strathclyde University**, tel:(0141) 553 4148, have more accommodation during the summer and at Easter but they are mostly quite pricey. Baird Hall on Sauchiehall St, tel:(0141) 332 6415, and Clyde Hall on Clyde Place, tel:(0141) 221 1219, are reasonable options.

Craigendmuir Park Campsite, Campsie View, Stepps, tel:(0141) 779 4159. Open all year. £6 a tent. Trains leave Queen St train station regularly for Stepps station (12-minute trip).

Strathclyde Country Park, 366 Hamilton Rd, Motherwell, (01698) 266155. Out of town but in a nice area. £3.50-£6.65, open April-October. Catch a bus from Buchanan Bus Station to Motherwell, ask to be dropped off at the entrance to the park, it's then about a 20 minute walk to the campsite.

B&Bs are in the Hillhead area beyond Glasgow University. Check with Tourist Information for their accommodation list.

Food

Glasgow does provide several opportunities for cheap eating. Gibson St, near the university and not far from the youth hostels, has Indian, Italian, fish and chips, kebabs and more. It's mostly cheap food. **Joe's Garage** just around the corner in Bank Street has half-price meals all evening, but what they don't tell you is that they're well over-priced to begin with. You'll end up paying about £3.50 for a main meal - pasta or pizzas.

Not necessarily great food, nor a great pub, but **Rufus T Firefly** on Hope St, near the West Regent St junction, has very cheap food during the day. Most of their meals cost around £3 and vegetarian food is also served. Rufus T Firefly was a zany character portrayed by Groucho Marx.

There are late night chippies on Sauchiehall St and Gibson St, a late night burger van at the bottom of Woodside Crescent, and even a van selling rather tasty crepes next to the Woodlands Rd petrol station.

Insomnia Cafe on Woodlands Rd near the Lynedoch St junction is open 24 hours and serves light and healthy meals at very good prices. You can buy alcohol in their delicatessen next-door (until 10pm) and have it with your meal. An internet cafe, **Java**, is on the corner of Park Rd and Gibson Street.

For vegetarians there is the **Vegville Diner** at 93 St Georges Rd, just near the Woodlands Rd junction. It's bright, cheerful and serves great food. The **Bay Tree Vegetarian Cafe** on Great Western Rd (near the Park Rd junction) has vegan and vegetarian dishes while **Cafe Alba** at 61 Otago St, off Great Western Rd, is open until 5pm only, Mon-Sat, and is mostly vegetarian.

NIGHTLIFE

Glaswegians are super-friendly and love to talk, and the best place to meet them is in the pub. If you don't understand what they're saying (they've got strong accents) just nod your head a lot and you'll be all right.

Pubs

Pub hours in Glasgow are disappointingly short - always open till 11pm, sometimes till midnight, but never after (unless the jazz festival is on in which case pubs <u>might</u> be open until 1am). You can get drinks after midnight in the clubs, but the solution to the problem is simply to start drinking earlier.

- in the city centre -

For quiet drinks in a lovely atmosphere, try **Cafe Gandolfi** on Albion St (near Bell St) or the **Tron Theatre's** restaurant/bar on the Trongate (it's the nicer of the theatre's bars). They both serve delicious food but it's not cheap enough for this book. A bit more lively is **Blackfriars** on Bell St, with bar meals and live music most Fridays, Saturdays and Sundays. The **Brewhouse** on John St and **McChuill's** on the High St regularly have live and free music.

The true folky pubs of Glasgow are the **Scotia Bar** on Stockwell St and the nearby **Victoria Bar** on Bridgegate. They often have music but are, at any time, a good place to hang out with the locals. The Scotia in particular is an institution. If you want a late drink, around the corner and upstairs is a pool hall that stays open till 2am. It may cost £1 after midnight.

The **Horseshoe Bar** on Drury Lane, not far from Central Station, has the longest bar in the world (it's in the Guinness Book of Records). Very cheap pub lunches, an interesting crowd and good beer make this old pub a cracker.

Along Sauchiehall St there's the tasteful cafe/bar **Nico's** and the popular **Gate**, and for anyone with a nose-ring or a tattoo there's **Nice and Sleazy**, which is as it sounds. Also try the candle-lit **Brunswick Cellars**. These four bars are all open till midnight. Heading further away from town along Sauchiehall St and near the Kelvingrove Art Gallery & Museum is **The Brewery Tap** - a good pub serving a wide range of beers.

- Woodlands Road and Byres Road -

The ever popular **Halt Bar** on Woodlands Rd has varying kinds of bands playing most nights. There are two rooms - one for listening to the music, the other for talking in. The next pub down the road looks dull from the outside but is wonderful inside. Try saying its name -**Uisge Beatha**- after a few pints. Uisge Beatha is Gaelic for 'Water of Life' and it's from 'Uisge' that the word whisky comes. As for pronunciation, it's probably 'ooshge-bay', though everyone seems to say it differently. These pubs are open till 11pm but till midnight on Fridays and Saturdays.

Byres Rd has a few studenty pubs, but highly recommended is the small cobble-stoned Ashton Lane, beside Hillhead Underground Station. It is fairly quiet early

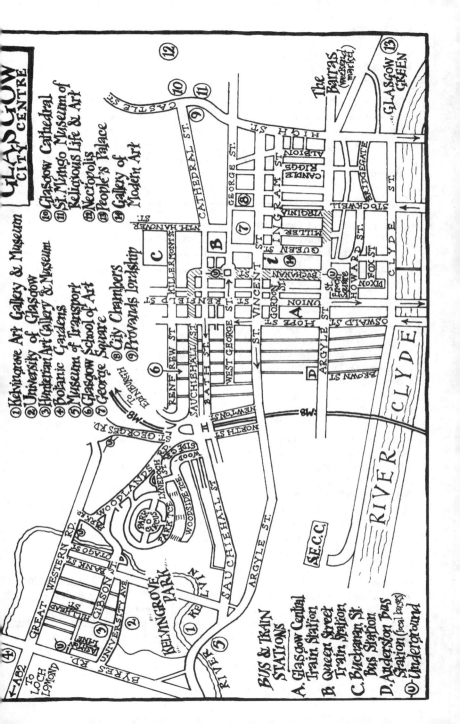

in the week but by the weekend turns into a hugely popular night-spot. Start at **Jinty McGuintys** for the best Guinness in town and occasional folk music, while the **Cul-de-Sac** and the **Ubiquitous Chip** both have good upstairs bars.

For Country & Western music and dancing - Glasgow-style - head for the **Grand Ole Opry** on Govan Road, south of the River Clyde and a taxi ride from the city centre. At weekends only. Yeehah!

Ceilidh dancing is alive and well in Glasgow with two venues, the **Riverside** on Fox St and the **Renfrew Ferry** at Clyde Place, having very popular ceilidhs every weekend; £5.

THE LIST is a fortnightly events magazine covering Glasgow and Edinburgh, available in newsagents for £1.90. Listings include films, music, theatre, dance, comedy, art and clubs.

Clubs

Recent legislation restricting clubs in the city centre has meant you have to be inside by 1am and they are closed by 3am.

Despite these restrictions, Glasgow does have some great clubs. For more mainstream music there's **The Garage** and **Reds** on Sauchiehall St or try the long-established **Cleopatra's** (Clattypats to Glasgow folk) on Great Western Road; £2-£6. At the weekend the **Glasgow School of Art** runs a few clubs which are very popular with students; £2.50-£5.

Also recommended is the **Cathouse** at 15 Union St, **Velvet Rooms** on Sauchiehall St, and **Trash** on Pitt St; £2-£7. **Fury Murrays** on Maxwell St has a varied selection of music which should suit most tastes; £2-£5 to enter. There are plenty of clubs to investigate - check the magazine 'The List' for details, or just ask some locals for a recommendation.

A good tip for any clubbers - hang about in any of the bars on Sauchiehall St from about 10pm and should anyone come round handing out flyers for a nightclub ask them if they have any free passes - they often do. Another bonus is that many of the clubs have cheap drink offers, e.g. vodka and mixer or a bottled beer for £1.

Cinemas

Cinemas in the city centre include the **Odeon** cinema on Renfield St, tel:332 8701, and the **ABC** filmcentre at 298 Sauchiehall St, tel:332 9513. These both have the latest mainstream releases. The **Glasgow Film Theatre (GFT)** on Rose St, tel:332 8128, shows international films and has an excellent reputation. The **Grosvenor** in Ashton Lane at Hillhead, tel:339 4298, is a small cinema in the university area. There are other cinemas in Glasgow mentioned in 'The List' but you need a car and a street map to get to them.

Music venues & theatres

The largest of Glasgow's rock venues is the **SECC**, tel:248 9999, but for bands not quite so big there's the excellent venue of the **Barrowland** on the Gallowgate, tel:552 4601. For up-and-coming touring and local bands there is **King Tut's Wah Wah Hut** on St Vincent St, tel:221 5279.

Glasgow has numerous theatres. The **King's Theatre** in Bath St, tel:227 5511, the **Royal Concert Hall** in Sauchiehall St, tel:227 5511, and the **Theatre Royal** in Hope St, tel:332 9000, have more classical and mainstream interests while the **Tron** on the Trongate, tel:552 4267, the **Tramway** on Albert Drive, tel:227 5511, and the **Citizen's Theatre** in Gorbals St, tel:429 0022, have more contemporary and adventurous productions (on the whole). Up-to-date information in the 'The List'.

Shopping

The major department stores are along Sauchiehall St and Argyle St. Buchanan St is also a shopping area, but is more up-market - wander into the attractive Princes Square shopping centre even if you can't afford anything. Byres Rd and Great Western Rd have less commercial shopping. There are small grocery shops open into the evening on Woodlands Rd.

Barras market

Definitely worth a wander through is the large and unusual weekend market called the 'Barras'. Very down-to-earth, it's not a trendy market but one with absolutely everything in it, with plenty of bargains and typical friendly Glaswegians trying to sell their wares. It's located around the Gallowgate to the east of the city centre. It's a huge market - you can't miss it - on Saturdays and Sundays only, during the day.

Second-hand shops

Sauchiehall St has several charity shops on it, while Byres and Great Western Rd have more student-orientated clothes shops. A good second-hand bookshop is **Caledonian Books** at 485 Great Western Rd, but **Bargain Books** on Sauchiehall St and Gordon St (opposite Central Station) always have cheap new books (not a huge selection though).

Supermarkets

Glasgow has two city centre supermarkets, **Somerfield** in Howard St near St Enoch Shopping Complex, and **Tesco**, along the pedestrian precinct of Argyle Street. A bit more expensive, but central, is the food hall in **Marks & Spencers** on Sauchiehall St. In the West End there is **Safeway** on Byres Rd near the Great Western Road junction.

Looking for flats

A few shops along Byres Rd and Great Western Rd have notices in their windows advertising accommodation. This can often be a much quicker and cheaper way to find a flat than through local newspapers.

USEFUL ADDRESSES

GLASGOW CENTRAL TRAIN STATION, Gordon St, tel:0345- 484950 (24-hr service). Trains to and from the south of Scotland, and England, plus some slow trains to Edinburgh. Left luggage facilities.

QUEEN ST TRAIN STATION, leads onto George Square, tel:0345- 484950 (24-hr service). Trains to the north and Edinburgh. Left luggage facilities.

BUCHANAN BUS STATION, Killermont St, tel:0990-505050 (8am-8pm daily). Buses throughout Scotland and down to England and Ireland. Also to Glasgow Airport. Left luggage facilities.
Glasgow's local buses depart from **Anderston bus station**, Argyle St, tel:226 4826.

GLASGOW UNDERGROUND, tel:226 4826. Glasgow's modest underground of a one-loop tube line is the only one in the U.K. apart from London's. 65p is the fare no matter how many stops and an all-day pass, known as a 'Heritage Trail' ticket, costs £2. Operates 6.30am-10.30pm Monday-Saturday; 11am-6pm Sunday. Waiting time between 4-8 minutes.

POST OFFICES
Glasgow's main post office is at 47 St Vincent Street and is open 8.30am-5.45pm Monday-Friday; 9am-7pm Saturday. The post office closest to the youth hostels is at 533 Sauchiehall St. For information call 0345-223344.

BANKS
Bank of Scotland (main branch), 110 St Vincent St. Open 9am-5pm, M, T, Th, F; 10am-5pm Wed.
Royal Bank of Scotland (main branch), 98 Buchanan St. Open 9.15am-4.45pm.
Clydesdale Bank (main branch), 150 Buchanan St. Open 9.15am-4pm M, T, W, F; 9.15am-5.30pm Th.
Barclays Bank (only branch), 90 St Vincent St. Open 9.30am-4.30pm M,T,W,F; 10am-5pm Th.
Lloyds Bank (only branch), 12 Bothwell St. Open 9am-5pm M,T,Th,F; 9.30am-5pm Wed.
National Westminster Bank (only branch), 14 Blythswood Square. Open 9am-5pm M,T,Th,F; 9.30am-5pm Wed.

TRAVEL AGENTS
Campus Travel, 122 George St, tel:553 1818, and at the University Hub, Hillhead St, tel:357 0608.
STA Travel, Strathclyde University Students' Assoc., 90 John St, tel:552 8808, and at 184 Byres Road, tel:338 6000.
Trailfinders, 254 Sauchiehall St, tel:353 2224.

FOREIGN EXCHANGE

Outwith banking hours several places exchange money but at a higher commission rate.

Tourist Information, 35 St Vincent St. See Tourist Information listing for opening hours.

Thomas Cook at Central Train Station, Gordon St, tel:221 6611. 8am-7pm M, T, W, Sa; 8am-8pm Th, Fr; 10am-6pm Sun. Another branch is nearby at 15 Gordon St. 9am-5pm M, T, W, F, Sa; 10am-5pm Th.

American Express, 115 Hope St, tel:226 3077. 9am-5pm M, W, Th, F; 9.30am-5pm Tue; 9am-12 midday Sat.

CAR RENTAL

A. M. K. Self Drive, 279 Clarence Drive (in the West End), tel:334 3044.£18 daily/ £90 weekly. Minimum age 23 years.

Arnold Clark, 10-24 Vinicombe St (off Byres Road), tel:334 9501. £18 daily/£126 weekly. Minimum age 23 years.

BICYCLE RENTAL

West End Cycles, 16 Chancellor St, Partick, tel:357 1344. £10 a day, £45 a week. May-September only.

TAXIS

Glasgow-Wide Taxis, tel:332 7070.

CAMPING SHOPS

Graham Tiso's are in Buchanan St close to Tourist Information. Several others are along Sauchiehall St.

 Hitching from Glasgow - see **Hitching**, Chapter 17.

The Glasgow National Telephone code is (0141)

11. The South

South of the busy metropolises of Glasgow and Edinburgh lies the beautiful and peaceful landscape of the 'Lowlands' - however the hills and mountains which stretch from east to west defy this title. You will find here delightful coastal scenery as well as some of Scotland's most attractive villages, especially the capital of Galloway, Kirkcudbright.

Here is Robert Burns' country, too, and the story of his life can be traced from his birth in Alloway to his early death in Dumfries. Further east is the region known as the Borders the historic castles and abbeys of which were extremely vulnerable to attack from the neighbouring English.

Ayr & Alloway

Refined and peaceful, Ayr sits beside the sea, one hour south-west of Glasgow. The town devotes itself to keeping the memory of Scotland's beloved poet Robert Burns alive, as it was in Ayr and nearby Alloway (where he was born) that he spent a good part of his life. The Burns trail starts here but, even putting Burns memorabilia aside, Ayr is an attractive and interesting seaside resort. With a population of about 50,000 it's an active place, and for backpackers there's one of the most impressive SYHA hostels.

Ayr has a lovely long white sandy beach for you to stroll along, from where you can see the island of Arran and the Kintyre Peninsula. Make sure you go to the end of the pier for the view back towards Ayr, and look out to sea for the island of **Ailsa Craig**, also known as 'Paddy's Milestone'- it marks the halfway point, by boat, between Belfast and Glasgow. Include Ayr's harbour on your walk too, as there are good boats here to look at. Just wandering about Ayr is pleasing enough with some attractive streets and buildings, the area between the High Street and the Esplanade being the most appealing.

The lovely **Auld Brig** across the Ayr River dates from the 13thC. In the late 18thC, as the second bridge was being built across the Ayr nearby, Burns wrote a vindictive poem predicting the second bridge's collapse and, true enough, in the 19thC it collapsed during flooding while the Auld Brig withstood it all.

i **Tourist Information**, tel:(01292) 288688, open all year, is situated in Burns Statue Square near the train station.

It's just a couple of miles south to the small village of **Alloway**. Robert Burns was born here and the **Burns Cottage and Museum** has an interesting introduction to this well-loved and famous poet. The entrance fee is £2.50/£1.25, but this will also get you into the **Burns Monument and Gardens**, a 10-minute walk or so further along the main road. You can climb up into the Burns Monument to survey the surrounding area (in particular the Brig o' Doon) and in the statue house you can see Burns' pals from the pub. Afterwards, wander over to the Brig o' Doon and then back up to **Alloway Kirk** (Burn's parents are buried there) to complete the Burns circuit.

Whilst in Alloway, it's important to know about Burns' rollicking tale of 'Tam o' Shanter'. The naughty Tam makes his way home after a good night in the pub in Ayr, via the spooky Alloway Kirk (a ruin even in Burns' day), and after events there makes his escape across the Brig o' Doon. For more details, read the poem or go to the **Tam o' Shanter Experience**, near Alloway Kirk, where for £2.50/£1.25 you'll see a slide show on Burns plus a dramatisation of 'Tam o' Shanter' on three large video screens. (A combined ticket for Burns' Cottage, Burns Monument and the Tam o' Shanter Experience costs £4.25/£2.)

Bikes are available for hire from the youth hostel on Craigweil Road, and a suggestion is to cycle south along the coast to Culzean Castle and Turnberry.

Buses to Ayr depart from Glasgow's Buchanan Street Bus Station every hour and trains from Glasgow Central Station every hour.

Ayr SYHA, Craigweil Road, tel:(01292) 262322, £7.75/£9.25, open 27/2-31/10. A splendid-looking building on the beach front. Sea views from the upper floors. Bike hire available.

Camping - Crofthead Caravan Park, 2½ miles east of Ayr off the A70, tel:(01292) 263516, open April-September, £5-£7 for 2 people.

ROBERT BURNS

Robert Burns, Scotland's most loved and respected poet, lived a short but eventful life from 1759 to 1796. Mostly over-sentimentally portrayed as a dreamy, romantic soul he was in fact a robustious, fun-loving and down-to-earth character who worked hard as a farmer for most of his life. His private life was aflame with scandal and he spent many a drunken evening at the pub. Proud and nationalistic, Burns wrote only in the Scots tongue and upon publication of his first book of poems was an immediate success. Still today his birthday (Jan 25th) is celebrated by Scots world-wide - a 'Burns Supper' involves the reading of his poem 'To A Haggis' followed by the stabbing of the notorious beastie. For the best introduction to his work, read the spirited and terrific tale of 'Tam o' Shanter' (but get a book with a glossary) or learn the words to 'Auld Lang Syne' for Hogmanay.

Heading South along the Coast

Dunure is a simple fishing village which has some quaint houses, a ruined castle and an interesting coastline to the south. There's nothing totally amazing about it but it's nice anyway - if you're cycling, stop here for a quick look and an ice-cream on your way to Culzean (pronounced Cull-ain) Castle.

Culzean Castle and Country Park - this tremendous castle set on the clifftop certainly looks impressive even if it only dates back to the relatively recent 1777. The exterior and the main gardens (palm trees in Scotland!) are exquisite, and the country park has plenty to offer walkers and nature lovers. When the tide's out, you can explore caves below the castle. The castle's interior has some attractive features including the 'saloon', the oval staircase and, believe it or not, a display about the former American President, Ike Eisenhower, who was once a regular visitor. The entrance fee is £6.50/£4.40 for the castle and country park, £3.50/£2.40 for the country park only (at 563 acres, the grounds warrant some exploration). The castle is open from Easter-October, the grounds are open all year.

About 3 miles south of Culzean Castle is the world-renowned golf course of **Turnberry**. The enormous hotel behind it is breathtaking and at about £200 a room, so are its prices.

Heading North along the Coast

Along the coast are a number of towns offering attractions for lovers of harbour scenes and sandy beaches. **Prestwick**'s airport will go down in history as the only place in Britain Elvis Presley ever set foot, and while **Irvine** is not a pretty place there is the **Scottish Maritime Museum** whose exhibits include the world's oldest clipper ship, a relic from the tea-trading days. The seaside resort of **Saltcoats** is a favourite with Glaswegians on a sunny day, and adjoining **Ardrossan** is the main departure point for the ferry to Arran.

Further up the coast is **Largs**, an attractive town and site of a famous battle where the Vikings were sent packing by the Scots in 1263. There is a Viking museum, Vikingar, which has a fancy audio-visual exhibition (designed for school-groups really); £3.50/£2.50, open all year. They also have a cafe and gift shop. The big event on the Largs calendar is the Viking Festival and fireworks held in 1998 from 29 August-6 September. You can stay in budget accommodation at the **Largs Tourist Hostel**, 110 Irvine Road, tel:(01475) 672851, £8 per person (twin rooms available). You can also catch a ferry to the island of Arran from Largs (see **Arran**).

Arran

Mountainous to the north with gentler hills to the south, Arran can be either a challenge to the adventurous or a place of rest for the adventure-shy. Scattered with villages of charm and serenity, there are walks from the very easy to the very difficult, sites of historic interest going back thousands of years and overlooking it all, the much-climbed mountain of Goatfell.

The island can be reached from Glasgow so easily that it's a perfect choice for anyone with limited time, but if you do have more time it is a place to get to know well and slowly. Either way you won't be disappointed. A good time of year to visit is between 9-15 April when the Arran Folk Festival is on.

Getting around Arran is quite easy as it has a good regular bus service. On the other hand the island's size and SYHA locations make it conducive to cycling, so consider hiring a bike for a few days when you first arrive.

The major ferry point of the island is at **Brodick**. It's a quiet, touristy town set around a bay, looking up at Goatfell. Although Brodick could be described as a transport hub, there are several interesting things to do and a night here wouldn't be wasted. **Brodick Castle and Grounds** are a pleasant one-mile walk from the town. The castle contains a display of wealth - silver, porcelain, art and furniture - but you might be less interested in going when you discover the price is £4.80/£3.20. Just seeing the castle from the outside and entering the superb gardens for £2.40/£1.60 is a better deal; NTS, open Easter and May-October, gardens open all year.

On the way to Brodick Castle is the **Isle of Arran Heritage Museum**. It's a local history museum in an 18thC croft. It's of some interest and cheap, but perhaps not essential to your visit. Further along the main road towards the castle is the Island Cheese Co. which makes all sorts of cheeses on the premises. Try the whisky variety, buy a packet of oatcakes, a bottle of Scottish wine and head off for a picnic.

There are two fine walks which begin a couple of miles up the road south to Lamlash. From the Cnoc na Dail car park you can walk across the Clauchland Hills enjoying fine views, and then returning to Brodick along the coast - one of Arran's stone circles is at the beginning of the path. Alternatively there is a walk inland to Glen Cloy which also leads you back to the town. Both walks are several miles long and you'll need reasonable footwear.

There are three places to hire bicycles in Brodick. They all offer similar deals, but **Brodick Cycles** (opposite the village hall) is slightly cheaper. There's also a mini-golf course just near the Brodick Boat and Cycle Hire; only £1 a round.

Tourist Information is located at the pier, tel:(01770) 302140, open all year.

There is no hostel in Brodick but several **B&Bs**. A **campsite** is located 2 miles out of town in a delightful location up Glen Rosa - Glen Rosa Farm Site, open April-October, tel:(01770) 302380, from £ 4 per tent.

Goatfell, Arran's highest mountain is 2866ft high and from its peak are terrific views of the surrounding Scottish mainland. There are no goats - the name of Goatfell is derived from the Gaelic and means 'windy mountain', which should warn you of the conditions at the top. There are several paths up to the summit but the most used ones begin just near Brodick Castle and at Corrie, a village 6 miles north of Brodick. The trek up it is a strenuous one and you should have all the correct walking gear for the trip - hillwalking boots, warm clothing for the summit and, definitely, a map. It will take roughly 5 hours. Tell someone in the town where you're going and what time you're coming back, don't go alone and be careful.

The North

Toward the north of the island lies the most dramatic terrain of Arran so the trip to **Lochranza** is definitely worthwhile. Lochranza lies peacefully on the shore of the loch with a ruined castle at its forefront and overshadowed by hills. It is perhaps Arran's most outstanding village and you should really make the effort to get there. From Lochranza there are excellent walking opportunities, in particular the signposted walks to the Fairy Dell and Ossian's Cave. The road leading to these paths also gives you the best view of the village, so take your camera.

You can also visit the **Isle of Arran Distillery** and go on one of their guided tours for £3.50/£2.50 (these prices might be going down). Open all year.

For food, the Lochranza Hotel serves bar meals all day, and if you're looking to hire a bicycle there's a place just near the youth hostel.

 Lochranza SYHA, tel:(01770) 830631, Grade 2, £7.75/£9.25, open all year except 4/1-28/1. **Lochranza Golf Camping Site**, tel:(01770) 830273, £7 for 2 people, open Easter-October.

The West

On the western side of the island are the sleepy towns of **Machrie** and **Blackwaterfoot**, which are not interesting in themselves, but essential places to visit for the sites around them. The **Machrie Moor Standing Stones** are 1½ miles along a path away from the main road (ask the bus driver to stop at the site rather than take you to the village). These stones are the remains of five circles arranged over 3,000 years ago - some of the magnificent red sandstone monoliths are so large that they tower over you. If you're impressed with these you might wish to seek out the other stone circle in the area at **Auchagallon**, a mile north of the village of Machrie. Machrie, by the way, has a tea-room and a golf course - and that's it. The friendly owners will allow you to leave your backpack at the tea-room while you walk to the standing stones.

If you have enough time you could always walk from Blackwaterfoot along a coastal path toward Machrie (or vice versa). This route has lovely views of the Kintyre peninsula and along the way you'll find the King's Cave, where King Robert the Bruce was supposed to have observed a determined spider battling against the odds, a sight which was said to have inspired him to reclaim the Scottish throne. Several caves are thought to be the king's, but you never know, this could be the one.

 For accommodation try **Burncliff** where, in a comfortable old farmhouse, you can get bed and breakfast for £10. (Ask if you can use their kitchen.) They have a lounge with an open fire, a TV and games. You share the house with the owners so it's very cosy, tel:(01770) 860245, half a mile from Blackwaterfoot on the String Road, open all year except around Christmas. Apart from Burncliff, accommodation on this side of the island is severely limited (unless you have a tent), so you'd be best to return to Brodick in the evening or head up to Lochranza.

The South

Although generally tamer than the north, the south of the island is still very pleasant. The modest community of **Lamlash** looks out across Lamlash Bay to the striking **Holy Island** and you can take the boat to the island for about £5.

From Lamlash there are walking paths - take the one from the back of the town to Benlister burn, or from the north of the town to Dunn Fionn, the site of an Iron-Age fort.

For food, the Drift Inn has lunch and evening bar meals and a beer garden.

 There are a few B&Bs but nothing very cheap. Campers can stay at the **Middleton campsite** just south of the town, tel:(01770) 600255, £2.50 per person plus £1/£1.50 a tent, open mid-April to mid-October.

The other SYHA hostel on the island is in the town of **Whiting Bay** and this makes the town a common stop for travellers. The town itself may not be so impressive but there are some good walks to take from here. Just beside the youth hostel is the beginning of an easy path which leads to the Glenashdale Falls with a detour to the Giants Graves.

Whiting Bay SYHA, tel:(01770) 700339, Grade 2, £6.10/£7.60, open 27/2-31/10.

Kildonan is a very small village at the south-east corner which has fine views out to Pladda lighthouse and the island of Ailsa Craig. There's also a ruined castle but it's not very exciting. The South Bank Farm Park and Tea Room (open Easter-September) is near Kildonan (a couple of miles along the road to Kilmory) and can be fun for an afternoon. All sorts of rare breeds of animals co-habit here on this working farm and there are sheepdog demonstrations twice a week.

Accommodation again is limited but there is a campsite which is open all year; £3 per person, including showers, tel:(01770) 820210.

Getting to Arran

Taking the train to Ardrossan from Glasgow is the quickest and most convenient way to the ferry. Trains that link up with ferry times leave Glasgow's Central Station about 5 times a day and cost £4.10 single. The ferry from Ardrossan to Brodick costs £6.70 return per person and taking a car with you is an extra £38.50 return. Depending on how much driving you intend to do, it could be cheaper hiring a car on the island. A ferry operates from the north of Arran at Lochranza to Claonaig on the mainland from April to mid-October (£3.65 single, plus £16.65 for a car). This can make an attractive alternative to Ardrossan's ferry for leaving the island, but be warned, the public transport services from Claonaig going north are haphazard. Getting to Oban looks easy on the map but you'll need to change buses three times and none of the timetables are designed to connect - ask at Tourist Information for up-to-date timetables. From mid May - 25 September a ferry service leaves Largs at 10.55am on Mondays, Wednesdays and Fridays, £4.35 single/£7.40 return for a foot passenger plus £22 single/£38.50 return for a car.

Getting around Arran

Stagecoach run buses frequently around the island as well as some runs (though usually much slower) by the postbus. Ask Tourist Information for timetables.

Cars can be rented from **Arran Transport** at Brodick pier, tel:(01770) 302121, £25-£30 for 24 hours, £14-£19 for part of the day.

There are only three banks on the island, two in Brodick (both with card machines) and one in Lamlash. Petrol stations are sparse, so fill up your tank when you find one (there's a garage at the pier in Brodick).

Galloway

It seems almost every town in Galloway is an enchanting and delightful place, situated amongst rolling hills or along a glorious stretch of coastline. Many historical sites, including standing stones, a stone circle, castles and monuments, make the region an explorer's paradise.

Public transport links the main towns but cycling is the best way to travel, with umpteen places to hire a bike. There are a few youth hostels and what seems like hundreds of campsites. B&Bs are everywhere, of course.

The largest town of the area is Dumfries, and Stranraer in the west is the only port in Scotland with ferries going to Northern Ireland.

Stranraer gets a lot of bad press, but there are worse places to get stuck waiting for a ferry. While not necessarily recommended as part of your itinerary, it is a perfectly reasonable place to break your journey to or from Ireland. **Tourist Information** is on Harbour St, tel:(01776) 702595, open all year. Stranraer has **B&Bs**, a campsite (**Aird Donald Caravan Park**, London Road, tel:(01776) 702025, open all year, £3.70/£5.70), eating places and pubs.

FERRIES TO IRELAND - See Getting to Scotland, Chapter 16.

West of Stranraer

Most visitors whizz through Stranraer as quickly as possible and miss the peninsula to the west called the **Rinns of Galloway**. This small tail of the Scottish mainland makes an unusual detour with rich rewards.

The seaside fishing village of **Portpatrick** on the west coast is a true gem and has fantastic coastal walks. This attractive and sheltered village has several food places and pubs and even a mini-golf course. The unique and old-fashioned shop Smugglers Cove is ideal for browsing. Portpatrick marks the beginning of the 340km (212 miles) walk east called the **Southern Upland Way**, but if you're not feeling so energetic, just walk the start of it which heads a few miles north along the coast (there is no Tourist Information office so if you'd like the relevant Southern Upland Way 'Short Walks' leaflet pick it up in Stranraer). Heading south of the town you'll find the ruined **Dunskey Castle**.

Portpatrick has no youth hostel, but the campsite, **Galloway Point Caravan Park**, tel:(01776) 810561, open Easter to October, is half a mile south of the town, nicely laid-out and well-situated to start your coastal exploration; £6. Dunskey Castle is within easy walking distance.

Buses for Portpatrick leave Stranraer five times a day, but not at all on Sunday.

If you can, make your way down to the **Mull of Galloway**, the southernmost tip of Scotland. There are beautiful views from the cliffs here.

the Southern Upland Way

Although it has a much lower profile than the West Highland Way, this route from coast to coast is in fact much more challenging. It is 212 miles/340 kms long (which means about two weeks' walk). Starting from sea level, the path rises and falls many times to a maximum height of 710m (over 2,000ft) as it tends to cut across rather than run along the glens. Many stretches are very remote so planning is essential and it is advisable to walk from west to east as this is the prevailing wind direction. An official guide to the Southern Upland Way by Ken Andrew is available in two parts, the west and the east sections. Alternatively, Tourist Information offices have some 'Short Walks' leaflets recommending certain stretches as well as a list of budget accommodation along the route.

East of Stranraer

A pleasant town to visit is **Newton Stewart** and not only does it have the most easily accessible (by public transport) youth hostel in the region, it is a superb touring base, especially for cycling.

In the town, there is a local history museum in a former church (£1, open April-October) as well as **Sophie's Puppenstube and Doll's House** on Queen St (open all year, £2.50).

Newton Stewart's long main street runs parallel to the river, until eventually the old bridge takes you over to the adjoining and more historic village of **Minnigaff**. This is where the youth hostel is located and from there you should take the pleasant easy walk up to Old Minnigaff's church.

Mountain bikes can be hired anytime of year from Belgrano in Church Lane, tel:(01671) 403307, £6-£10 daily and £25 weekly. Should you head north of Minnigaff, a small road will take you to the **Wood of Cree Nature Reserve** and on to **Glen Trool** in the **Galloway Forest Park**. Follow the signs to **Bruce's Stone** where there is a magnificent panoramic viewpoint (Robert the Bruce was victorious in battle here). There is also the **Galloway Deer Museum** - free entry and open Easter to mid October.

Another bike trip is along the A75 southeast to **Carsluith Castle**. Beyond that you will find the mysterious **Cairn Holy** - two Neolithic burial cairns.

i Newton Stewart is a busy town with many shops and banks. **Tourist Information** is on Dashwood Square; open Easter to October, tel:(01671) 402431.

 Minnigaff SYHA, Newton Stewart, tel:(01671) 402211, Grade 3, £6.10/ £7.60, open 20/3-31/10.

Campsite - **Creebridge Caravan Park**, tel:(01671) 402324, £4/£6, open March-October, over the bridge and 300yds on the right. Some caravans to rent.

Wigtown is another attractive town with a free museum displaying its local history. There is also a short walk from the centre of town to the **Wigtown Martyr's Stake,** with a plaque explaining their sad demise. Inland from here along the B733 road is the 19-stoned circle of **Torhouse**, and to the south of Wigtown is the **Bladnoch Distillery** offering free tours and a free sample of whisky.

Further south are the towns of **Whithorn** and the **Isle of Whithorn**. St Ninian brought the message of Christianity back to Whithorn from Rome in AD397 and began his quest to convert the local peoples. Ninian's church and shrine became a destination of pilgrimage for many centuries (today the pilgrimage is more commonly to the Isle of Iona off Mull, from where Columba also converted pagans to Christianity, but 150 years later than Ninian).

The **Whithorn Priory and Museum** tells the story, as does the visual show of the **Whithorn Dig and Visitor Centre**. Those interested in archaeology must visit the dig as archaeologists are busy excavating the area, which has buildings dating back to the 5thC. Informative staff are only too willing to answer any questions; £2.70/£1.40. The Isle of Whithorn is not an island any longer and its port is a very modest one but it provides enjoyable views and a lovely short walk to St Ninian's Chapel.

Kirkcudbright (pronounced kir-<u>koo</u>-bree) is the most outstanding and beautiful of Galloway's towns and full of attractively painted 18thC houses. Kirkcudbright sits at the mouth of the River Dee and well deserves its standing as the capital of Galloway. The impressive ruin of **MacLellan's Castle** is right in the town centre and has a low entrance fee of £1.20/90p, but it is possibly sufficient to just look at from the outside. Nearby the **Hornel Art Gallery and Library** in Broughton House has the original and beautiful paintings of Edward A. Hornel on display. Hornel was a very successful artist in his time and lived in this house for many years until his death in 1933. Take this opportunity to acquaint yourself with his work and afterwards take a walk through the gardens; £2.40/£1.60, open April to October from 1pm-5.30pm everyday, NTS.

The **Stewartry Museum** in St Mary Street is an old-fashioned museum filled with curious exhibits relating to the social and natural history of the area; £1.50/75p, open March-October. You can see artists at work in the **Tolbooth Art Centre** on High St and the **Harbour Cottage Gallery** on Castlebank, for £1.50/75p.

 Tourist Information is at Harbour Square, tel:(01557) 330494, open Easter to October, and can give you details of the many **B&Bs** in the town.

 The **Silvercraigs Campsite**, Silvercraigs Rd, tel:(01556) 502521, £6-£8.15 for up to four people, is open Easter to mid-October.

The slightly larger town of **Castle Douglas** is pleasant, sufficient for all supplies and makes another good touring base. It is convenient for buses and has several sights that you can easily get to.

Threave Castle is two miles from town, with part of the fun in just getting there. A farmland path leads from the castle car park for 10 minutes or so, then at the water ring the bell and wait for the boat to pick you up and take you across to this interesting ruin. Commanding views from the hall, and a man still in the dungeon; £1.80/£1.30 includes boat-trip, HS, closed winter. Back at the car park, grab a cup of tea and some cheap food at 'The Bothy'.

A mile south is **Threave Gardens**. These delightful gardens are well tended by the students of the Threave School of Gardening, but unfortunately are a bit expensive at £4/£2.70, NTS.

 Castle Douglas' **Tourist Information** is at Markethill, in the car park, tel:(01556) 502611, open Easter-October.

You can hire a bike from **Ace Cycles** on Church St, tel:(01556) 504542, £10 a day.

 Campsite - **Lochside Caravan Site**, tel: (01556) 502521, £7.10/£8.70, overlooking Carlingwark Loch, open March-October.

The **Galloway Sailing Centre**, 10 miles north of Castle Douglas on the A713 road, provides budget accommodation, Loch Ken Parton, tel:(01644) 420626, £7.50 (bring your own bed linen or it will cost extra). A few buses go from Castle Douglas past here every day.

From Castle Douglas take your bike and head south-east for **Rockcliffe** - just a small village but in an interesting location at the seaside. Walk up to the **Motte of Mark**, the site of an Iron-Age fort, for sweeping views of the coast, and at low tide you can walk across to Rough Island, which you can see from the motte. There is an easy cliff-top walk to the larger village of Kippford, but the whole area is ripe for coastal walking, so should you choose to camp here (at Rockcliffe's campsite) there's much to keep you busy by foot.

Orchardton Tower makes another fine destination for a cycle trip. Charming and still in excellent condition, this is Scotland's only circular tower house, dating from the 15thC; free to enter.

North-west of Castle Douglas, **New Galloway** is another lovely town and is a popular tourist destination. St John's Town of Dalry and Balmaclellan are smaller but equally attractive.

Accommodation may be a bit pricey with only a few **B&Bs** and there's no campsite, but you could head to the **Kendoon SYHA**; no phone, Grade 3, £4.65/£6.15, open 20/3-3/10, tucked away on the B7000 road about 8 miles north of New Galloway. Convenient for walkers on the Southern Upland Way, but public transport users might be frustrated - the Dumfries to Ayr bus gets the closest to it (about a mile from the hostel).

Dumfries

The bustling town of Dumfries is placed around the waters of the Nith. Four handsome bridges span the river as the water flows over the 18thC caul (or weir) on its way out to sea. With several museums and pretty sights it is an attractive town, which celebrates the memory of Scotland's national bard Robert Burns, who spent the last six years of his life here. From Burns statue at the top, past the Midsteeple and on toward the celebrated home of Robert Burns, Dumfries' long pedestrianised High Street is a pleasure to stroll down (more town centres should be like this). Numerous shops will try and tempt you with their wares, but so will two historic pubs and to these you should certainly weaken. Both the **Hole in the Wa'** and the **Globe Inn** were frequented by Burns 200 years ago, but the Globe was his favourite and parts are exactly as they were in his time. As you enter, the room to your left is where Burns whiled away hours with his pals, and upstairs is the bedroom where he supposedly had an affair, and later a child, with the Globe's barmaid of the time - an unorthodox shrine to say the least.

Burns House in Burns Street is where the poet spent the last three years of his life. Although modest in size, this home was the best Burns lived in and it was here that he died at the age of 37. Just prior to his death Burns was sent to the seaside to bathe in icy Scottish waters as a cure for gout, but in fact he had rheumatic fever, and this harsh and totally inappropriate treatment certainly hastened his death. The museum is free and open all year (closed Sundays and Mondays, October-March). **Burns Mausoleum**, in the churchyard nearby, is a respectful shrine depicting the romantic image of an angel looking down upon the 'ploughman poet'. Across the river is the **Robert Burns Centre** which presents an absorbing exhibit on Burns' life, and provides an excellent introduction to this complex man. The display is free but it costs £1.20/60p if you want to see the audio-visual display on either Burns or the town of Dumfries; open till 8pm April-September (Sundays 2-5pm), and open Tuesday-Saturday till 5pm from October-March.

Dumfries Museum and the **Camera Obscura** are situated in an 18thC windmill tower, a unique building with sweeping views. The museum is free and filled with an intriguing assortment of displays of life in the surrounding area, from excavated Stone-Age tools and weapons to information on witch trials. Also look for the Sacred Stones display in the basement. The Camera Obscura was converted from a windmill tower in 1836 and still operates today. It is the oldest Camera Obscura in Scotland and is dramatically cheaper than Edinburgh's - it's only £1.20/60p to enter and open April-September.

Dumfries' last museum is inside the town's oldest house, the **Old Bridge House** at the riverside beside Devorgilla Bridge. It's just a small building with a small collection, the most interesting section being the old dentist surgery; free to enter and open April-September.

A signposted walk along the riverside called **Burns Walk** is pleasant and easy.

Historically Dumfries is very important because it was here that Robert the Bruce slew his rival John 'The Red' Comyn inside Greyfriars Church, and he was excommunicated for this act. Greyfriars church (which stands on the site of the original) is opposite the statue of Burns at the top of the High Street.

There are no youth hostels or campsites in Dumfries sadly, so it's time to splash out and stay in a B&B. There's many to choose from - ask **Tourist Information**, Whitesands, tel:(01387) 253862, open all year.

Buses to Dumfries leave Glasgow or Edinburgh three times a day from Monday to Saturday, and twice a day on Sundays; £6.40 single/£8 return. Stranraer to Dumfries buses go three times daily; about £5 single. Catching a train from Glasgow is expensive at £15.90 single/£19.30 return.

You could also take a day-trip to the lovely town of **New Abbey**, home of the impressive rose-coloured ruin of **Sweetheart Abbey**. Inside is the tomb of Devorgilla Balliol in memory of whom the abbey was named. After the death of her husband, Devorgilla carried his embalmed heart with her everywhere in a small casket. Today she and his heart lie peacefully here. It's open all year and admission is £1.20/90p, HS. The quaint village is lovely to walk through and the **New Abbey Corn Mill** has been excellently restored. It's one of the few remaining mills in Scotland, and even if you don't go in, wander round the back for a look at the wheel; open all year and £2.30/£1.75 to enter, HS (an Abbey and Corn Mill ticket costs £2.80/£2.10). The town also has an interesting museum of costume in **Shambellie House** which is set in lovely grounds; £2.50/£1.50 to enter, open April-October. Coffee and snacks can be bought at either the coffee shop opposite the abbey or Shambellie House. Pub lunches are available from pubs in the village.

The other option outside Dumfries is the magnificent ruin of **Caerlaverock Castle**, 9 miles south along the B725. Built in the 13thC, this moated triangular castle is a treat and easily evokes colourful images of the past; £2.30/£1.75, HS. If you visit in winter, you could have a look for the 12,000 geese that live in the **Caerlaverock Nature Reserve** nearby.

The Borders

The Borders region of Scotland is a peaceful and beautiful place. Amongst its rolling hills and fertile lands are the historic abbeys and scenic spots which provided inspiration for the Borders' favourite son, Sir Walter Scott.

Stretching across the land are the Cheviot Hills, providing a neat divide between those two old rivals, England and Scotland. Ferocious battles were waged in the Borders region where the Scots fought hard to protect their land from determined and persistent invaders.

The four famous abbeys - at Melrose, Kelso, Dryburgh and Jedburgh - founded in the 12thC, lie in magnificent ruins today and highlight the area's turbulent past. They were constantly attacked during Border raids and finally destroyed in the 16thC. This was at a time when the English King Henry VIII had tried to marry the child Mary, Queen of Scots, to his son Edward, hoping to obtain the Scottish throne by doing so. Mary's mother, however, would not allow this to happen and Henry was furious. He set in motion a wild campaign of destruction and the Borders region took the brunt of these attacks. The campaign came to be known as the 'Rough Wooing' and Henry's popularity in Scotland understandably took a nose-dive. Although the English can be blamed for much of the destruction throughout the Borders' history, there was much havoc caused by rivalling Border families, owing allegiance to neither Scotland nor England.

Melrose, Abbotsford

The landscape of the Lowlands is tamer than the Highlands of the north, but provides ample opportunities for walking. Passing through the Borders is the 'Southern Upland Way', a coast-to-coast walk of 340 kilometres/212 miles.

With such fertile and manageable soil, the region is well-cultivated and a fair proportion of Scotland's agricultural produce comes from here. There are only a handful of hostels (and no independent ones), but they are all remarkable places to stay either for their unique locations or their views. If you happen to be in the region in June/July ask about the 'Common Ridings', a traditional horse-riding event held in several towns throughout the Borders. The Hawick Common Riding is the most controversial as women have only just been allowed to ride with the men!

The attractive town of **Melrose** sits by the ruins of its impressive Abbey. Not only does it make the ideal place to stay for backpackers (it's the only Borders town with a youth hostel), it also makes a good base for exploring the surrounding area. **Melrose Abbey**, due to constant raids by the English, has spent much of its life in ruin. What we see today dates from around the 15thC although the abbey was actually founded in 1136. It is a splendid structure with numerous historic tales attached to it, the most famous being that the heart of Scotland's mighty King Robert the Bruce was buried here (a casket believed to contain his heart was unearthed for inspection in 1996). There is a modest museum in the Commendator's House and the entrance fee is £2.80/£2.10, HS.

Melrose has a few museums which you may wish to visit - the Trimontium Exhibition (on Roman life in the area), the Melrose Motor Museum and a Teddy Bear Museum - but if these don't tempt you, take a relaxing stroll down to the River Tweed. For a more challenging walk, however, you can head for the **Eildon Hills**.

Melrose's **Tourist Information** is in the Square, open Easter-October, tel:(01896) 822555. To get to Melrose from Edinburgh you need to take a bus to Galashiels and change buses there.

Melrose SYHA, Priorwood, tel:(01896) 822521, Grade 1, £7.75/£9.25, open all year. From the hostel there's a terrific view of the abbey. Take the East Port off the main square, onto the High Road and it's signposted to the left.

Three miles outside Melrose is Sir Walter Scott's house, **Abbotsford**. He bought the property when it was only a simple farmhouse, and built in its place the grand mansion we see today. Scott was a keen collector, particularly of anything relating to Scotland's history, and the exhibits contained here are remarkable - included are Rob Roy's sporran, a glass tumbler that belonged to Robert Burns with one of his poems engraved upon it and a mask modelled from the skull of Robert the Bruce. There is also the door of Edinburgh's Old Tolbooth Prison, a prison which featured prominently in one of Scott's novels, 'The Heart of Midlothian'. When this Tolbooth of the Royal Mile was demolished in 1817, Scott requested the front door and this is all that remains of the original building (you'll never find the door - ask a guide). Scott's own desk and chair are still in the beautiful library. Open mid-March to October, £3.50. Afterwards wander down to the River Tweed and meet the horse who lives there. The bus to catch from Melrose to Abbotsford is the Galashiels bus that goes via Tweedsford.

Dryburgh Abbey is the most elegantly situated of the four Border abbeys. Set amongst fine trees and away from any traffic, it is a tranquil place. The stone has a lovely pinkish hue and within it you will find the tombstone of Sir Walter Scott. Also look for the room with the magnificent echo, just off the cloister; £2.30/£1.75, HS.

If you are driving in this region make sure you go to **Scott's View** on the B6356 road a few miles east of Melrose. This vista of the Eildon Hills was Walter Scott's favourite, and even when Scott's horses were leading his funeral cortege to Dryburgh Abbey in 1832, the horses rested at this place out of habit.

Kelso is a pleasant town with a fine and spacious square as well as another of the famous abbeys. Although the Kelso Abbey ruins (free) are the least impressive of the four, this town can still make an agreeable stop.

The mansion of **Floors Castle** can be reached by a 20-minute walk from the town. It is a splendid-looking building and achieved recent fame for its appearance in the film 'Greystoke - the Legend of Tarzan'. The castle is still lived in today and subsequently only a few rooms are open to the public; open 10 April-25 October. The £4.50/£3.75 admission fee to enter the house and gardens (£2 for the grounds only) may deter some of you - for a free view of the castle go to Kelso Bridge near the abbey.

Tourist Information on the Square tel:(01573) 223464, is open Easter-October. There's no youth hostel in town but there is the **Kirk Yetholm SYHA**, 6 miles south-east of Kelso along the B6352, tel:(01573) 420631, Grade 2, £7.75/£9.25, open 20/3-31/10. It's essentially a walker's hostel as it is at the end of the Pennine Way. Kelso has many **B&Bs** but most are expensive.

Jedburgh

The beautiful ancient Royal Burgh of **Jedburgh** has to be the pick of the Border towns. Its layout is reminiscent of Edinburgh with its long High Street branching off into numerous closes, a 'herringbone' effect typical of ancient Royal Burghs and believed to be advantageous in defence.

Its major attraction is **Jedburgh Abbey**, a magnificent and imposing ruin. Included in the £2.80/£2.10 entrance price is an interesting video which concentrates on the lives of the monks who once inhabited it, making comparisons with life in the modern day Pluscarden Abbey (which is east of Inverness); HS. An excellent view of the abbey can also be obtained from the Abbey car park, further down from the entrance.

Mary, Queen of Scots House in Queen Street is the residence where Mary stayed during a Court of Justice session. She almost died of a fever here, too. This museum describes the events in her tragic life and costs £2/£1, open mid-March to November.

Jedburgh's **Castle Jail and Museum** is at the top of the Castlegate, and is the other major attraction of the town. Although the castle is no more, a jail built in the year 1800 now stands on its site. Cold and depressing conditions were a fact of life for many prisoners here until the establishment was closed down in the late 19thC. The cost of £1.25/75p to enter is good value for its insight into 19thC penal conditions and reform; open March-October.

i Jedburgh's **Tourist Information** is open all year and situated near the Abbey, tel:(01835) 863435. There's no youth hostel but many **B&Bs**, and a campsite (tel:(01835) 863393, £6/£9, open March-October) is along Edinburgh road opposite the Jedburgh Woollen Mill.

There are very few youth hostels in the Borders region but you could try **Broadmeadows SYHA**, tel:(01750) 76262, Grade 3, £4.65/£6.15, open 20/3-3/10, 5 miles from Selkirk off the A708. Buses go once a day from Selkirk.

Traquair House is one of several grand houses in the Borders region but this one deserves a special mention. Said to be the oldest inhabited house in Scotland and now open to the public, you can easily enjoy an hour or two here. They brew their own ale - a tradition of the house that goes back hundreds of years and they also have a maze for you to get lost in. It is said that Bonnie Prince Charlie passed through the gates at the end of the avenue in front of the house in 1745 and the Earl of Traquair at the time avowed the gates should not be opened again until a Stewart monarch sat on the throne - they have been kept shut ever since. The house is open everyday 11 April-30 September (Fridays to Sundays only in October), costs £4.50/£4, grounds only £1.75, and is situated a mile south of Innerleithen.

The Borders Coast

Some of the most spectacular coastal scenery in Scotland is on the eastern coast. The nature reserve at **St Abbs Head** a mile north of the fishing village of St Abbs, is a birdwatcher's dream with thousands of seabirds breeding here in the summer. Extensive cliff paths make a visit here an exhilarating experience at any time of year.

The village of **Coldingham**, a mile inland from St Abbs, has the ruins of a 13thC priory to seek out, and there is a youth hostel nearby, **Coldingham SYHA**, tel:(018907) 71298, Grade 2, £6.10/£7.60, open 20/3-31/10, just 4 miles from the village.

Further south is the village of **Eyemouth**, a fishing community still busily making its living from the industry and thus the harbour is the centre of activity. Eyemouth's history contains the horrific incident in 1881, when 129 Eyemouth fisherman at sea in a fleet of ships were drowned in a violent storm. The Eyemouth Museum was established as a memorial 100 years after the disaster, one that would have understandably devastated the local community. Inside the impressive Eyemouth Tapestry depicts the event; open April-October, £1.

12. Western Isles

Ancient stone circles, white sandy beaches, rugged mountains and wide open moors give these islands an air of natural and mystical beauty. Some might find the desolation and the weather conditions challenging both mentally and physically, but the rewards are rich for those who endure.

Situated on the outer reaches of Europe, these islands seem almost forgotten by tourism. The locals are friendly and accommodating but maintain a fierce guard over their Hebridean way of life. Gaelic is widely spoken, the roads are mostly single track and everything shuts down on a Sunday.

A holiday here can reveal to you a whole assortment of fascinations.

Lewis, for example, is built on rock which is amongst the oldest in the world at 2,900 million years, about one third the age of the universe. There are no less than 28 known prehistoric monuments including the wondrous Callanish Stones, castles, brochs and old deserted villages scattered about this beautifully wild and peaceful landscape.

There are quite a number of hostels around the islands including four run by the Gatliff Trust. Although appearing in the SYHA handbook, the Gatliff Trust is a separate organisation. Their hostels are very basic and cheap, and can be great fun as there's no miserable

Map labels:
Butt of Lewis (Rubha Rabhanais)
Barvas (Barabhas)
Carloway (Carlabhagh)
Callanish (Calanais)
Stornoway (Steornabhagh)
to Ullapool
LEWIS
Hushinish (Hisinis)
Rhenigidale
Harris
Tarbert (Tairbeart)
BERNERAY
Leverburgh
Otternish
NORTH UIST
Lochmaddy
to Skye
BENBECULA
Howmore
SOUTH UIST
Lochboisdale
Ludag
ERISKAY
BARRA
to Oban
Castlebay
to Oban

warden hanging around. One thing most of the hostels seem to have in common (apart from Stornoway and Lochmaddy) is that they're located in very obscure places which is great once you're there but getting to them without a car can be difficult.

Camping is, weather permitting, very free and easy. There are, of course, many B&Bs plus the occasional hotel. Note that all Lewis and Harris roadsigns are in Gaelic only.

Lewis

Stornoway (Steornabhagh), the capital of the Western Isles, is a busy and bustling town and is surprisingly large by Highland standards. It has many amenities and shops to prepare yourself for onward travel.

Although there's not a lot to see in Stornoway there is the **Museum Nan Eilean** (Western Isles Museum) on Francis Street. Something sadly lacking from this museum are the curious **Lewis Chessmen** which were found in Lewis but are housed miles away in the Museum of Antiquities in Edinburgh and the British Museum in London (they do, however, have 3D images of them on computer). These chessmen were discovered in Uig in 1831 when a Lewis man fled from what he thought was a hive of elves - he had, in fact, unearthed a fabulous collection of 12thC Norse chess pieces carved from walrus ivory. Of interest, too, is the **An Lanntair** art gallery in the Town Hall. Both the museum and the gallery are free and open all year. It's a pleasant walk through the castle grounds to Lews Castle, built by a tea and opium trader (not open to the public). For a lovely panorama, walk to the Lewis Memorial, 2 miles out of town. The harbour provides some entertainment with many comings and goings and the occasional seal.

i **Tourist Information**, on Cromwell Street, tel:(01851) 703088, open all year, can provide you with a wealth of ideas and advice on how to get to many sites of beauty or interest and the other islands. It is advisable to buy the detailed map depicting these.

A minibus leaves Stornoway at 2pm Monday-Friday in the summer and will take you to see the sights of Lewis, including Callanish; a 3½ hour trip for £6. There are other tours that depart from Stornoway - see Tourist Information for details.

Stornoway Hostel, 47 Keith St, 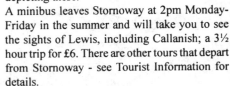 Stornoway, tel:(01851) 703628, £8/£8.50 a night (includes breakfast), open all year, but book ahead from December-February. Very cosy with friendly owners. 2 miles outside Stornoway at Laxdale is a **campsite**, tel:(01851) 703234, open April-October, £6.50-£9.

If you feel like an adventure, consider hiring a bike in Stornoway from **Alec Dan**, 67 Kenneth

King

Lewis Chess Piece

St, tel:(01851) 704025, for as little as £3.75 and up to £7.50 a day, and cycling 14 miles to Callanish (Calanais). Either return the same day or continue on to spend the night at the lovely Gatliff Trust Hostel at Garenin near Carloway (Carlabhagh) on the west coast. Return to Stornoway the next day by the circular route through Barvas (Barabhas), side-tracking up the road towards the Butt of Lewis (Rubha Rabhanais) if you have the inclination.

Car Rental: There are several places which offer car hire but the cheapest are Loch's Motors, South Beach St, opposite the bus station, tel:(01851) 705857, £18 daily/£95 weekly, and Lewis Car Rentals, Bayhead St, tel:(01851) 703760, £21.15 daily/£124.55 weekly.

Callanish Standing Stones

These magnificent and awe-inspiring standing stones are testament to a lost civilisation, 4,000 years ago. They cannot fail to impress deeply, casting a spell over the beautiful environment in which they are set (free to visit and unrestricted). In Gaelic - Calanais.

The whole area is rich with archaeology and history. Visit **Carloway Broch** at Dun Charlabhaigh, a mere 2,000 years old but still highly impressive with gorgeous scenery as a backdrop. Nearby lie the silver, sandy beaches of Dalmore and Dalbeg. Basic accommodation is available at the **Garenin Gatliff Trust Hostel**; £4.65, open all year.

North along the A858 is the **Black House Museum** which costs £1.80/£1.30 and is open all year; HS. This type of housing was once common in the Hebrides - thick walls packed with peat and a thatched roof. Visiting the Black House makes you realise just how essential peat was, and still is, to the islanders' lives. The Isle of Lewis is covered with peat stacks.

The **Butt of Lewis** is the northern most tip of the island. Don't expect to see a man named Lewis exposing his backside to the wind, because there's only a lighthouse, some birds and a feeling that you've reached the end of the A857.

Ten miles south of the Butt of Lewis is the **Galson Farm Bunkhouse**, tel:(01851) 850492, £8, open all year.

One of the most fascinating discoveries on the Isle of Lewis are the **Beehive Dwellings**. They are ancient stone structures resembling igloos. Archaeologists are still not sure how old they are, or whether they were used solely for shelter. You'll need a map to track them down. Take the B8011 from Garynahine (west of Stornoway). About 10 miles down the road you'll come to a blue parking sign on the right. Now backtrack about 100 metres and on your left a small river begins just near Loch Suirstavat. Follow the river and, nestled between two hills, Caultrashal Beag and Ben Mohal, are the deserted dwellings. The hour-long walk on the boggy moors is worth it.

Rook

Lewis Chess Piece

The only sound in the air is that of golden eagles and finding the buildings is like discovering one of Lewis' best kept secrets.

The **Raven's Point Hostel** at Kershader, tel:(01851) 880236, is open all year, £5.85-£6.95 a night.

A particularly beautiful free camping site on Lewis is off the B8011 on the way to Cnip at the Traigh Na Bevie dunes. The beach is long, white and sandy and there are even toilet facilities. At Eilean Fraoich is another great campsite, tel:(01851) 710504, 18 miles from Stornoway on the way to the Butt of Lewis. It's open May-October, £3.50-£7.50, and you get a self-catering kitchen, laundry facilities and additional blankets if required (hot showers 20p extra). Harris tweed is also woven on site.

Harris

Harris is the most mountainous part of the Western Isles, with spectacular rugged scenery, making for some good hill-walking. The beaches are quite stunning with vast white stretches of sand. By the way, Lewis and Harris are separate islands in every way - except geographically.

Harris' main village **Tarbert** (Tairbeart) is small and uneventful and the ferry from Skye arrives here. There is a **Tourist Information**, open from Easter to October, tel:(01859) 502011, a post office and some wee shops to purchase any essentials.

The **Rockview Bunkhouse**, tel:(01859) 502211, costs £8.50 a night and is open all year. Bike rental is available at the hairdresser, tel:(01859) 502271, for £5-£6 a day.

An interesting day's trekking in North Harris can be had up Glen Ulladale. Turn off the Hushinish (Husinis) road just before Amhuinnsuidhe Estate, walk up past the dam and continue into the wild, beautiful landscape until you reach Srom Ulladale, the highest cliffs in Britain.

The road down the west coast of Harris should not be missed as it passes beautiful beaches, particularly Scarista. If you make it past the small ferry port of Leverburgh (An T-ob), have a drink at the Rodel Bar and visit St Clements Church. The road back up the east coast to Tarbert is called the 'Golden Road' and is the home of Harris tweed weaving, which can be watched at Plocropol.

Drinishader Hostel, tel:(01859) 511255, £7, open all year. To get there travel south of Tarbert for about two miles, then turn left and go another couple of miles along the Golden Road.

Stockinish SYHA, tel:(01859) 530373, Grade 3, £4.65/£6.15, open 20/3-3/10. At Rhenigidale is another **Gatliff Trust Hostel**, £4.65, open all year. The hostel is located 6 miles east of Tarbert by foot or 13 miles by road. A taxi-bus operates to Rhenigidale twice daily during the school-term however you must phone ahead and book; tel:(01859) 502221 for times. Don't forget to take plenty of food.

Connecting Harris to her southerly neighbouring islands is a ferry service. The chief destination is North Uist but tiny Berneray makes a great island-hopping stop.

BERNERAY

This tiny island, lying just off North Uist, is a gem that is a must for your holiday. The houses in Berneray are concentrated near the harbour forming the main settlement. The bay beyond has a thriving seal population with perhaps 50 visible at any one time, some lying on the rocks and others playing, jumping right out of the water. They are plentiful here because there is no competition from humans as it is too shallow for boats to fish. The island is well populated with otters, too, but more patience is required. The entire west coast consists of an unforgettable stretch of sand and dunes.

The island has two shops - one of which sells booze (there's no pub) - a post office, two **B&Bs** and the spartan but ideal **Gatliff Trust Hostel**; £4.65, open all year. Berneray can be reached by boat from Otternish on North Uist for 90p, so you need to catch the ferry from Leverburgh on Harris to Otternish first.

NORTH UIST

Teeming with archeological sites and blessed with those fabulous white sandy beaches, North Uist is an island full of possibilities - a patchwork moorland of tiny lochans and peat bogs to the east coast, on the west a string of seaside hamlets set back from the glorious sands.

Lochmaddy is the main town where the ferries arrive from Skye, and buses leave to the south. It has a **Tourist Information**, tel:(01876) 500321, open Easter-September, shop, post office, pub and bank. Cars can be hired to travel the Uists, tel:(01870) 602191 or 602818. The **SYHA hostel** is the big white house, the first turning right from the ferry terminal, tel:(01876) 500368, Grade 2, £6.10/£7.60, open 15/5-31/10. However, a good place to stay is the **Uist Outdoor Centre**, tel:(01876) 500480, £6/£8, open all year, which offers, as well as accommodation, courses in sub-aqua diving, rock climbing, waterskiing, canoeing and hill-walking. The Outer Hebrides are known as the best place in the British Isles for diving due to unparalleled visibility of 35 metres, and this centre organises dives in sheltered sea lochs, by offshore islands, night

· Grey Seal ·

dives and wreck dives (including the S. S. Politician; see **Eriskay**). Alternatively you can stay at **Taigh Mo Sheanair** (in English - My Grandmother's House), a renovated croft house at Claddach Baleshare, tel:(01876) 580246, £8-£9 for a bunkbed, £4 to camp, open all year. Three to four buses per day go along the main A867 road and it's then one mile to walk to the hostel.

A few miles west of Lochmaddy visit the sites of **Pobull Fhinn**, 24 standing stones in an oval shape, and the **Barpa Langass**, probably the best preserved of all the Uist chambered tombs, built in the second or third millenium BC. If you can, take a torch.

Other impressive remains can be found all over North Uist, particularly at **Dun An Sticir**, an 18-metre wide broch.

To get to North Uist from Harris, Caledonian MacBrayne ferries leave Leverburgh for Otternish; £4.30 single, car £20.20, motorbike £10.10, bicycle £1.

BENBECULA

Like the Uists this island has beaches to the west and a myriad of lochans among the peaty land to the east. Climbing its hill Ben Reuval will give you a fine view of the whole island and beyond. It has its share, too, of archeological sites. However Benbecula's beauty has been partly compromised by its military base.

The island is linked by road to both North and South Uist and by air (expensively) to Stornoway, Barra and Glasgow; tel:0345 222111 for flight information. The main centre is at Balivanich which has a bank, shop, post office and pub. Lionacleit in the south has a museum, cafe and huge swimming pool. The coastal road connecting these two communities offers the better variety of scenery; otherwise the main road passes through the centre of the island. There is a **bunkhouse** at 22 Balivanich, tel:(01870) 602522, £8.50/£7.50, open all year. Three-four buses go past the hostel each day.

SOUTH UIST

South Uist is the hilliest of the southern Outer Hebrides but the hills lie to the empty east with its rocky shores. The main road, however, runs along the much flatter and well-populated western side of the island. It passes many hamlets and dozens of turnings leading to small communities. A map of the island will reveal the many standing stones, chambered cairns, brochs and other remains. The west coast is virtually one long tremendous beach and indeed if you have the inclination, and the weather is accommodating, you should consider walking the beach as your means of transport.

At the top of the island lies **Loch Bee**, renowned for its population of mute swans, and **Loch Druidibeg**, a vast breeding area for Greylag geese. Between these waters, on the slopes of **Ben Reuval** (a different one to the Ben Reuval on Benbecula), is a modern statue to Our Lady of the Isles. The view from here is good but further up this hillock is 'Space City' (you'll understand the nickname when you see it) and from here on a clear day you can see the Scottish mainland, Skye, and St Kilda to the west. What's more, if you're feeling lazy you can drive up this hill. While in this area stay at the delightful **Howmore Gatliff Trust Hostel**, a mile from the main road near the beach; £4.65, open all year. If you're travelling along the main road be sure to take the turning near Bornish to the Rubha Ardvule promontory for a splendid view of the coast. To the south of this turning is the **Kildonan Museum** which gives you an idea of South Uist life in the past and highlights some of the historic sites worth visiting; £1, open July-September.

At the bottom of the island at Pollachar near the standing stones is the local inn, not to be passed by. Towards the end of the road you can catch a wee passenger ferry from Ludag to Barra which is brilliant fun if the weather's wild - bobbing around on a small fishing boat between the islands.

i **Lochboisdale** is of no great interest but is the main port for Barra and Oban and has a post office, shop, bank, cafe, hotel, B&Bs and a **Tourist Information**, tel:(01878) 700286, open Easter-October. On the ferry look out for the ruin of the 13thC castle on Calvay island, a few minutes' sail from the pier.

To travel through these southern islands the bus leaves daily (not Sundays) to Lochmaddy - but don't rush. There is also a **postbus** and **car hire** (£25 daily/£141 weekly, tel:(01878) 700267).

ERISKAY

Eriskay is a tiny island lying between South Uist and Barra and should not be missed as it has a charm all its own. It shot to fame in the 1940s when a ship, the S.S. Politician, was wrecked on its coast. The ship was carrying thousands of cases of whisky which were 'rescued' by the locals to the chagrin of the exciseman, as depicted in the excellent book 'Whisky Galore' by Compton Mackenzie. While on the island visit St Michael's church and the beach before having a dram in the pub.

The boat to Eriskay leaves from Ludag five-eight times a day in summer, less frequently in winter, and costs £1, plus £1 for bicycles, tel:(01878) 720261 or 720216 for sailing times.

BARRA

Last, but by no means least, Barra hangs at the southern end of the Western Isles. It's a gorgeous island and will keep you busy with an assortment of delightful corners to visit. The 14-mile circular road conveniently takes you around with a couple of possible diversions either at the north end towards Eoligarry, including the wonderful cockle-shell beach, or south to Vatersay, a small crofting community.

Castlebay is the main town - and guess what? It has a castle in its bay. It has all the basic essentials plus a friendly, positive atmosphere. A boat will take you to the castle for about £1.50 and visiting the castle itself costs £1. Take a hike up Ben Heaval at the back of the town or hire a bike. Don't take a car to Barra or your holiday will be over in half an hour.

i **Tourist Information**, tel:(01871) 810336, open Easter to mid-October, will provide you with plenty of ideas plus accommodation info - there are no hostels here but plenty of free camping.

To get to Barra from South Uist a ferry runs between Ludag and Eoligarry four times daily in summer, twice daily in winter, for £4.50 single, bicycle £2, tel:(01878) 720238 - phone ahead to reserve a place in the summer as it can get very busy. The Caledonian MacBrayne ferry goes from Lochboisdale to Castlebay, but not every day so check timetables, for £4.90 single, car £27.50, motorbike £13.75, bicycle £2. Castlebay is also where Caledonian MacBrayne ferries from Oban arrive.

Getting To The Western Isles

There are three ferry services which leave from Ullapool, Uig and Oban. They go to and fro on most days, connecting the islands with the rest of Scotland and are run by **Caledonian MacBrayne**, tel:(01475) 650100.

Ullapool-Stornoway - single passenger £12 (£20.55 return), car £54 (£91 return), motorbike £27 (£45.50 return).
Uig-Tarbert or Lochmaddy - single passenger £7.85 (£13.40 return), car £37 (£63 return), motorbike £18.50 (£31.50 return).
Oban-Castlebay or Lochboisdale - single passenger £17.30 (£29.50 return), car £61 (£104 return), motorbike £30.50 (£52 return).
Mallaig-Castlebay or Lochboisdale - single passenger £12.75 (£21.70 return), car £45 (£77 return), motorbike £22.50 (£38.50 return).
Car and motorcycle prices do not include passenger fees. Bicycles £2 extra.

Buying an Island Hopscotch ticket rather than buying each ticket separately can save you a small amount of money, however, you must study a Caledonian MacBrayne brochure to see which Island Hopscotch combination suits you best. It's a very good idea for cyclists because bicycles can be taken aboard for free with these tickets. An Island Rover ticket covering all Caledonian MacBrayne ferry crossings costs £39 for 8 days and £56 for 15 days. Again, this is good for cyclists as bicycles travel for free.
The alternative is flying - from Glasgow or Inverness to Stornoway, Benbecula or Barra. This is usually very expensive, however, **British Airways**, tel:0345 222111, sometimes have special return deals that work out quite cheaply. Generally speaking booking 14 days in advance is cheaper.

Getting around the islands

Undoubtedly the most convenient way is by car - your own if you can afford all the ferry charges or, of course, they can be hired at various locations and most firms will drive the car to the ferry for you to collect (car hire firms listed in main text). There is a comprehensive but infrequent bus service augmented by the postbus. The bus can be frustrating at times, especially when it means that you have to wait half a day or longer at a ferry port.
Cycling is the most admirable method and the one that gives you the truest feel of the islands (every bump). The islands are relatively flat, except for Harris - however the wind is a factor to be considered.
Hitching is immensely unpredictable. Generally speaking the locals are very good at picking you up but at certain times and in certain places there is so little traffic.
Between the islands the ferries run six days a week, sometimes seven. The main company is **Caledonian MacBrayne** but there are also smaller (cheaper) ferries taking different routes, mentioned in the text.
A public transport guide to Skye and the Western Isles covers ferry and bus timetables for £1 and is available from Tourist Information Centres or from the Public Transport Section, Highland Council, Glenurquhart Rd, Inverness, IV3 5NX.

13. Orkney

Orkney's ancient burial tombs, massive standing stones and prehistoric villages mark the beginning of a 5,000 year journey. Jumping aboard the ferry to get here can be the beginning of a great adventure as there is so much to see and do. With the possible exception of the Nile Delta, Orkney is reputed to have more ancient monuments per square mile than any other part of the world.

The early Pictish inhabitants and the later Vikings have both left remarkable evidence of their existence, the Norse language in particular having a strong influence. The main towns proudly display 12th, 15th, 16th and 17thC architecture while the immense natural harbour, Scapa Flow, has become a diver's paradise with several of the 74 scuttled WWI German warships at its bottom. Orkney is an excellent place to see the Northern Lights, particularly in the late autumn, as well as puffins throughout the summer.

The word Orkney is believed to come from the Celtic 'Ork' meaning 'the young pigs', possibly a tribal nickname, and the Norse 'øy' meaning 'islands'. To call Orkney 'the Orkney Islands' or even the 'Orkneys' is in fact tautology but a mistake commonly made. There are 67 'øy', 10 main ones but numerous smaller ones and they are mostly flat with the exception of Hoy and Rousay, which have dramatic cliffs and Orkney's only really hilly terrain.

Mainland

The major island, possessing the two largest towns of Kirkwall and Stromness and a fair proportion of the historic sites, is always referred to as the 'mainland'. For information about individual places in Orkney there are good and extremely helpful leaflets available from the Tourist Information offices in either Stromness or Kirkwall.

STROMNESS

Taking the ferry from Scrabster will take you past the island of Hoy, viewing the impressive pillar the **Old Man of Hoy** and the sea cliffs, rising to over 1100ft at St John's Head. Just before docking you round the point of Ness and Stromness appears, clinging to the hillside that has provided a sheltered port. Stromness is a delightful town with narrow, paved streets, hostel accommodation and several shops.

i **Tourist Information**, tel:(01856) 850716, open all year, faces the ferry terminal and provides a heritage guide pamphlet detailing the town and its history. However if you're in the tourist office make sure you visit the Orkney display (it's at the back and not apparent at first glance) - videos of Orkney can be put on by request. The town centre is easy to get around and although there's not a lot to do the **Stromness Museum** on the main street deserves some of your time; £1.50, open all year. The **Pier Arts Centre**, which has a permanent collection of 20thC art together with temporary exhibitions, is also worth visiting and is free to enter.

A particularly good time to visit Stromness is when the **Orkney Traditional Folk Festival** takes place - in 1998, 21-24 May. It's also an ideal place to stay while exploring Orkney's most renowned and remarkable sites - Skara Brae, Maes Howe and the Ring of Brodgar.

Walks around Stromness

For a bird's eye view, take the easy walk up the hill behind Stromness, **Brinkies Brae**. Climb up through the town's curiously-named lanes and then follow the granite dykes to the hilltop. The views include Scapa Flow (where the British fleet was moored in two wars and the German fleet was scuttled in 1919) and the hills and cliffs of Hoy to the south. For a longer walk, head south through the town, through the campsite and out past the golf course along the seashore. From here follow the old road around the coast past the gun emplacements (both in and out of the golf course), positioned there to protect Hoy Sound from past invaders. The friendly seals bask on the rocks looking across at the two main hills of Hoy (Ward Hill and Cuilags). After 20 minutes, a road winds back towards town. Ten minutes further on, a track and the local cemetery appear. Perched by the seabank and surrounded by a 4-foot high wall, this provides a respite from the wind and a look back at Orkney's past families. Further on is sandy Warbeth beach from where you can head back along the road to Stromness. The road ascends and provides superb views over Scapa Flow, Flotta, Burray and South Ronaldsay before descending into Stromness. Alternatively the coast can be followed from the beach, passing the farm of Pow, alternating between bank and rock to Breckness and the massive Black Craig. Offshore, you will see the sea-swept Kirk Rocks, the grave of many ships.

Browns Hostel, 45 Victoria St, tel:(01856) 850661 open all year, £7.50/£8. A crammed but cosy independent hostel with intimate views of the main street, just 3 minutes from the ferry.

Stromness SYHA, Hellihole Rd, tel:(01856) 850589, Grade 2, £6.10/£7.60, open 20/3-31/10. Adequate hostel in an unfortunately named street (the name actually comes from the old Norse for 'Holy Well').

Point of Ness Campsite, tel:(01856) 873535, £3.50-£5.50, open May-mid-September, 1½ miles west of the pier.

The Coffee Shop at the laundrette on Ferry Road is small and slightly genteel but good. **The Cafe,** with its windows overlooking the harbour is an ideal place to watch the world go past over a cup of coffee, but is a bit more expensive. It's just along the main street past the horse trough. The **Peedie Coffee Shop** in Dundas Street serves good mince rolls, coffee and cakes with pink icing. The **Ferry Inn** and the **Royal Hotel** have the best bar meals. A bakery, delicatessen, Chinese takeaway and mini supermarket all line the main street.

Around Stromness

Note that Historic Scotland has a £9/£7 joint entry ticket for Skara Brae, Brough of Birsay, Maes Howe, the Broch of Gurness and the Bishop's and Earl's Palaces. If you go to all of these places you save £2.10.

A living village 5,000 years ago, **Skara Brae** was swallowed by sand until uncovered during a hurricane in 1850 and excavated in 1927. It is Northern Europe's best preserved prehistoric village, a tight warren of stone houses joined by stone passages and covered alleyways, containing beds, fireplaces, shelves, grinding stones, tools, a workshop and household artefacts. It's in immaculate condition and lies about seven miles north of Stromness. An information centre tells you more about the site's history; £4/£3, HS, open all year. Just off the path to Skara Brae lies the haunted 17thC mansion, **Skaill House,** which is included in the price of your ticket. Hiring a bike can make a good option for transport - just beware of the wind gusts.

Situated 4 miles from Stromness beside the main Kirkwall-Stromness road, **Maes Howe** is Orkney's most famous tomb, built about 4,500 years ago. The tomb is 7m high and 35m wide, and the set stone slab interior is lit by the mid-winter sun as it sets between Hoy's hills. The interior is covered by runic writing from Viking grave robbers (graffiti basically), which includes a Nordic Dragon (looking a bit like a horse) and comments about beautiful Scandinavian maidens (some things never change); £2.30/£1.75, HS, open all year.

Within sight of Maes Howe, on a thin bridge of land between the lochs of Harray and Stenness, are the **Stones of Stenness** and the **Ring of Brodgar**, two ancient monuments around which there is a silent mysterious aura. The older monument, the Stones of Stenness, was once a circle of 12 stones of which three remain. Brodgar is much bigger and staggeringly impressive. The circle spans some 103 metres and has 36 of its original 60 stones; free.

Although more difficult to get to without transport, the west coast of Orkney offers miles of cliff-top walks with the chance to view tens of thousands of seabirds. Between Stromness and Skara Brae are the sea-cliffs of **Yesnaby** with its two-legged sea castle and isthmus fortification of the **Brough**. Beyond the Bay of Skaill lies **Marwick Head**, an RSPB bird reserve, with its cliff top memorial to Lord (Your country needs you) Kitchener who was lost offshore during WWI. The north-west corner of the mainland, Birsay, was the first burial place of St Magnus. It has a wealth of historic and ancient buildings including a once splendid 16thC palace built by Robert Stewart, Earl of Orkney and, on the tidal island of the **Brough of Birsay**, early Christian and Viking ruins complete with central heating (£1).

The area of Evie is overlooked by wind generators on the hills and is mostly visited for the **Broch of Gurness**. This is the best of Orkney's brochs, probably built in the first century. It served as a defence tower for the surrounding village until the 5thC

· Standing Stones ·

when it was apparently abandoned, but it was later inhabited by both the Picts and the Vikings; £2.30/£1.75, open April-September.

In Evie village is the **Evie Hostel**, tel:(01856) 751208, prices from £5, open March-October, or the smaller **Eviedale Bothy**, tel:(01856) 751254 or 751270, open May-September, £5 per bunk (bring own sleeping bag). The bothy has a campsite, £3 a tent plus £1 per person.

KIRKWALL

The islands' capital Kirkwall is one of the best-preserved examples of an ancient Norse town. Originating from a Christian settlement, it has a history of both noble and religious conflicts. The central landmark, **St Magnus Cathedral**, built of magnificent red sandstone, has housed Sunday services since 1137. It is open to the public Monday-Saturday (and for attending services on Sunday) and is free to enter. To the south of the cathedral is **Earl Patrick's Palace** (1606), a superb ruin and fine example of French Renaissance influence on Orcadian architecture. The adjacent **Bishop's Palace** is a much older building first constructed in the mid-12thC. A ticket for £1.50/£1.10 gets you into both palaces; open April-September.

The **Tankerness House Museum** has the most comprehensive exhibition on Orkney life; £2 (free for students and in winter), open all year.

Visitors to Kirkwall at Christmas or New Year should not miss the opportunity to see, or take part in, the Ba'. One of very few ancient ball games still played, it is a wild and frantic rugby scrum, with no rules and no maximum number for the two teams, the 'Uppies' and the 'Doonies' - 300 players is not unusual. Very much a team game, the object is to get the Ba' (ball) to the goal, a wall at the upper end of the town for the Uppies or into the sea at the harbour for the Doonies. Two games are played on both Christmas Day and New Year's Day. If you play, be prepared to buy new clothes afterwards.

Kirkwall's **Tourist Information** is in Broad St, tel:(01856) 872856, open all year.

Walks around Kirkwall

Tourist Information offers a pamphlet detailing a walk through the town, pointing out the main points of interest. If you're staying at the SYHA hostel on Old Scapa Road turn left as you leave the building and follow the road for 15 minutes to the seashore. To the right you'll see the Scapa distillery (not open to the public). Walk along the shore towards the wharf past the modern harbour department building to a shed beside the road. Inside is a memorial to the battleship the Royal Oak and 800 of its crew. The ship lies just offshore having been torpedoed by a German submarine in 1939. Now a war grave, it is marked by a naval wreck buoy and overlooked in the distance by the oil terminal flare stack on Flotta. From the shed continue to the right to look at the boats at the harbour or turn left, taking New Scapa Road and Wellington Street, back to the hostel for a round trip of about an hour.

Also leaving from the youth hostel, turn up nearby Glaitness Road for a walk up **Wideford Hill**. Continue along the roadside until you have almost rounded the hill, then just before the road descends towards Finstown, look for a narrow path up some concrete steps on the right. The path follows a fence so is easy to find. Follow this path as it ascends the hill but before reaching the crest take a left down to a cairn located high up the slope. This tomb provides great views down over the Bay of Firth, and is a good example of a tomb with side chambers. Continue up to the hilltop for panoramic views of Orkney and the Scottish mainland. Return to Kirkwall via the vehicle track found on the top which will bring you back to Glaitness Road. It's about a three-hour walk.

There is also a shorter but possibly more enjoyable walk that can be taken. Follow the main street up the between the Cathedral and the Palaces for a mile (following the signs for South Ronaldsay) and you will come to the **Highland Park Distillery**. Conducted tours are available for £2, but this includes an excellent audio-visual presentation of Orkney and whisky production and a dram; open all year.

Midsummer madness comes to Orkney in the form of the **St Magnus Festival**, a six-day feast of the finest music, drama and dance with top rate performers from all over the world. Try about 40 performances in six days - it can be done, just! Contact Dorothy Rushbrook, tel:(01856) 872669, for details of the '98 programme, running from 19-24 June. Book accommodation well ahead.

For a cheap snack or a coffee, just across from the Cathedral, is the **St Magnus Cafe**. Also reasonably-priced are **Trenabies** and the **Pomona Cafe.** You can have Indian or Chinese food or try the **International Takeaway** on Bridge Street for Orkney's speciality, fried patty and chips. The pubs offer bar meals at lunchtime and in the early evening. You can browse around the stalls in the arcade in Bridge Street and enjoy good, traditional food at the **Anchor Cafe**.

The town has a wide choice of shops providing everything you might wish - locally-made silver and gold is available from the original Ola Gorie collection, or from Ortak. Try Robertson's tasty Orkney Fudge and you can even get a traditional straw-backed chair to keep the draughts away in winter.

 Kirkwall SYHA, Old Scapa Rd, tel:(01856) 872243, Grade 1, £7.75/£9.25, open 27/2-31/10. Clean and well equipped, 11.30pm curfew, ten minutes' walk from Tourist Information.

Peedie Hostel, Ayr House, Ayr Rd, tel:(01856) 874500, £9.50, open all year. A new independent hostel.

Pickaquoy Campsite, 150m south-west of the foot of the hill coming down into Kirkwall, tel:(01856) 873535, £3.50-£5.50. Open mid-May to mid-September.

East of Kirkwall

Lying 9 miles east is Deerness where there is **The Gloup** - a sea-cave that has collapsed leaving a large blowhole and archway to the sea. From here you can walk around the cliffs to the north and back in a round trip (2-3 hours). This passes the **Brough of Deerness**, possibly the site of a Celtic monastery, standing on an isolated rock 5 minutes' walk past The Gloup. Look out for the Covenanters' Memorial on the east coast.

South Isles

To the south-east of the mainland lie the islands of **Lamb Holm, Glims Holm, Burray** and **South Ronaldsay**, now joined to the mainland by the **Churchill Barriers**, set to protect the British fleet during WWII. Just across the barrier lies the **Italian Chapel**. In 1942, 1,000 Italian prisoners were kept here and built this charming chapel from scrap metal and concrete - whatever they could get their hands on really. Note the lights made from bully beef cans. It's well worth a visit and free. Each summer (in 1998, 15 August) the village of St Margaret's Hope is host to the 'Festival of the Horse', an unusual ploughing match. The local girls dress up in their finest horse harness and compete for the prize as the best dressed 'horse' while the boys test their skills with a miniature plough on the sands at Herston.

Continuing south brings good views of Flotta and the oil terminal. To the east of the ferry terminal at Burwick lies Isbister Farm, home to the **Tomb of the Eagles**. The people who inhabited this area 5,000 years ago entombed their dead with, amongst other things, eagles, possibly the totem animal of their clan. Unlike most other historic sites it lies on private land, the owners of which offer colourful guided tours showing the chambered tomb (where 300 bodies were buried), a Bronze-Age house and the museum in their farmhouse. You're allowed to hold many of the ancient artefacts, such as the skulls of Stone Age man, their tools and eagle bones; £2.50 entrance fee, open all year (summer months 10am-8pm, winter 10am-noon).

North of the tomb lies Halcro Head; it's a good walk there, showing cliffs and rock formations. Continue along to Windwick Bay to rejoin the road.

 Wheems Bothy, Eastside, South Ronaldsay, tel:(01856) 831537, £5, open April-September, 2 miles east of St Margaret's Hope. This is an organic farm which has some food for sale.

Herston Hikers Hostel, South Ronaldsay, tel:(01856) 831208, £4, open all year. Very basic accommodation with an open fire and stove, but *no* hot water and you must bring your own sleeping bag.

HOY

Another of the South Isles is Hoy, the largest island after the mainland. It has the most dramatic terrain of Orkney with sensational sea-cliffs and the rock pillar, the Old Man of Hoy. You could make a day-trip to Hoy returning to Stromness at night but with two hostels, Hoy makes a good stopover. The ferry from Stromness arrives at Moaness pier. On landing, head up and round to the right of the hill ahead. This is **Ward Hill** the tallest in Orkney at 1563ft and between it and the other peak of Cuilags is a rough track which will lead you to **Rackwick**, a small hamlet situated around a beautiful bay at the end of a deep valley. There are great views and the path leads past what little is left of the ancient native tree cover.

Out of Rackwick lies a popular trek up to the **Old Man of Hoy**, Hoy's most famous landmark - a rock stack that reaches 450ft into the sky. Further along, the sea-cliffs are excellent for birdwatching. You can walk along past **St John's Head**, a high sheer cliff, and back to Moaness, although this is probably too much if you want to return to Stromness the same day. Coming back from Rackwick, walk along the road through the dramatic little valley to the southern side of Ward Hill. Stop to see the **Dwarfie Stane**, a rock-cut tomb thought to be unique in Britain. Near the end of the road you pass the most northerly forest in Scotland - well, a forest by Orkney standards.

The rest of Hoy is the only real wilderness in Orkney and provides a trek across the hill tops to Lyness, a naval base during the wars. The **Scapa Flow Visitor Centre**, just a couple of minutes' walk from the ferry terminal, sheds light on Orkney's role in both World Wars; £1.50, open all year. South of Lyness lies the picturesque bay of Long Hope, guarded on the north and south headlands by **Martello Towers** - the southern one at Hackness with its associated Battery is open to the public. At the far end of the bay is the splendid late 19thC mansion of **Melsetter House** (not open to the public). Beyond Long Hope in South Walls lies **the Longhope Lifeboat Memorial** erected to commemorate the loss of the lifeboat crew in 1969.

North Hoy (Moaness) SYHA, tel:(01856) 873535, Grade 2, £6.10/£7.60, open 2/5-11/9. Near the pier. Bring your own sleeping bag.

Rackwick SYHA Outdoor Centre, tel:(01856) 873535, £6.10/£7.60, open 14/3-11/9. Bring your own sleeping bag.

Burnmouth Bothy, down near the beach in Rackwick, free and always open. Very basic - you need your own bedding and a sleeping mat - either sleep in the house or camp outside.

The ferry from Stromness to Moaness runs three times a day in summer, twice in winter for £2.30 single (bicycles £1.10). If you're short on time, a bus to Rackwick meets the morning ferry and returns in time for the afternoon ferry, tel:(01856) 791263 (they also have a taxi service). From Lyness a ferry runs about five times a day to Houton on the mainland (sometimes via Flotta) for £2.30 single (bicycles £1.10) and from there a bus connects with Kirkwall; Peace's Coaches, tel:(01856) 872866.

North Isles

Shapinsay

The highly-cultivated island of Shapinsay is one of the most visited in Orkney but perhaps due simply to its proximity to the mainland. The ferry arrives at small **Balfour** village, standing in front of the gatehouse to the 19thC **Balfour Castle**. The village was built for the workers on the Balfour Estate in the 19thC and is separated from the castle grounds by a ring of trees. A tower marks the end of the village but the gatehouse is now actually a pub - pop in for a pint. The castle is open May-September, but only on Wednesdays and Sundays. This is the highlight of the island (the village also has a small coffee shop and museum at the Smithy - summer only), although to the far south-east lies Castle Bloody (a chambered cairn, in fact) and impressive sea-cliffs. A standing stone is just inland from here and to the north are the remains of the Broch of Burroughston from where you're likely to see seals. Ferries leave from Kirkwall about five times daily; £2.30 single. To see the island you really need a bike, which costs £1.10 to bring on the ferry from Kirkwall.

Rousay, Wyre and Egilsay

The largest of these three islands, Rousay, contains numerous sites of archaeological significance including the largest and possibly the best cairn in Orkney, **Midhowe Cairn**. It is covered by a protecting stone building, the tomb being rather fragile; free. Nearby is **Midhowe Broch**, an Iron-Age broch and walled enclosure you are free to wander through. There are splendid views of the holy island of Eynehallow, lying in the channel between Rousay and the mainland. Midhowe is on the west coast about 5 miles from the ferry and en route you can visit several small tombs on the roadside, all open. These are **Taversoe Tuick, Blackhammar** and the **Knowe of Yarso**. Just past Westness House a path leads to the shore and then north to Midhowe. This is known as the **Westness Walk** and information about the archaeological sites along this mile-long stretch is set out in a leaflet available from Tourist Information. If you're cycling around Rousay, the road, which circles the island, goes beyond Midhowe and leads to the Loch of Wasbister within which is a crannog, or artificial island, built in the early Iron Age. The west coast's cliffs are a popular spot for birdwatching.

Rousay Hostel, Trumland Farm, tel:(01856) 821252, £6/£8.50, open all year. The hostel is situated on a working farm which might just need helpers - you receive bed and board. Phone ahead and see. There is a campsite on the same premises.

The much smaller islands of **Wyre** and **Egilsay** also have archaeological sites to visit. **St Magnus Church**, close to where St Magnus was martyred, dominates the landscape of Egilsay with an unusual tower almost 50ft in height; free.

· **Puffin** ·

Cubbie Roo's Castle on Wyre is said to have been built in the 12thC by the mighty Viking Kolbein Hruga (or Cubbie Roo). The ruin is surrounded by a circular ditch and nearby is **St Mary's Chapel** which also dates from the 12thC (both free).

To get to these islands a ferry departs from **Tingwall** about six times a day to Brinyan village on Rousay, mostly continuing on to Wyre and Egilsay (both request stops - ask when you board). Rosie Coaches, tel:(01856) 751227, run buses between Kirkwall and Tingwall which meet the ferries. The hostel in Evie is just a short walk from the Tingwall ferry point.

Stronsay

'The Island of the Three Bays', Stronsay, lies 90 minutes by ferry from Kirkwall. This low-lying island's main features are its long white and sheltered beaches. In contrast, it also has the Vat of Kirbister, one of the finest 'gloups' in Orkney. Also of interest are the old kelp kilns on the smaller island of Papa Stronsay.

Inganoust, tel:(01857) 616314, is a basic bothy on an organic farm, with water, gas cooker and toilet (no shower), £3. Check out the **Old Telegraph Office** seal watch hide, the only one in north-west Europe.

The ferry leaves Kirkwall for Whitehall, an old herring fishing station on Stronsay, once or twice a day; £4.60 single, bicycle £1.70.

Eday

One of Eday's main claims to fame is that the stone quarried here went to build St Magnus Cathedral in Kirkwall. It was also the place of capture of John Gow, a notorious 18thC pirate. The island has many chambered cairns - Vinquoy and Huntersquoy to the north of the island being the best of them. The impressive Stone of Setter stands 15ft high about a mile away. Quite a hilly island, you can obtain good views from the tops of these hills to the scattering of islands all around.

Eday SYHA is located at London Bay, tel:(01857) 622283, Grade 3, £4.65/ £6.15, open 1/4-29/9.

Ferries go from Kirkwall to Eday at least once a day (except Sundays), £4.60 single, £1.70 bicycles. They may go via Stronsay.

Westray and Papa Westray

Westray is the largest of the northern isles and has a rich variety of places to visit. Formidable **Noltland Castle** stands west of the fishing village of Pierowall and along the cliffed western coastline is the Gentlemen's Cave where noble supporters of the failed Jacobite rebellion hid. The entire island is a good place to spot birds, particularly from **Noup Head** with its lighthouse, while **Stanger Head** on the eastern coast is ideal for viewing puffins between May and August. Common and grey seals are often seen and also whales occasionally. The world's shortest scheduled flight of less than two minutes goes from Westray to the smaller Papa Westray.

Papa Westray means the 'island of the priests' and has 8thC and 12thC chapels to confirm this. It features the **Knap of Howar**, the earliest standing houses in Europe. Like Skara Brae, it was uncovered by a severe storm, but, though an older site, it is not so famous. Ask about a boat-trip to the even smaller island of **Holm of Papay** to visit the chambered cairns there, the South Cairn in particular.

Papa Westray **SYHA hostel** is two miles south of the ferry at Beltane House, tel:(01857) 644267, Grade 1, £7.75/£9.25, open all year.

Ferries to Westray go at least once a day through the summer, £4.60 single, bicycles £1.70, but onward trips to Papa Westray, £2.30, are less frequent so check timetables for details. The Westray ferry terminal is at Rapness, some 10 minutes' drive from Pierowall. For bus tours/car hire, contact Mr Harcus, tel:(01857) 677450. A shuttle bus from Pierowall connects with the Papa Westray sailings, tel:(01857) 677432.

Sanday

Sanday's magnificent white sandy beaches plus important historic monuments make the island a delight should you choose to visit. Sanday means literally 'sandy isle' and these lovely, secluded beaches are possibly the best Orkney has. Numerous seals and sometimes otters can be seen and sadly whales have occasionally beached themselves here. **Quoyness Chambered Tomb** at Elsness is another of Orkney's splendid Neolithic sites dating to 2000 BC. The large main chamber leads off into six small cells; free. This ancient burial site is actually one of hundreds on the island. To the north at the **Tofts Ness Prehistoric Funerary Complex** there are 500 burial mounds all likely to be excavated thoroughly in the future. A wrecked German WWI destroyer can be seen at low tide in the Bay of Lopness plus further north is a wartime radar station.

Accommodation is limited on Sanday but if you have a tent you can camp, just ask the landowner first.

Ferries depart from Kirkwall once or twice a day, £4.60 single, £1.70 bicycle.

North Ronaldsay

The most remote island of Orkney, North Ronaldsay, attracts fewer visitors but it has some rare features to be proud of. Standing on a migration crossroads, the island is hugely popular with birdwatchers during the summer months as the birds make their way to Iceland, Greenland and Scandinavia. North Ronaldsay is surrounded by a dry-stone dyke and living outwith the wall are the island's unique breed of seaweed-eating sheep. Look out for **Matches Dyke**, one of two 3,000-year-old stone and earth dykes which divide the island. North Ronaldsay has only one weekly sailing and even then it's 'weather permitting'; £4.60 single, £1.70 bicycle.

Getting to Orkney

BY FERRY

P&O Scottish Ferries, tel:(01856) 850655, have sailings from Scrabster to Stromness for £14/£15 single, £28/£30 return (10% student discount). Sailings are twice daily (6am and midday) Monday-Friday and midday on Saturday through the winter. The summer schedule has extra sailings each day with one on a Sunday. A set one or two day-return ticket is £15, and a two-five night stopover return costs £21. It costs £65-£77 return for a car and this is not including driver's and passengers' fares. P&O in Aberdeen, tel:(01224) 572615, also have more expensive crossings from Aberdeen to Stromness that depart once a week in winter, twice a week in summer, an 8-10 hour ride, £37-£40 single/£74-£80 return (10% student discount).

John O'Groat's Ferries, tel:(01955) 611353, offer a £22-£25 return fare from John O'Groats to Burwick from May to September. There is a free connecting bus every afternoon from Thurso railway station to connect with sailings. If you're coming from Inverness the same company runs the **Orkney Bus** - £37 return includes the bus and ferry trips from Inverness-John O'Groats-Burwick and back.

BY AIR

British Airways or **British Airways Express** offer flights from Edinburgh, Glasgow, Inverness, Aberdeen and Wick to Kirkwall Airport, tel:0345 222111 or (01856) 873457. As a price guide, from Edinburgh it costs about £149 single and £122 return (if you stay over on a Saturday night). From Wick it's about £32 single and £30-£46 return (depending on when you book). Phone them for details because they have varying cheap deals.

Getting around Orkney

A bus and ferry public transport travel guide to 'North Highland and Orkney' is available for £1 from Tourist Information Centres or from the Public Transport Section, Highland Council, Glenurquhart Rd, Inverness, IV3 5NX.

BY BUS (Note - no bus services on Sundays)

Peace's Coaches, tel:(01856) 872866, run many bus services from Kirkwall to Stromness. This route passes the Ring of Brodgar, Stones of Stenness and Maes Howe. Peace's also go from Kirkwall to Houton and Kirkwall/Stromness to Dounby.

Causeway Coaches, tel:(01856) 831444, run from Kirkwall to St Margaret's Hope, 2-4 times a day.

Deerness Bus Service, tel:(01856) 741215, from Kirkwall to Deerness, once a day.

Rosie Coaches, tel:(01856) 751227, from Kirkwall to Tingwall 3-5 times daily, Evie and the Broch of Gurness twice daily.

Wild About Orkney, tel:(01856) 851011 (or contact Tourist Information in Kirkwall or Stromness) run a variety of day and half-day tours from January-December, specialising in archaeology, wildlife and folklore tours. Prices from £6-£17. They can provide a door-to-door service and they also run tours to Hoy, £23/£20.50.

Go Orkney, tel:(01856) 871871, also provide full-day and half-day tours around Orkney from March-October taking in the major monuments - Skara Brae, Ring of Brodgar and Maeshowe - with prices ranging from £6/£4 to £12/£10. They also run tours to other parts of Orkney. You can travel with luggage and bicycles on their bus and if you book in advance they can organise reduced-price ferry travel.

BY FERRY

Inter-island ferry sailing is simply a matter of working out the timetables which are available from Tourist Information or Orkney Ferries, Ayre Rd, Kirkwall, tel:(01856) 872044. Prices are either £4.60 or £2.30 single depending on the distance, likewise inter-island trips cost £2.30 or £1.15.

Steve Mowat Boat Operator, tel:(01856) 850624, operate a service from Stromness to Moaness (the only service to Moaness) on Hoy for about £2.30. June to September - three sailings daily from Monday to Friday and twice daily at weekends. October to May - twice daily, Monday to Friday only.

BY AIR

British Airways Express, tel:(01856) 873457, provide frequent, expensive but quick flights to Eday, Sanday, North Ronaldsay, Papa Westray and Westray. It is necessary to book ahead.

BIKE RENTAL

Cycle Hire, 54 Dundas Street, Stromness, tel:(01856) 850255, £5-£8 a day.

Patersons Cycle Centre, Tankerness Lane, Kirkwall, tel:(01856) 873097, £7-£8 a day.

CAR RENTAL

Brass's Self Drive, Pierhead Office, Ferry Rd, Stromness, tel:(01856) 850750, £32.90 daily/£164 weekly.

Peace's Car Hire, Junction Rd, Kirkwall, tel:(01856) 872866, £30 daily, but cheaper per day the longer you hire.

14. Shetland

These islands are like nothing else in Scotland. Remote, dramatic and windswept they can be cruel to travellers, yet they reward the adventurous like few places in the world can. There is life here aplenty - folk music, fishing, oil and the old crofting traditions - yet there is space too. Skies so big, horizons so long and the midnight sun so amber - this is the land of sea and of wind and of living. The islands have some of Scotland's most significant and exciting prehistoric ruins, most importantly the Iron Age Mousa Broch and the excavated settlements at Jarlshof. Shetlanders, often refusing to be called Scots, say theirs is a Viking land. Scandinavian influence began around the 8thC, and

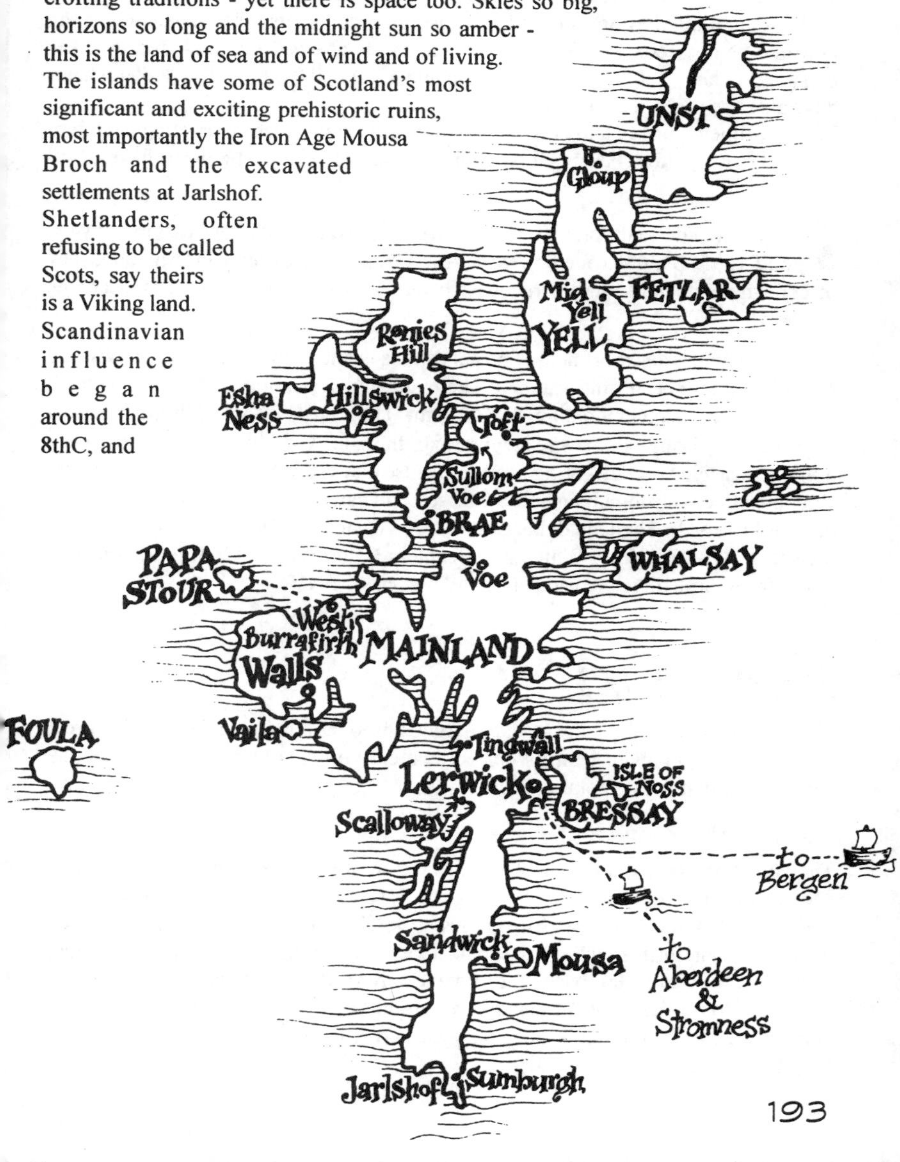

UNST

Gloup

Mid Yell

FETLAR

YELL

Ronies Hill

Esha Ness

Hillswick

Toft

Sullom Voe

BRAE

PAPA STOUR

Voe

WHALSAY

West Burrafirth

MAINLAND

Walls

Vaila

FOULA

Tingwall

Lerwick

ISLE OF NOSS

Scalloway

BRESSAY

to Bergen

Sandwick

Mousa

to Aberdeen & Stromness

Jarlshof

Sumburgh

193

although the islands came into the Scottish crown in 1468, it was not until the 17thC that Scottish institutions firmly stamped themselves upon their Norse predecessors.

The archipelago has over a hundred islands of which 15 remain inhabited. Most of the stable population of 23,000 live on the largest island called (predictably) Mainland. The two most remote islands are Foula and Fair Isle.

Wildlife is another of the main attractions. There are eight National Nature Reserves in the islands and they are some of the most important spots for birdwatchers in the northern hemisphere. The Shetlanders themselves are well outnumbered by other creatures, notably 330,000 sheep, 300,000 fulmars and 250,000 puffins. Killer whales have also been seen recently in great numbers.

The coastline is rugged and crenellated, there are many caves penetrating deep into the cliffs and golden beaches that even in summer you are likely to have all to yourself.

i The Shetland Islands only **Tourist Information** is at the Market Cross in Lerwick, tel:(01595) 693434, open all year. Apart from bus and ferry information, they offer a what's-on guide and currency exchange. Be patient if the ferry has just come into town.

There is an assortment of hostels on the islands and virtually all of these are in very beautiful locations. There are also six camping böds on Shetland, providing basic accommodation for £3 a night. They must be booked through Tourist Information - bring your own sleeping bag, though. And although you obviously don't need a tent you must bring everything else that you would take when camping. Böds are effectively mountain huts by the sea, and have been chosen for their location or their history. In Shetland dialect a böd was a basic house for fishermen. They are located at Whalsay, Voe, Whiteness, Scatness (Dunrossness), Yell and Eshaness. Apart from these there are campsites and numerous B&Bs.

Mainland

The best thing to do about the capital, Lerwick, is to leave it immediately. It's a great town, but to appreciate it in its correct context you should go and discover the countryside first before coming back.

South of Lerwick

The island of **Mousa** is not inhabited but is one of the most admired in Shetland. **Mousa Broch** (a defensive fort) which stands sentinel over it, is one of the finest prehistoric landmarks in the British Isles as notable for its elegance as for its age. It is a circular fortress which rises and tapers 40ft high, commanding excellent views over the watery approaches. It's not the only broch in Shetland but indisputably the best. Mousa lies opposite Sandwick and, although the monument is free, you must arrange with Tom Jamieson to take you across in his boat; tel:(01950) 431367, June-September.

Sumburgh Head is one of the prettiest spots in Shetland. Here is the archaeologist's dream site of **Jarlshof**. A wild storm in 1905 peeled back the sand dunes revealing extensive remains of 3,000 years of continuous inhabitation - a Bronze-Age village, an Iron-Age broch and an entire Viking settlement. A visitor centre displays the fascinating history of the site; £2.30/£1.75, open April-September, HS. Keep walking north around the bay from Jarlshof and you reach Scatness. Walk down Scatness along to a signed footpath to get to the **Ness of Burgi**, a honeycomb prehistoric fort.

There is a camping **böd** at Scatness, Dunrossness, close to Sumburgh, £3 a night, open April-October, complete with shower.

North of Lerwick

The north mainland is the most formidable and perhaps the most satisfying corner of Shetland. Here are the big hills and the most deeply clefted voes. The village of **Voe** is central enough to make a touring base for the north and west. It has splendid views and the camping **böd** here, The Sail Loft, is in a beautiful situation; £3 a night.

Brae, one of the largest settlements in the islands, though nothing special, is friendly, has good shops and is the public transport hub for buses to Lerwick and the north isles. There is a **campsite** (tel:(01806) 522563, £3.50-£9, open April-September), an indoor swimming pool and several pubs.

Just beyond town is the **Mavis Grind**. In Shetlandic dialect 'grind' means gate and this thin spine of rock is all that separates the Atlantic from the North Sea. Continue toward the Sullom Voe oil terminal which is an awe-inspiring and confusing site. You can see the towering flares from a long way off and they light up the night sky for miles around.

Rønies Hill is the highest spot in Shetland, rising to nearly 1500ft. It is not difficult to climb (though you should wear waterproof boots) and the views from the summit are spectacular.

North Roe feels even more remote than some of the outer isles. It has a fine bay and harbour, a shop and an excellent beach north of the village at Sandvoe. The main reason to visit North Roe, however, is to continue onward on foot to **Fedaland**. This is one of the best hikes in Shetland, being both accessible and beautiful. Follow the A970 as far as it goes to Isbister and continue straight on up the hill and over the gate. If the weather is good you might consider bedding down in one of the ruined haaf (fishing cottages). Keep on walking as far as you can go to the point of Fedaland.

Hillswick is one of the archetypal Shetland communities with a sense of permanence and an air of the magic of story-telling and legends of the sea. It comes as no surprise to hear that mermaids were reported in the waters around Hillswick this century. There is a shop here and you must take refreshment in **Da Booth**, the oldest tavern in Shetland.

Continuing along the B9078 you will find perhaps the best (and most remote) camping böd close to the sea cliffs at Eshaness. 'Johnny Notions' **böd**, £3, open April-October, is named after the local inventor who also pioneered inoculation as a medical treatment. There is no electricity here so bring some candles and listen to the sea crashing on the cliffs (to get there follow the road as far as Braewick and turn right toward Hamnavoe - well signposted from there). Hike to the cliffs at Eshaness, don't get too close to the edge and revel in the cacophony of birdlife. Follow the coast around to the **Holes of Scraada**, great blowholes demonstrating the immense hydraulic strength of the sea.

West of Lerwick

The village of **Walls** (pronounced Waas) has the air of a place to which more was promised, and perhaps it will come to fruition, for in the waters west of Shetland, new and plentiful basins of oil have been discovered. Voe House **Böd** in Walls costs £3 a night. There's a cheery and well-stocked shop, and Walls' annual show in July is one of the largest in the islands.

Ask around in Walls to see if it is possible to get a lift on a lobster boat out to **Vaila Island** which sits out from Walls, and must be one of the most eccentric islands in Scotland. The old Haa (country home) was built in 1696 and was sold in 1893 to a wealthy Yorkshire industrialist, Herbert Anderton, who proceeded to rebuild the place in extravagant (and very un-Shetland) baronial style.

The village of **Sandness** is like Walls in many respects, self-sufficient with great views over to Papa Stour and several large Haas notably Melby House (private). Good for a day trip. The A971 from Walls to Sandness is an excellent cycle route, especially on a sunny day.

The delightful island of **Papa Stour** has a population of just 40 and has in the past advertised for new families who might want to commit themselves to living on the island (how about it?). Interesting Viking remains are being excavated here continually. There is no hostel and in fact staying at Mrs Holt-Brook's **B&B** by the beach is your only option, tel:(01595) 873238, £16-£19. It's well worth it, though. Ferries to Papa Stour leave from West Burrafirth.

Whiteness and **Weisdale** are just north-west of Lerwick. If you hike or drive west on A971 from Tingwall airstrip to the crest of the hill you can enjoy one of the finest views in Shetland down Whiteness voe (fjord). On a clear day you can see Foula - and on a filthy day take shelter in the bar of the Westings Hotel. Hike or drive down the hill until the road meets the water, take the sharp left turn along the east side of the voe and keep going until the road peters out, then you will see the delightful **Böd** of Nesbister, £3 a night, but if it cost twice that price you would not begrudge it. As with all camping böds the facilities are basic (no electricity in this one) but there is a beach where otters and seals sunbathe, and on midsummer nights Whiteness Voe is one of the most likely places to catch sight of porpoises. Climb up the Nesbister hill and at the top find the Broo Loch for great views, or check out the old kirk. The kirkyard dates back to the Viking period and one man interred there was so unsure of his religious persuasion that he was buried with a Valhalla axe in one hand and a Christian cross in the other.

Continuing on toward Weisdale, stop at the Hjaltasteyn Silver workshop. Even if you can't afford anything the owners are very friendly and will take the time to explain the intricate Norse designs.

Almost directly west of Lerwick is **Scalloway**, the most Nordic connected settlement in Shetland, which had close ties to Norway during the last war. There is a museum and the ruined **Scalloway Castle**, built by Earl Patrick Stewart, a cruel man who later died for his excesses.

You could take a side trip to **Burra** (buses from Lerwick or Scalloway), a fascinating island with a pure white beach beyond the hamlet of Papil.

LERWICK

Once you have seen it in context as the functional busy capital of the islands, Lerwick looks at its best and just because it is the most northerly town in Scotland doesn't mean it lacks zest.

The history of Lerwick is relatively simple. It grew in the 18thC because the Dutch needed a base for their herring trade, and since the arrival of oil the town has grown rapidly. The centrepieces of the town are the old Hanseatic streets that peel off the harbour, and the harbour itself. It is here that the great babble of Shetland can be heard - not only Russians, but Japanese, Bulgarians, Norwegians and Icelanders abound when the fishing is good.

· Viking Longship ·

Up Helly Aa is an event unique to Shetland. It is a spectacular fire festival complete with Viking Longship acted out by a jarl (earl) and his retainers, together with hundreds of supporters, or guisers, dressed in topical fancy dress. The largest Up Helly Aa is held in Lerwick and it lightens the winter sky on the last Tuesday of January each year. The participants spend a year preparing for this major event in the Shetland calendar. A torchlit procession ends with the burning of the (full-sized) longship in the town park and is followed by a night of revelry in 'halls' around the town. Unfortunately it is difficult for visitors to get a ticket to the 'halls' unless you have friends or can influence people well in advance.

The **Shetland Museum** offers the visitor a collection of great interest and charm. Among the highlights are the displays on Pictish and Viking sites and a narwhal tusk (a delicate coiled ivory taken from that elusive Arctic whale, which in medieval times gave credence to the legend of the unicorn). Also exhibited are replicas of the St Ninians Isle treasure (the real pieces, to the annoyance of many Shetlanders, are in Edinburgh) and displays on the old whaling, fishing, crofting, and knitting lifestyles. The museum is located in Lower Hillhead Street, open Monday-Saturday, admission free. Lerwick's **Town Hall**, built in 1884, is opposite the museum and has interesting stained glass windows depicting Norse sagas; free.

Fort Charlotte was built to protect the islands from the Dutch in 1665-67; free, always open.

The **Böd of Gremista** is not one of the sleeping böds, but the birthplace of Arthur Anderson (one of Lerwick's most famous sons who founded the P&O Shipping company in 1837), and has been converted into a museum on his life and the progress of Shetlanders at sea. To get here, head out of Lerwick on the north road, take a right after the power station; free.

Clickimin Broch (just take the south road out of town past the Clickimin sports centre) is a squat version of the Mousa broch sitting beside a small loch. Its situation is now hemmed in by large suburbs - better at night when the lighting flatters it.

If you are pushed for time or are fed up with Lerwick then the quiet of the island of **Bressay** is your most accessible tonic. Head for the north shore of the island (keep to the road and then cut along the pebble beaches), which has excellent sand beaches and views of the Out Skerries on a clear day (beware the stench of the fish meal plant). Behind Bressay is **Noss**, one of Shetland's eight nature reserves. Noss is best reached on one of the two official tours that operate out of the inner harbour several times a day in the summer. Both can be booked at Tourist Information. Try going on the Dunter which is run by Dr Jonathan Wills, one of the great characters in Shetland (everybody knows him - he once ran the radio and was a journalist on the local newspaper). He does various tours including under the cliffs of Noss, and if there are several of you the tours can be tailored; from £10. Laerling run the other tours to Noss for £10.

Lerwick SYHA, King Harald St, tel:(01595) 692114, Grade 1, £7.75/ £9.25, open 3/4-1/10.

Clickimin campsite has good facilities, tel:(01595) 741000, £5.90-£8, open May-September.

There are a multitude of **B&Bs** of which Tourist Information has details.

Being a fishing town, Lerwick has no shortage of places to eat and drink. **Da Noost**, the **Potato Shop** and sundry chip shops, Chinese and Indian takeaways, almost all on Commercial Street, will fill the belly for a good price. Several well-stocked supermarkets sell fresh bread and a selection of wine, cheese and salami. If you are not a shy individual ask one of the fishermen on the trawlers once they've docked for a fish, and then cook it up yourself for dinner. Almost certainly they will - herring is sold in tonnes and one small fish won't be missed. Make sure they are pelagic boats (that is fishing herring or mackerel).

The **New Harbour Cafe**, behind the Thule bar, is a good place for a snack. Other cheap eats include **The Havly** at the Norwegian Seaman's Mission (immediate left after Presto supermarket on Commercial Street) which has fresh filter coffee, Norwegian cakes and Norwegian newspapers. Further along, the stunningly ugly **Royal Mission for Deep Sea Fishermen** runs a fully-fledged cafe and has pool tables and showers. Further along still is the **Viking Bus Station Cafe**, quite good as cafes go, modern, clean with good chips.

Up the lane from Tourist Information is the pub the **Lounge**, which is one of the most important folk music bars in Europe and where sessions, though with a casual air, often find their way onto television or record. If you are exceptionally lucky, the fiddler to end all fiddlers, Aly Bain (a Lerwick man), might be playing. If not, chances are someone else worth listening to will be, especially at weekends. You could also try **Captain Flint's** on the Esplanade, recently opened in the style of a pirate's ship. At the other extreme but not to be missed is the grotty but delightful **Thule** bar right on the harbour front (sad, grey concrete exterior opposite the town lavatories). Among hard-drinking Shetlanders this is a place of legend - beware of the Russian fishermen when they get too drunk! On Friday nights these both get very busy. At times there are more Russians, Latvians, Bulgarians etc., living on the factory ships than there are residents in Lerwick.

The Outer Isles

Just watching the large and modern boats sail in and out of Symbister harbour on **Whalsay** is fascinating. You can stay at the Grieve House **Böd** (£3, well-signposted out of Symbister, no electricity) which was once the home of one of Scotland's foremost poets, Hugh MacDiarmid. MacDiarmid was a genius, but did not care for Whalsay - you will probably think differently. There is a golf course on Whalsay which hosts midnight sun golf in the height of summer.

If even smaller islands take your fancy, try an overnight trip to the **Out Skerries**, a remarkably industrious fishing community perched on a fistful of low lying and pretty skerries (rocky islands).

The island of **Yell** has many charms and a warm community with it. Most visitors drive along the windswept and god-forsaken main road cutting through peat bog and conclude that the rest of the island is the same - not so. If you take any of the smaller coastal roads you will see some of the finest bays in Shetland, especially at Hamnavoe and Otterswick. Yell is rich in wildlife with one of the largest otter colonies in Scotland and is a good place to spot whales and dolphins. A lost walrus once washed up in these parts. To really enjoy Yell take a hike up the west coast through the Lumbister Wildlife Reserve. On the east coast take the coastal walk from Burravoe to Mid Yell. There is a camping **böd** at Windhouse Lodge, Mid Yell, £3 per night, open April-October - this one has a shower. There are various **B&Bs** on the island.

For the traveller **Unst** is probably the most interesting island in the traditional sense. Not only is it the most northerly, but there is also Muness Castle, plenty of rotund

Shetland ponies and a large, ultra-modern airforce base. Birdwatchers will want to head for Hermaness National Nature Reserve, the first landfall for weary birds migrating down from the Arctic. From the point you can see the Muckle Flugga lighthouse. For those of a romantic bent, do not miss the ruined kirk at Lund. It would be difficult to find a more seductive church ruin. Examine the graveyard for graves of shipwrecked sailors - there are plenty of German and Spanish ones, but the Shetland graves are the most touching. The **Gardiesfauld Hostel** in Uyeasound, tel:(01957) 755311, is a historic building that has been refurbished, open May-September, £6.95. For meals and a warm fireside chat try the **Baltasound Hotel**.

Fetlar was described as the garden of Shetland but now has a rather forlorn look about it; however, on a fine day it can be exquisite. An interesting feature on the island is the Muckle Funziegord dyke which divided the island in half. For accommodation there is the **Garths Campsite**, tel:(01957) 733227, £3.60-£6.60. Alternatively Mrs Boxall will arrange transport from the ferry to her **B&B**, tel:(01957) 733227, £15.

The island of **Foula** could command a whole book of its own (and several have been written). The islanders still use the Julian calendar and lead a remote and hardy life, even by Shetland standards. The island is 14 miles from the mainland and small, but so hilly it seems bigger. The back of the hill of Kame drops 1,220ft straight into the sea.

The **Fair Isle** rises up from one of the roughest stretches of sea in the world and though its cliffs rise up for 700ft, waves and sea spray sometimes crash right up onto the island itself. A trip to Fair Isle is something not to be missed as there is an otherworldly quality about the island. Its postage stamp size holds a richness of human life and on its cliffs rest a parade of birds. This is a popular spot for birdwatchers who migrate from around the world to watch the flight of puffins at close quarters. The Fair Isle is also famous for its unique knitting patterns. Accommodation should be booked in advance. Prices are inevitably higher but worth it. Try the **Fair Isle Lodge**, tel:(01595) 760258, £25 bed and board, with weekly rates available. No camping is allowed on Fair Isle.

Getting to Shetland

Shetland is not as isolated as you might think, being the gateway to the north Atlantic. Whether you choose to fly or sail the connections are excellent, but be warned - it is a long way and there are almost no bargain tickets to be had.

BY SEA: The main route is the five times weekly P&O ferry from Aberdeen leaving from the city centre docks at 6pm, Monday to Friday, and getting into Lerwick at 8am the following morning; £49-£55 single, £98-£110 return. From Stromness on Orkney the ferry costs £37-£40 single, £74-£80 return. Contact <u>P&O Scottish Ferries</u> in Aberdeen, tel:(01224) 572615. If you are coming from Norway, there is a summer-only service from Bergen, £45-£63 single or alternatively Bergen-Shetland-Aberdeen for £85-£103 single with which you can stop over in Lerwick as long as you wish. (10% student discount on all P&O ferries.)

BY AIR: For those who suffer sea-sickness flying is recommended. Most flights are routed through Aberdeen; for reservations contact British Airways, tel:0345 222111. Flying from Aberdeen to Lerwick can cost as much as £127 return however they sometimes have special offers where the price can be as little as £79 return. Widerøe run a summer only service from Bergen to Shetland, on Thursdays and Sundays - check fares with a Travel Agent or Lerwick Tourist Information. If you are in Orkney you can get a half-price flight to Shetland if you book a Shetland B&B in advance through Orkney Tourist Information. This discount makes the flight only slightly more expensive than the ferry - and you're in Shetland in less than an hour. This offer is available going from Shetland to Orkney too. All flights are subject to airport tax, an extra £5 each way, £10 for international flights.

When You Arrive: The chances are that you will arrive at either the Holmsgarth ferry terminal in Lerwick or at Sumburgh airport. If you fly into Sumburgh your first view of Shetland will confirm every good comment about the islands. The planes dip low over Sumburgh head with its whitewashed lighthouse and beaches curled around the airstrip - it's very exciting. Holmsgarth, however, is a dour and functional ferry terminal which will make you wonder why you came - ignore first impressions. The one mile hike from the terminal to the centre of town is depressing as it seems to pass all the ugliest buildings in Lerwick. Fear not, though - this is the worst Shetland gets.

Getting Around Shetland

The ideal way to get around is a hire car but if your budget won't stretch that far a bicycle is fine. Public transport can be scarce but luckily the Tourist Board produce an excellent transport timetable which gives times and prices of all bus, ferry and air routes within the islands. Shetlanders are generous to hitchhikers but on country roads cars can be few and far between.

BY BUS: Various private companies operate bus services so it's best to go straight to Tourist Information and get up-to-date timetables. All the main settlements have bus connections to them and most buses will co-ordinate with ferries, but be very careful not to get stranded.

BY FERRY: These inter-island ferries are an experience in themselves and of course are crucial to the outer isles. Unst, Yell, Fetlar, Bressay, Whalsay and Skerries are served by efficient ro-ro ferries. Foula, Fair Isle and Papa Stour have smaller craft. All the ferries are subsidised and foot passengers travel cheaply.

BY BICYCLE: There are supplements for taking bicycles on ferries but they are usually minimal and sometimes not enforced. The good aspects to cycling in Shetland are the excellent uncrowded roads and splendid views. A böd holiday might be the best option for cyclists. The problem, of course, is the weather. Wind can play havoc even with skilled cyclists. The least windy time, fortunately, is in the height of summer. In Lerwick the main bicycle hire is at Grantfield Garage, beside the ferry dock, North Rd, tel:(01595) 692709, £6 a day, £30 a week.

CAR RENTAL: John Leask, tel:(01595) 693162; Bolts , tel:(01595) 693636 and Star Rent-A-Car, tel:(01595) 692075.

BY AEROPLANE: British Airways Express operates from Tingwall airport (close to Lerwick), tel:(01595) 840246, to Fair Isle, Foula, Skerries, Papa Stour. Much better for those who don't like rough sea crossings (and they can be rough) and reasonably priced. Eight people to a flight with the postbag on your knee.

15. History of Scotland

Not only has the 2,500-million-year-old land that is today called Scotland spent most of its 'life' in the southern hemisphere, it was once attached to North America and for a while stood separated from the rest of Britain by an ocean. Over millions of years, it slowly drifted northwards through the hot equatorial regions and on its way experienced intense volcanic activity, the results of which have given Scotland its distinctive landscape. Having settled in its northern location, Scotland spent much of the next two million years under ice and the slow-moving but powerful glaciers also had a profound effect on the land we see today.

The ice finally receded about 10,000 years ago and life came to the region. The exact arrival date of human settlers is unknown but we do know they have lived here from at least 4000BC.

Scotland's numerous prehistoric remains stand well upon the world's stage. The Isle of Lewis's Stones of Callanish were created at roughly the same time as England's Stonehenge and Orkney's Maes Howe, a 20-ft high chambered cairn from 3400BC, predates the pyramids of Egypt!

Little is known about Scotland's Neolithic inhabitants. The purpose of the various stone circles and standing stones they erected are still largely a mystery but some of the most telling remains belong to the settlement of Skara Brae on Orkney. This Stone-Age village was kept perfectly intact for thousands of years beneath the sand, until a violent storm revealed its existence in 1850. This provided an amazing opportunity to gain some insight into the living conditions of Scotland's prehistoric settlers, showing a self-sufficient and close-knit community.

The first peoples of Scotland to be identified are the 'Beaker' people who lived about 3-4,000 years ago and were so named after the many cups, or beakers, buried in the tombs of their dead. Apart from this, however, little is known about them.

During the Iron Age the Celts arrived in Scotland. Today we can observe their hill-forts but also, more fascinatingly, their brochs. A broch is a tall, circular defensive tower, unique to Scotland, intricately constructed and most common in the north. It is presumed the community actually lived outside the tower but sheltered inside it in times of attack. The Celts dominated

Scotland in these early times and it was only with the Romans' decision to invade in the first century AD that their way of life came under real threat.

Although the Romans established a fort at Cramond near Edinburgh, they underestimated the determination of their opponents in the north and eventually gave up their quest to conquer this country they called Caledonia. They built the Antonine Wall between the Forth and Clyde rivers to keep the troublesome Highlanders at bay but this barricade was constantly attacked. The Romans eventually retreated to their other barrier across the north of England, Hadrian's Wall, and as the Roman Empire fell into decline many troops were recalled to Europe. The Romans finally left Britain in about AD400 and due to their relative lack of success in the north left behind little trace of their existence there.

With the departure of the Romans, the identities of the different races residing in Scotland come to the foreground. There were four peoples - the Picts, Scots, Britons (all Celtic) and the Angles. The Picts were the most powerful, occupying most of the mainland, while the Britons occupied the south-western region and the Angles, the south-east. It was the Scots, however, who were to bring Pictish domination to an end.

The Scots came from Ireland and settled in the western coastal areas. After many years of fighting, the Scots King Kenneth MacAlpine finally claimed the Pictish throne in AD843, uniting the Picts and Scots in a new kingdom named Scotia; approximately two hundred years later the Angles and the Britons also succumbed. It was at times an uneasy alliance but the races eventually merged, partly because they needed to fight the menace of incoming marauding Vikings, but also because of the influence of a new religion sweeping Europe at this time - both St Ninian (in about AD397) and St Columba (in AD563) had arrived in Scotland with the intention of converting the heathen locals to Christianity.

At the time of Kenneth MacAlpine, there was a stone slab referred to as the 'Stone of Destiny' on which a new Scottish King was seated (rather than crowned). MacAlpine moved the stone to Scone, just north-east of Perth. (In 1296 the English King Edward I stole it and took it to Westminster Abbey in London. It remained there for 700 years until 1996 when it was finally returned to Scotland and it now lives in Edinburgh Castle.)

One of the most significant aspects of the Celtic races was the importance they placed on the family unit. The Highland tribes were divided into large groups called clans ('clan' comes from the Gaelic word for 'descendants') and the chiefs of these clans inspired, and indeed demanded, intense loyalty and devotion. Clan members took the name of their leader - many were in fact actually related to him but others took their name from the chief of the land they occupied. Mac or Mc means 'son of', and it is to this Scottish custom that millions of MacLeans, MacLennans, MacKenzies, MacDonalds and many more, the world over, owe their names.

When Scotland's four races united in 1034, the ruling King was Duncan I, who was eventually killed by his cousin Macbeth. Macbeth reigned successfully and relatively peacefully for 17 years (Shakespeare's version was mostly fiction). He was eventually slain by one of Duncan's sons, Malcolm, who was to reign for an even greater length of time - 36 years. While Macbeth had ruled from the north, near Inverness, Malcolm's base was Dunfermline and then later Edinburgh, this choice resulting in Edinburgh becoming the Scottish capital.

Malcolm married the Saxon princess Margaret, and their long reign marked an end to Gaelic domination and the beginning of English influence. Malcolm was the first king to speak English and Margaret introduced the ways of the English court, much to the disillusionment of some of their subjects.

Feudalism was slowly introduced into Scotland by their son King David I, who gave large estates to Norman families. To the north-west, however, the clan system was still firmly established and the feudal system helped create a long-standing division between the Gaelic speaking Highlanders and the Scots-English speaking Lowlanders.

Despite growing English influence upon Scotland's monarchs they often fought bitterly with England, determined to keep their own land and sometimes to gain some more.

The other major force within Scotland came from the north. The Vikings first invaded Scotland in the late 8thC and by the 13thC they occupied Shetland, Orkney, the Hebridean islands and some of the far north mainland. The Scots King Alexander III brought about the final confrontation against the Norse King Haakon and his army in 1263 at the Battle of Largs. Haakon was forced to retreat from the Hebrides and the mainland. Orkney and Shetland remained Scandinavian, however, until the 15thC, and the Norse influence is still evident in these parts today.

Alexander's death in 1286 and the death four years later of his granddaughter and heiress (Margaret, the Maid of Norway, a child who never saw Scotland) left the throne empty. The events which followed belong to a crucial period in Scottish history. The Scots nobles asked the English King Edward I to decide which of them could claim the throne. As Edward had designs on Scotland he chose John Balliol, expecting him to be a puppet king he could easily control; eventually, however, Balliol turned against him. Edward then invaded, defeated Balliol and the Scottish nobles and imposed English rule.

In response, the outraged Scots rebelled, led by the fearless William Wallace, a man not of noble birth, who was forced to gather his army without the help of the Scottish nobility. In a superb display of military leadership Wallace's outnumbered men defeated the English at Stirling Bridge in 1296 and Wallace was acknowledged as Guardian of Scotland. After a later defeat at Falkirk, however, Wallace was forced into hiding for seven years before finally being betrayed and handed over to the English. He was hung, drawn and quartered in London for his treasonous (according to King Edward) acts.

Robert the Bruce became the next hero to fight for Scottish independence. Bruce was of noble birth and simply claimed the throne in 1306. He too was forced into hiding for some time but he returned to finally defeat the English decisively at the Battle of Bannockburn in 1314. Scottish independence was finally accepted by the English in 1328, just one year before the death of King Robert the Bruce.

Bruce's heir, David II, lacked nearly all of his father's heroic qualities and almost handed the Scottish throne to England on a silver platter by agreeing that should he die childless the throne would pass to Edward III. Not surprisingly the Scottish nobles were opposed to this and rejected the idea. Upon David's death, the throne was handed to his nephew (and Bruce's grandson), Robert Stewart, who became the first in the long line of Stewart monarchs.

The Stewart monarchs of the next 200 years mostly came to the throne during their youth and were mostly called James (except for three Roberts and a Mary). While each was raised to adulthood, Scotland was controlled by appointed regents. Such regencies were usually periods of great instability and the noble families of the time gained much strength and power, most notably the Douglases.

James I, when heir to the throne, had been sent to France for safety at the age of 12, but was captured by the English en route and spent 18 years captive in the Tower of London. Upon his return as king he did much to assert his authority over the powerful noble families but naturally this won

him enemies and he was eventually killed by them. James II was spared by his subjects but was unfortunately killed during a battle when one of his own siege guns exploded next to him. James III, was so unpopular with the nobility of the day that they dethroned him and proclaimed his son king.

James IV fought with the French against the English and, although he was a very popular king, he unwisely attacked England at the Battle of Flodden in 1513, where he, as well as 10,000 men, were slaughtered.

Lion Rampant

His son James V became king as an infant, but when he finally took the throne he retained his father's sympathies with the French and married Mary of Guise. This union firmly established the Scottish monarchy's faith as Catholic, infuriating King Henry VIII of England as it conflicted with his desire to abandon the Catholic church altogether. James V was an eccentric leader who sometimes liked to mix among his subjects disguised as one of them. Just days before his death he was told that his wife had given birth to a girl, Mary.

Mary, Queen of Scots was sent to France to be raised as a Catholic and in relative peace. (French influence altered the spelling of her surname from Stewart to Stuart.) Upon her return at the age of 18, Scotland was in the midst of the Reformation, with opposition to the Catholic church at its highest. Although most Highlanders retained their Catholic belief, many in the south had embraced the ethics of the Protestant Church. Mary was forced to battle it out with the vociferous reformer, John Knox. Mary's husband Lord Darnley was later murdered, and due to a suspicion that Mary was involved in the plot, together with public outrage at her over-hasty remarriage to the Earl of Bothwell, she was forced to abdicate in favour of her son, James VI. Mary fled to her cousin Queen Elizabeth of England for protection but was instead imprisoned for 19 years before being beheaded.

Her son James did nothing to save her life and upon Queen Elizabeth's death he inherited the English throne. He quickly moved his court to London to become James I of England and thus the crowns of Scotland and England were united. The year was 1603.

Although the battles for the throne were not entirely over, the focus of debate swung towards religion. Charles I tried to enforce his Episcopalian beliefs (to have the church governed by bishops appointed by the king) upon a mainly Presbyterian population who wished their church to be governed only by elders of the kirk. In opposition to Charles' plans, thousands of Scots signed the National Covenant, an agreement to resist any imposition of Episcopalian ways.

In the meantime, England was having a Civil War which left Charles beheaded and Oliver Cromwell in power. Scotland responded to these events by proclaiming Charles' son, Charles II, king. Cromwell's reply was to invade, so in 1650 Scotland was once again occupied by an English army. This occupying force withdrew 10 years later when Charles II was crowned King of Great Britain. Charles, who had previously supported the Covenant, then turned on the Scots and tried to enforce episcopacy again.

Under the next monarch, King James VII/II, who was a Catholic, Covenanting became a punishable crime, forcing Covenanters to worship in secret or face execution (and thousands did), in a period which became known as the 'Killing Times'. James was the last Catholic monarch to reign before being forced to abdicate by his daughter Mary and her husband,

William of Orange. Supporters of the deposed and exiled monarch became known as the Jacobites (from the Latin 'Jacobus', which means James) and a large proportion of them lived in the Highlands. William was so concerned about these rebellious Highlanders that he forced the clan chiefs to swear allegiance to the throne. One chief, MacIan MacDonald, who accidentally missed the deadline, paid dearly for his unpunctuality. The government saw this as a justifiable reason for ridding themselves of one of the many troublesome clans of the north and arranged the massacre of the MacDonalds of Glencoe. The Campbells of Glenlyon were ordered to carry out the deed. Having been welcomed into the MacDonalds' homes, the Campbells rose in the night to slaughter their hosts. The Campbells' act of betrayal has not been forgotten to this day.

It was around this time that the parliaments of England and Scotland were joined in the Treaty of Union of 1707. There was much fury and outrage at the prospect, but Scotland was in such a weak position financially, that there was little choice. All major government decisions from then on were made in London.

There had been several Jacobite uprisings to reclaim the throne for James VII/II's son, James Edward Stuart, but it was James' grandson, Prince Charles Edward Stuart, or Bonnie Prince Charlie, who made the most memorable attempt. Charles came to Scotland from the continent to regain the throne for his father. His army got as far as Derby, with London in reach, but lack of numbers forced their retreat and their final defeat came at the Battle of Culloden near Inverness in 1746. He spent five months on the run from the authorities, finally returning to Europe and the Stuart (formerly Stewart) claim to the throne went with him. Following the defeat at Culloden the government sought to suppress the Jacobites forever. The clan chiefs' powers were effectively stripped from them and the carrying of weapons, the wearing of the Highland dress and even the playing of the bagpipes was banned. By the time the ban was lifted, after almost 40 years of intense persecution, the Highlanders were a diminished and defeated people with any evidence of Jacobite support completely wiped out. Most left for the growing industrial cities of the south or emigrated overseas.

Even more were to leave during the Highland Clearances. This barbaric episode in Scottish history occurred when landowners, realising the potential for profit, evicted tenants from their land and replaced them with sheep. Thousands lost their homes and by the mid-19thC many parts of the Highlands and Islands were virtually deserted.

In the south of the country, however, in striking contrast, an exciting and unique surge of intellectual activity was taking place. This period came to be known as the Scottish Enlightenment and spans roughly a century until the mid-19thC. Philosophers (such as David Hume and Adam Smith), poets (Robert Burns and Allan Ramsay), writers (Walter Scott), artists (Henry

Raeburn) and architects (Robert Adam) all flourished and Edinburgh in particular became a city at the forefront of European progress.

Glasgow was also to have its time of prominence, trading with the Americas in tobacco (mainly). The city grew significantly in size and wealth and once the tobacco era ended the city continued to prosper leading in the industrial fields of cotton, iron and steel. Ship-building in the 19thC and early 20th was the River Clyde's domain.

The 19thC also saw a major change in attitude toward the Highlands. Walter Scott's novels did much for promoting Scotland, and Queen Victoria's enthusiasm for the beautiful countryside helped increase its popularity.

Since the turn of the 20thC Scotland's history has been more or less parallel to that of the rest of Britain. Two World Wars brought the country its share of grief and toil as it played its full part. The demise of the British Empire caused a massive reduction in the country's once proud maritime contribution to the world.

The main Scottish issue of interest today is the question of independence from England. In 1997 a referendum asked the Scottish people if they wanted their own Scottish parliament - the answer was a resounding "yes". The parliament will be located in the capital Edinburgh and will be operating in the next couple of years. The British Parliament in London will still make decisions for Scotland in matters concerning the United Kingdom, but the Scottish parliament will determine most matters at home. To many this is the solution to the Scots' long-running grievances with Westminster while to others it is the first major step on the road back to Scottish independence.

16. Getting to Scotland

FROM IRELAND

Northern Ireland to Stranraer

Three slightly different ferry services operate many times daily all year. The cost of a single crossing is about £23-£27. If you have a student card or Inter-Rail Card the price is £12-£18.

Of the ferries, **Seacat**, tel:0345-523523, is the fastest and takes you direct from Belfast, with a connecting bus from the city centre or station. The two other ferries, **Stena Line**, tel:(01776) 702262, and **P&O European Ferries**, tel:(01581) 200276, embark from Larne. They are grander and the journey is more cruise-like. On all these routes bicycles are free. Cars are about £120/£160, motorbikes £37-£50 - if you have a vehicle, phone around for the best price. **Scottish Citylink** buses run from Stranraer to Glasgow for £12. A 'Young Scot' card or a 'Smart Card' will give you a third off. A through bus and boat ticket from Belfast to Glasgow costs £32. Alternatively **Western Buses** provide a cheaper service from Stranraer to Glasgow at about £8 full fare, but it takes much longer.

Travelling by train, the normal fare from Stranraer to Glasgow costs £19.50 single/£28.40 return. There is a through boat and train ticket from Belfast to <u>any station in central Scotland</u> for about £35 single (full fare) which might be best for those ineligible for discounts.

Linking Donegal and Derry (Londonderry) with Glasgow is a private bus company - **Seda O'Donnell** - which operates 4-6 days per week, everyday in July and August; £33 single from most places in Donegal County, £30 single from Derry. Their pick-up point in Glasgow is not the main bus station but just opposite the Citizen's Theatre in Bedford St; phone (0754) 8114 (Ireland) or (0141) 631 3696 (Scotland and Northern Ireland).

Flights from Dublin

Dublin to Prestwick - from £54 single/£61 return . Excellent value. Telephone Ryanair on (01) 609 7800 (Ireland), 0541- 569569 (Scotland and U.K.).

FROM THE CONTINENT

Across the North Sea

Bergen, Norway to Shetland, Scotland

Only one ferry sails direct to Scotland from the continent - **P&O Ferries**' summer-only Bergen-Shetland-Aberdeen which costs £45/£63 to Shetland and £85/£103 through to Aberdeen (motorbike £32/£38, bicycle £6/£7). Under-26 - 20% discount. Tel:(01224) 572615 (Britain), (555) 48600 (Norway). Ideal for Norwegians and those who like to get well off the beaten track. On this route you can jump ship in Shetland for as long as you wish before continuing to Aberdeen. Alternatively you could continue to the Scottish mainland through Orkney (which will cost about £50/£60).

Bergen (and Stavanger) to Newcastle, England

Colour Line, tel:(0191) 2961313 (Britain), (555) 48660 (Norway). Operates all year. The highest prices are in July at £85-£95 but they are sometimes as cheap as £20 in winter with a 50% student discount.

Gothenburg, Sweden to Newcastle

Scandinavian Seaways, tel:(0191) 2936262 (Britain), (31) 650600 (Sweden). From 4 June to the end of August only, once a week. This company operates totally different fares on each side of the North Sea. In Newcastle a return ticket booked 21 days in advance costs £170/£208 (a single not booked in advance is £136-£162). In Gothenburg there seems to be no such discount. The price is 825/1125kr single and they offer a 15% under-25 discount.

Ijmuiden, Netherlands to Newcastle
Scandinavian Seaways , tel:(0191) 2936262 (Britain), 20-6116615 (Netherlands). Service operates from February to December. £30-£58 single and £30-£84 for a mid-week return. Students get a 25% discount.

Hamburg, Germany to Newcastle
Scandinavian Seaways, tel:(0191) 293262 (Britain), (40) 3890371 (Germany). From May to September only. Again different fares on different sides of the sea. £84/£124 return 21 days in advance, or in Germany 197 DM/282DM return - 20% student discount and ask for a four-berth cabin as this is even cheaper.

Hamburg, Germany to Harwich, England
Scandinavian Seaways (same telephone number and different fares idea as above). Operates all year. £64/£124 return booked 21 days in advance or in Germany 129DM/282DM return - 20% student discount and ask for a four-berth cabin as this is even cheaper.

Rotterdam, Netherlands to Hull, England
P&O North Sea Ferries, tel:(01482) 377177 (Britain), (0181) 255500 (Netherlands). All year service. £36/£45 single, £18/£23 for students or under-26. 14-hour overnight trip. A bed costs an extra £12 (or £35 for a group of four).

Zeebrugge, Belgium to Hull
Same service and prices as above. Tel:(050) 543430 (Belgium).

Crossing the English Channel

About half a dozen companies sail the English Channel on many routes many times a day. The normal single fare is about £25, however, it can be even cheaper in the off season. The single ticket is usually the price of a 5-day return too (which you could buy to give away or sell). If you have an Inter-Rail card, **Stena Line** and **Hoverspeed** give 50% reductions, **P&O** 30%, **Sally Line** 35%. Also ask for student/under-26 discounts. In winter there are some very cheap day returns so always check their various prices - and at any time of the year ask the price of a day return.

If you are travelling from any train station in the Netherlands and are under 26, consider buying a BIJ ticket straight through to London which might be only a little more than the ferry from Hook of Holland to Harwich.

Car prices vary greatly according to the time of year, day of the week and even time of day and you should phone around as the Channel Tunnel is having some effect on prices. Also note that you can cram up to nine people (yes, nine) into a car on most routes with little or no extra charge, so offering lifts can make a great saving. Motorcyclists do well with the **Sally Line** charging about £30, or £42 with a passenger (cheaper than without a motorbike). **Stena** also offer a good deal for motorcycles with 2 people in the off-peak times - £36-£42, again cheaper than the normal passenger fares. So foot passengers, maybe you should pretend you've got a motorbike and then forget to drive it onboard. On all these boats bicycles are free.

Cross Channel Ferry Companies

Stena Line, (tel:0990-707070 Britain, 35063903 France, 174-389333 Netherlands) - Hook of Holland-Harwich; Calais-Dover; Dieppe-Newhaven.
Hoverspeed, (tel:(01304) 240241 Britain, 0590-1777 France) - Calais-Dover; Boulogne-Folkestone.
P&O Ferries, (tel:0990-980980 Britain, 21460440 France) - Calais-Dover; Le Havre and Cherbourg-Portsmouth.
Brittany Ferries, (tel:0990-360360 Britain, 98292828 France) - Caen and St Malo-Portsmouth; Cherbourg and St Malo-Poole; Roscoff-Plymouth.
Sally Line, (tel:0990-595522 Britain, 28267094 France, 59559955 Belgium) - Ostend and Dunkirk-Ramsgate.

Cross Channel Boat-Train

The railways and other agencies offer continent to London tickets which conveniently include the ferry journey. If you are under 26 there is a BIJ ticket, often marketed under names like Transalpino, Go Trans 25, Euro Train, etc, which gives a sizeable discount.

The Channel Tunnel

Eurostar, being slightly overdrawn at the bank, are not offering any particularly cheap tickets for this service. The standard single to London is £83. The under-26 fares to London are, from Paris £84 return, Brussels £69 return, Lille £65 return, Calais £65 return. Ask for promotional fares, however, which may undercut these prices. For information telephone 0345-881881 (Britain), 49700175 (France).

Flying

Direct and indirect flights are too numerous to mention. Best to check at your local travel agent and student travel office for cheap deals. Scotland's international airports are **Glasgow**, tel:(0141) 887 1111, **Edinburgh**, tel:(0131) 333 1000, **Prestwick**, tel:(01292) 479822, and **Aberdeen**, tel:(01224) 722331. Glasgow airport, being the busiest, has some direct buses to other destinations, e.g. to Edinburgh, and once a day up the west coast to Fort William and Skye. Prices of buses to the city centres range from £1.20 to £3.50. If arriving at Prestwick Airport, ask about any discount rail offers available - they usually do a good deal with Britrail.

FROM LONDON

* If you are in London, information about Scotland can be obtained from the Scottish Tourist Board office at 19 Cockspur Street, not far from Trafalgar Square, tel:(0171) 930 8661/2/3.

Rail

Trains to Scotland leave London about once an hour mainly from King's Cross station (to Edinburgh and Inverness) but also, less frequently, from Euston station (to Glasgow). The journey takes a mere 4-5 hours, however a standard ticket is not cheap at £72 single to Edinburgh. If you travel at off-peak times and not on a Friday a Supersaver ticket will cost £63 single/£64 return. If you have to travel on a Friday, a Saver fare is £72 single/£73.50 return.

There are also a couple of different return fares which, if you book in advance, can make the journey quite affordable. For example, on the London-Edinburgh route, the Super Apex ticket costs £33 single/£34 return but must be booked at least two weeks in advance; the Apex fare is £47 single/£48 return, if you book at least one week in advance. (Both tickets are subject to availability and once you have booked you cannot change the travel times.) **British Rail** enquires - tel:0345-484950.

Coach

Buses depart from London mainly at around 10pm-11pm for a 8-9 hour overnight journey. By day they usually leave in the mornings. Prices are very reasonable but they do vary from £13-£15 single and £23.50-£29.99 return. **Scottish Citylink/National Express**, tel:0990-808080 or 0990-505050, and **Silver Choice** (tel: Thomas Cook on (0171) 930 6885) leave from Victoria Coach Station.

Backpackers Bus

An interesting alternative if you wish to include England in your holiday could be the **Slow Coach**, 38 Bolton Gardens, Earl's Court, London, SW5 0AQ, tel:(01249) 891959. They offer a jump-on jump-off circular route from London through Bath, Stratford-Upon-Avon, the Lake District to Edinburgh then back down through York and Cambridge to London for £99. It runs from April-October. It's good fun because you're travelling with like-minded people and you can stop off anywhere en route for as long as you wish.

Hitching

The best starting point is on the M1 slip road at Staples Corner near Hendon. To get to Staples Corner, catch Buses 32, 266, 112 or a 16 at Victoria Station/ city centre and change to a 32 at Cricklewood Broadway. The nearest tube station is Hendon but it then requires a bit of a walk. Probably the best route through England is up the M6 which branches west from the M1 north of London, as it is an easily followed continuous route with plenty of service stations.

Flying

The best deal is via Luton Airport with **easyJet**, tel:(01582) 445566, with three flights daily from £29 single (plus £5 tax). Seats at this price are limited, and other seats cost £39/£49/£69. These extremely cheap fares have created a bit of a price war, so check with the other companies for their best offer. The other companies whose flights leave Heathrow, Gatwick and Stanstead frequently are **Air UK**, tel:0345-666777; **British Midland**, tel:0345-554554 and **British Airways**, tel:0345 222111. easyJet, Air UK and British Airways fly to Edinburgh, Glasgow, Aberdeen and Inverness, but British Midland flies into Edinburgh and Glasgow only. Bear in mind the cost of transport to the various airports; Heathrow - £3.30 by underground, Gatwick - £5 by bus, Luton - £7 by bus, Stanstead - £9 by bus. At the other end, the buses to get into the city centre cost - Inverness, £2.30 (no Sunday service); Edinburgh, £3.20-£3.50; Glasgow, £2; Aberdeen, £1.20.

17. Getting around Scotland

By Bus

Bus travel is the cheapest form of public transport and has the most extensive cover of the countryside. A price guide is:

Glasgow to Edinburgh - £4.50 single/£6.50 return, £5.50 day return.
Glasgow to Oban - £9.80 single/£16.80 return.
Glasgow to Fort William - £9.80 single/£16.80 return.
Glasgow to Kyleakin (Skye) - £14.40 single/£20 return.
Fort William to Kyleakin (Skye) - £8.70 single/£11.20 return.
Fort William to Oban - £5.70 single/£9 return.
Edinburgh to Perth - £4.40 single/£5.90 day-return or £7.40 return.
Edinburgh to Inverness - £11.90 single/£20 return.
Edinburgh to Aberdeen - £12.10 single/£20 return.
Inverness to Kyleakin (Skye) - £8.50 single/£11.10 return.
Inverness to Thurso - £8.60 single/£11.50 return.

The major company is **Scottish Citylink** (linked with National Express) which operates the most important routes; however some smaller companies offer competitive rates. So, once given info about a bus time or price, ask if there are any other companies on the same bus route.

Scottish Citylink have an Explorer Pass which costs £30 for 3 days of unlimited travel, £60 for 5 days (out of 10), £90 for 8 days (out of 16) and £120 for 15 days (out of 30).

Before you buy a ticket you should consider the discount cards available if you are under 26. If you have a European Under-26 card you are entitled to a third off Scottish Citylink and Skyeways bus routes. If you do not have one of these and you are under 26 or a full-time student you can buy from Scottish Citylink a 'Smart Card' for £8 which entitles you to a third off the price of most National Express *and* Scottish Citylink buses (including their Explorer Pass). It can be bought in England and Scotland. Young Scot cards can be bought for £8 in Scotland only and will give you a third off internal Scottish Citylink and **Skyeways** bus routes. For bus information phone: 0990-505050 (local-call rate).

By Backpackers Bus

Several backpackers' bus companies operate in Scotland and they provide an excellent alternative to the normal bus service. The services that they offer which are of most interest to the independent traveller are the jump-on jump-off tours. The most popular stops are Edinburgh, Perth, Pitlochry, Aviemore, Inverness, Loch Ness, Kyleakin (on the Isle of Skye), Fort William,

Glencoe, Oban, Loch Lomond and Glasgow (other stops too). Travelling this way gives you the best of both worlds as you can stay as long as you wish in any particular spot and then get taken (door-to-door) to your next destination. What's more, it's all done in an easy-going cheerful manner with the driver giving an informal guided tour on the way, stopping intermittently to take in the scenery. It's also a great way to meet other travellers.

Go Blue Banana's thoroughly enjoyable and very popular jump-on jump-off tour operates up to seven days a week at a cost of £75. For those short of time they also offer two different fully-guided three-day tours - one focuses on the Isle of Skye, whilst the other is Inverness-based and goes further north. Both of these tours cost £69, run several times a week and are good fun. They also run a fully-guided six-day tour which combines both three-day trips (and more) and costs £129. There might be other tours operating in the summer and in winter they sometimes run ski and snowboarding trips. Go Blue Banana's excellent tours are guided by fun-loving Scottish drivers and for their three-day and six-day tours they make a point of only staying at independent hostels. Look for their minibuses painted with scenes from Scottish history. Visit their city centre shop at 16 High St, Royal Mile, Edinburgh, tel:(0131) 556 2000.

Haggis Backpackers offer a very high level of service on their jump-on jump-off tour which runs up to seven days a week, all year; and costs £75. They also offer three-day tours taking in some of Scotland's most spectacular scenery, departing from Edinburgh and staying in Skye or by Loch Ness, for £69. Their six day/five night tour will take you to some of the best places in the Highlands and the Isle of Skye, and costs £129.

Haggis tours are fully-guided by enthusiastic and entertaining, young, Scottish guides who will do their best to ensure you have a brilliant time in Scotland. All their buses are painted a distinctive bright yellow.

Drop in to their centrally located shop for a chat at 11 Blackfriars Street, Edinburgh, tel:(0131) 557 9393.

MacBackpackers is a company that provides backpacker tours staying in Scotland's Top Hostels. They also can arrange a holiday package staying at these hostels but with car hire as your mode of transport. Information can be obtained from the Castle Rock Hostel at 15 Johnston Terrace, Edinburgh, tel:(0131) 225 9666.

A recent addition to Scotland's backpacking transport businesses is **H2H Direct** which provides a hostel to hostel service at a competitive price. Call them on tel:(01463) 710858 for information.

For backpacker tours incorporating outdoor activities contact **Excellent Adventures**, tel:(0131)229 2233, New Heights, 134 Lothian Road. You can go hillwalking, climbing, abseiling, canoeing or rafting with their qualified guides. A three-day tour costs £75 but some hiring of equipment may cost extra (at reasonable prices). They plan to introduce five-day tours this summer.

By Train

Travelling by train is a very comfortable form of public transport and conducive to sightseeing, but also outrageously expensive. You can reduce your costs by purchasing an Inter-Rail or Britrail train pass before you enter Britain, but remember these passes come with certain restrictions and can be frustrating. Not only that, but the rail network in Scotland is not as extensive as you'd hope and you might (depending on where you go) find yourself with no alternative but to bus it. This is especially the case on the west coast, and, of course, there are no trains on the islands (except a miniature one). Basically, check how appropriate it is for your itinerary. A discount card you can purchase within Britain is the Young Person's Railcard for £18. You must be between 16 and 25 or a student, and the card will give you a third off the price of rail travel for 12 months (bringing rail prices to the approximate equivalent of a full-price bus ticket).

Just buying tickets at the station can be complicated and confusing. To follow are some examples of train fares and regulations attached to the particular route. (Return tickets are valid for one month).

Edinburgh to Inverness - £28 single/£33 return (not Fridays), £34.90 return (Fridays). £21 Apex return ticket booked at least 48 hours in advance.

Edinburgh to Aberdeen - £31 single/£35 return (not Fridays), £41.90 return (Fridays). £25 Apex return ticket booked at least 48 hours in advance.

Edinburgh to Stirling - £4.50 single/off-peak day return £6.60.

Edinburgh to Glasgow - £6.90 single/off-peak day return £8.

Glasgow to Stranraer - £18.90 single/£22.50 return (not Fridays), £27.50 (Fridays).

Glasgow to Fort William - £22 single/£29.60 return (any day).

Glasgow to Oban - £16.40 single/£22.20 return (any day).

Glasgow to Mallaig - £27.60 single/£36 return (any day).

Scotrail has various travel passes available -

Freedom of Scotland Travelpass - unlimited rail travel plus many discounts (bus, ferry, visitor attractions, etc). 8-day - £99; 15-day - £139; 8 in 15 days - £110.
Scotrail Rover - unlimited rail travel. 8 days - £90*.
Flexi-Rovers -
 Scotrail Flexi-Rover - 4 in 8 days - £62; 12 in 15 days - £119 * (few restrictions).
 North Highland Flexi-Rover - 4 in 8 days on northern rail lines centred on Inverness - £40 *.
 West Highland Flexi-Rover - 4 in 8 days on Glasgow to Mallaig and Oban lines - £40 *.

*Young Person's Railcard Holders are eligible for a third off the full price ticket.

Two rail routes show the rugged and magnificent scenery of Scotland at its finest. They are Inverness to the Kyle of Lochalsh, and Mallaig to Fort William (the latter route has steam trains in the summer) and even if you were normally travelling by bus either of these journeys would make a special treat. Scotrail information - phone 0345-484950 (24-hour service at local-call rate).

By Car

Having a car gives you the freedom to explore the quieter and often more beautiful back roads that a person on a bus can only dream about. Unfortunately hiring a car is a major expense unless you can club together with others. A rough guide for car hire is £20-30 a day in summer, though in winter it's sometimes as cheap as £95 per week (see Glasgow and Edinburgh car hire sections). You will need a current licence (your licence from home is OK) and need to be over the age of 21, sometimes older. You must drive on the left side of the road, of course - hopefully this won't be a problem for you. Virtually all hire cars have manual gears. All signs are indicated in miles. The speed limit in cities or towns is 30 miles per hour unless otherwise indicated. A black circle with a diagonal line on a white background means the city speed limit is lifted and you may increase your speed to 60mph. Only if indicated and on dual carriageways may you go up to 70mph.

Parking - if you follow these guidelines you should have no excuse for getting a ticket!

Most busy towns have metered or ticketed parking (about 20p for 20mins) between 9am and 5pm, Monday - Friday and 9am -12 noon on Saturday.

A double yellow line at the curb means you must NEVER park there.

A single yellow line is more complicated - a sign nearby will state certain busy hours (e.g., 8am-8.45am and 4.30pm-5.45pm) between which you must not park at all, other than that between 9am-5pm Monday-Friday, 9am-12 noon Saturday, you may park on a single line for loading or unloading (a few minutes) only, and after these hours there are usually no restrictions.

All passengers must wear a seat belt, unless there are none in the back seats.

Many of Scotland's roads are winding and unpredictable which makes overtaking a dangerous business - be careful and patient no matter how slow that caravan in front of you is going. Relax, you're on holiday.

When driving on single track roads there are widened passing places to allow traffic to pass and there is a certain etiquette to be aware of. If it is easier for you to do so, you should be the one to pull over and wait, or to reverse back. As the driver passes you, they will acknowledge your kindness with a wave of the hand and you should do the same back. Don't go overboard with your wave, though, be very casual or they'll spot you as a tourist. The passing places are not for parking in, and if a driver behind you is wishing to travel faster you must pull into the place and let them overtake. Taking your car by ferry to the islands can be very expensive; see section 'By Ferry'.

By Bicycle

Provided you're fit enough, cycling around Scotland not only allows the freedom a car brings but it gives you a much fuller experience as you can feel and smell the landscape and all at a leisurely pace. Although there are many quiet country roads perfect for cycling, there are also some established cycle paths, most notably the 'Great Glen Cycle Route' from Fort William to Inverness and the 'Glasgow - Killin' cycle route.

Transporting your bike to or around Scotland on the trains involves reserving in advance (on almost all routes) as there is limited space for bikes. A reservation costs £3 no matter the distance. Taking your bike on a ferry costs about £1 or £2 extra. Bike hire prices vary but it usually costs £10 a day and is cheaper by the week. For weekly hires phone around. One of the cheapest is at Edinburgh Cycle Hire, 29 Blackfriars Street, tel:(0131) 5565560, £50-£70 a week.

By Ferry

Numerous ferries offer transport to the islands. A price guide for a single person (no car) is:

Ardrossan to Brodick, Arran - £3.95 single/£6.70 five-day return.
Kennacraig to Port Ellen, Islay - £6.45 single/£10.90 five-day return.
Oban to Craignure, Mull - £3.25 single/£5.60 five-day return.
Mallaig to Armadale, Skye - £2.50 single/£4.25 five-day return.
Uig, Skye to Tarbert, Harris - £7.85 single/£13.40 five-day return.
Ullapool to Stornoway, Lewis - £12 single/£20.55 five-day return.
Scrabster to Stromness, Orkney - £14/£15 (10% off for students).

While taking a bicycle on a ferry is quite cheap (£1-£2 and sometimes free), taking a car on a ferry is a major expense. Prices can be £5 for a 5-minute journey or over £50 for a 3-hour journey, and that's not including any passenger's fares.

The main companies operating are **Caledonian MacBrayne**, tel:(01475) 650100, on the west coast, and **P&O Scottish Ferries**, tel:(01224) 572615, servicing Orkney and Shetland (also Norway). Many Tourist Information centres have these operators' 'Timetable and Fares' booklets. If you are going to more than two of the western islands you should check Caledonian MacBrayne's 'Island Hopscotch' offers and see if you can make a saving. Any sufferers of seasickness shouldn't worry as almost all the ferries are large and sway little (unless the weather's really bad).

Public transport travel guides including bus, train and ferry timetables are available for the Highlands. The four guides are 'South Highland', 'Inverness and Inner Moray Firth', 'North Highland and Orkney' and 'Skye and the Western Isles' and cost £1 each. They are available from Tourist Information Centres or from the Public Transport Section, Highland Council, Glenurquhart Rd, Inverness, IV3 5NX.

Hitching

Like everywhere, thumbing a lift in Scotland is excruciatingly unpredictable, but is generally speaking quite good. There are times, however, in mid-summer when almost every road has a hitch-hiker on it and the only people going anywhere are caravaners. Except for those days, it is usually a friendly, easy, happy-go-lucky form of transport (until you miss your plane home).

How to hitch: firstly, if it's important, make sure you are on the correct route to your destination. This is usually done by the use of a map, looking at sign-posts and asking the locals (but never ask just one, always ask about five and gain a consensus). If you have to take a bus from a city centre to the hitching place, ask at least three bus drivers, one inspector and several people on the bus or sure as eggs are eggs you'll be heading the wrong way - remember these people never hitch themselves. Secondly, make sure you're standing on the correct side of the road. Thirdly, look good or interesting or happy or intelligent or something.

Don't wear sunglasses (even in the rain) - and guys, be clean shaven, unless you've got a really impressive beard. Smile, but not menacingly. Contrary to popular opinion, it's good to hitch with a rucksack, as it lets the driver know you're a tourist and hopefully interesting and optimistic rather than a local who got out of bed too late to catch the bus.

The use of a sign is arguable. Sometimes drivers who otherwise would go past you will stop because it is exactly where they are going or the sign makes you look like you know where you are going and that's important to them. On the other hand, you sometimes miss out on lifts that are going part of the way. Importantly, if someone stops for you and you don't like the look of them, it's awkward to get out of accepting the lift if you have a sign which states where the driver says he is going.

Some useful sign ideas are: - 'Anywhere', or 'I tell good jokes', and when desperate, 'It's my birthday' (you might even get a drink out of it). Hitching seems safe in Scotland, however single women should take care and avoid the industrial parts of busy towns and cities.

* Any hitcher should always have the strength of character to refuse an offered lift if their instincts tell them to.

Hitching from Edinburgh

North to Perth, A90/M90 - the best spot to hitch is at Barnton Roundabout. Take buses 18 or 41 or quicker buses from the bus station-platform 'Queensferry'. Alternatively start hitching in town - walk out Queensferry Road; the junction with Belford Road is a reasonable place.

West to Glasgow, A8/M8 - take buses 12, 26, 31 or 86 to Drumbrae Roundabout, then walk out a few hundred yards (but not as far as the next big junction).

North-west to Stirling, M9 - same as to Glasgow but you'll definitely need a sign. Accept lifts to Newbridge roundabout if you don't mind standing at the very start of the motorway (this is technically illegal but usually OK).

East to Dunbar, A1 - take bus to Wallyford roundabout from the bus station.

South to England - it's highly debatable which road you should take as there is not one major route to either Newcastle or Carlisle. If you're heading for London then it's best to head through Carlisle to pick up the M6 motorway which is continuous all the way (with service stations). Probably the best option in any event is to hitch on the A7 which splits east or west at Galashiels, take buses 3 or 8 to the Butterfly World and stroll up to the roundabout. (There is a series of two further roundabouts which you could walk out to.) The other options are - for the A68, take bus 3A and alight at City Bypass junction, or for the A702, take buses 4, 7 or 15 to Fairmilehead. Stand at the roundabout at the bypass or walk out half a mile to where the A703 and A702 split. You must stand right at the junction, and don't walk further on as there's nowhere to stop for miles.

Hitching from Stirling

All directions - to Perth, Glasgow or Edinburgh by the M9 or to Callander and Fort William by the A84 - take a bus through Raploch as near as possible to the motorway roundabout or, walk; it's just over a mile north-west from the centre through a rough area. For Perth and Callander, walk on to the second roundabout. Edinburgh and Glasgow are initially in the same direction so a sign might be a good idea or you could accept a lift to the service station a few miles down this motorway close to where these two roads split.

Hitching from Perth

The city is about three-quarters ringed by motorway and, although you can try nearer the centre, it is better to head out to the requisite junctions on this ring road.

North to Inverness, A9 - take one of the many buses to Inveralmond roundabout.

South-west to Stirling, A9 - take a bus No. 7 to the Lovat Hotel, it's then still a bit of a walk to the roundabout but you can hitch on the way.

South to Edinburgh, M90 - take buses 17 or 18 and ask the driver to drop you at Friarton, you need to walk further but hitch as you go. The actual turning to Edinburgh is all too sudden from a driver's point of view so consider stopping to hitch before you reach it.

East to Dundee, A85 - in town cross the river and turn right. Start hitching as you walk - there are no buses to the roundabout which is about 1½ miles out. In places you have to cross the road as there is no footpath, but it's a nice refreshing walk.

Hitching from Dundee

West to Perth, A85 - take bus No. 76 to Invergowrie and walk up to the main road and roundabout.

South to St Andrews, A914 - simply stand just before the Tay Bridge, a stroll from the centre. It's not ideal but the alternative is a mind-numbing 1½ mile walk over the bridge. Take any short lift as there are a couple of better spots at roundabouts in the first four miles.

<u>North to Forfar and main route to Aberdeen, A929</u> - take buses 32 or 33 to Forfar Road and get out at the turning for Fintry.

<u>East to Arbroath and the coastal route to Aberdeen, A92</u> - take buses 26, 28 or 29 to the roundabout junction of Arbroath Road with Kingsway East and get out at Scott Fyffe Garage.

Hitching from Aberdeen

<u>North-west to Inverness, A96</u> - take bus 27 to Inverurie Road.
<u>South to Dundee, A92</u> - take bus 17 to the terminus at Stonehaven Road.

Hitching from Inverness

<u>North to Thurso and north-west to Ullapool, A9</u> - walk out Longman Road to the roundabout just before the Kessock Bridge. Only accept lifts under 20 miles if they'll drop you at a roundabout.

<u>East to Aberdeen, A96 and south to Perth, A9</u> - from Eastgate shopping mall walk out ¾ of a mile to the A9/A96 junction (second roundabout).

<u>West to Loch Ness and Skye, A82</u> - cross the main bridge in town and walk out about a mile to where the road crosses the canal (you can always try hitching on a boat), or you can start hitching just a few minutes from the town centre.

Hitching from Fort William

<u>North to Inverness and Skye, A82 and west to Mallaig, A830</u> - you can hitch after just a few minutes' walk across the small bridge after the Glen Nevis turning, but there's a lot of local traffic. The best place is 1½ miles further where these two roads split - buses to Caol and Corpach go to this junction.

<u>South to Oban and Glasgow, A82</u> - the best spot is simply at the roundabout at the south-west end of the shopping street. You can walk out a couple of miles but don't go further than the town limit as the road beyond is all bends.

Hitching from Oban

<u>North to Fort William, A828, or east to Crianlarich, A85</u> - just stand in town where the road starts by the Corran Halls at the bottom of the hill; be reluctant to walk up the hill as the road twists and climbs for miles.

Hitching from Glasgow

<u>North-west to Loch Lomond and Fort William, A82</u> - take buses 11 or 62 out Great Western Road to the junction with Kilbowie Road. Take any lift going as far as the roundabout at the top of Dumbarton (about eight miles further).

<u>South-west to Ayr and Stranraer, A77</u> - take buses 38 or 38A to Eastwood Toll. Unfortunately the M8 motorway passes right through Glasgow putting a lot of the serious traffic out of reach. For any directions eastward you could try

standing at any slip road with a sign but there's a lot of local traffic. Motorway junctions 15, at Castle Street, and 17 at St George's Cross, near the hostels, are probably the best. Otherwise the more definite places to stand are -

East to Edinburgh, A8/M8 - take buses 13 or 260 from Buchanan Street Bus Station to Bargeddie junction. It's a bit of a nightmare finding the correct slip road but once you do it's a good spot. Accept lifts to Harthill Services.

North-east to Stirling, A80/M80 - from Buchanan Street Bus Station take buses 36, 37, 39, 40 or 50 to Muirhead.

South to Carlisle/England, M74 - take bus 64 out London Road to the junction with Fullarton Road, then walk to the start of the M74. Accept lifts to Bothwell Services (6 miles further).

For hitching from London to Scotland see **Getting to Scotland**, Chapter 16.

Generally speaking this is an excellent way to traverse Scotland coast-to-coast through a whole medley of different environments. Quiet roads winding past cottages and meadows, easy canal tow-paths and quiet lochside forest tracks contrast greatly with punishing mountain trails and the accursed A82 main road. It is about 65 miles long but you can, of course, cycle just some parts of it. If you're staying in hostels you can find plenty en route at Fort William, Loch Lochy, Fort Augustus, Loch Ness-side, Drumnadrochit and Inverness. Unofficial camping places, of course, abound.

The southern half of the route is in the most part very easy and relaxing, however north of Fort Augustus as it runs along Loch Ness things are quite different with some very steep tracks and a busy road to contend with.

There is a free leaflet courtesy of Forest Enterprise available at relevant Tourist Information offices detailing each section. However, it omits a very pleasant easy section along the canal from Dochgarroch to Inverness. Also at Clunes on Loch Lochy be sure to side-track west towards Loch Arkaig, along the 'Dark Mile' taking in a lovely waterfall before reaching the Loch.

Suggested Itineraries

When you first arrive in a new country it can be difficult to know where to go with the time you have. This is a list designed to help you plan your holiday, though it is impossible to give anything other than a rough guide.

4 Days Holiday
Visit any 2 of

1 Week
Visit any 4 of

10 Days
Visit any 6 of

2 Weeks
Visit any 9 of

3 Weeks
Visit any 12 of

Edinburgh, St Andrews, Dunkeld/
Pitlochry, Glencoe, Oban

Braemar, Glasgow, Gairloch,
Skye, Inverness/Loch Ness

Orkney, Cromarty, Arran, North Skye,
Loch Lomond, Fort Augustus, Killin,
Glen Nevis/Fort William

Aberdeen (and Dunnottar), Ayr, Ullapool,
Jedburgh/Melrose, Lochinver, Kingussie,
Dufftown, Roy Bridge, Plockton, Mull

Western Isles, Islay & Jura, Pennan,
Stirling, Aviemore/Loch Morlich, Inverary,
The Trossachs, Banchory, Morar/Mallaig

In a MONTH you can cover many more places of interest -

    Shetland, Mull of Kintyre, Tongue & Smoo Cave,
      East Neuk of Fife, Coll and Tiree,
    North-East fishing towns - Findochty, Lossiemouth, Portsoy -
      Lochinver, Perth, Dumfries, Blair Atholl,
    Portpatrick, Whisky Trail, Culross, Callander,
      Cannich/Glen Affric, Ardnamurchan, Findhorn

Weather & Travel

Travelling in Scotland in any season has its advantages.

Spring is, of course, a wonderful time to visit with, from March onwards, all the usual trappings of flowers, melting snows and new-born lambs. Possibly the best month is May as it's usually quite dry, reasonably warm and has long bright evenings. Spring is also a time when tourists are still a novelty and the locals have plenty of time for you.

The **summer** season from June to September is naturally the favourite time to holiday in Scotland, with tourist numbers peaking in July and August. Temperatures are usually in the twenties, but remember, there is sometimes rain and worse - midges - so take some insect repellent on the west coast in particular.

Autumn offers perhaps the best scenery with the trees and the hills turning a rich variety of autumn shades, often with a sprinkling of snow on the mountain tops.

The weather in **winter** is a lot milder than you might expect (don't listen to London-based weather reports - they haven't a clue). Although there is always snow covering the mountains, the towns and cities of Scotland are seldom afflicted. Visually the land is superb and, with fewer tourists, winter is perhaps the best time to meet the locals.

There are a few Scottish weather quirks to know which might help you through your holiday.

Daylight hours are wonderfully long in the summer (often staying light from 4am until 10pm, even later in the Northern Isles) but short in the winter (from about 8am to 4pm).

If you're on the west coast and you're being rained on too much, consider moving east; the east is much drier - Inverness gets a miserly 25 inches of rain yearly, yet Fort William on the west gets about 90 inches. However, if there is too much sunshine on the North Sea, the east coast will become foggy. If you find yourself wandering the streets of Edinburgh or Aberdeen in a pea-souper, consider a short journey just a few miles inland (and uphill) - you'll often be surprised to find gorgeous sunshine. A general rule is that during westerly winds, the east gets the best weather and vice versa.

In winter, don't think that the further north you go, the colder it gets - the Isle of Skye is usually warmer than Edinburgh. And while the west tends to be warmer and wetter, the east is usually colder and drier - but check the daily newspaper weather forecast (the Scottish papers, not the English ones).

And if you find yourself complaining about the weather, then address your complaints to Mother Nature, but first remember that the rain in Scotland is FUN-RAIN. What's more, if we had consistent sunshine and high temperatures the country would be ruined, with concrete hotel blocks, discotheques and low class pizza restaurants on every inch of coastline. Besides, without rain where would we get the pure water to make the whisky?

18. Accommodation

HOSTELS

For many backpackers the most appropriate types of accommodation are the relatively inexpensive 'youth' or 'backpacker' hostels throughout the country. Usually providing dormitory accommodation they are great for meeting other travellers - especially good for those travelling on their own. There are two types, either 'Scottish Youth Hostels Association' hostels or 'Independent' hostels.

Scottish Youth Hostels Association

Eighty youth hostels throughout the country carry the SYHA logo. They are mostly donated buildings, ranging from the splendid to the basic. The SYHA used to classify their hostels as Grades 1, 2 or 3 but now grade them as either Superior, Standard or Simple. This is in relation to the facilities provided. In this book we have decided to stick with the Grade 1, 2 or 3 classification as it is more straightforward. Most town hostels will be Grade 1 or 2, with Grade 3 hostels being in more remote areas. Most small hostels are open from March to October only - the larger hostels may also be closed for some weeks in the years, so check carefully. A long-established organisation, part of the world-wide Youth Hostel Association (or Hostelling International), there is a membership procedure. You can either buy membership for your own country's YHA, or you can simply join the SYHA while here (sometimes this is cheaper than joining at home). If you have an international address SYHA membership costs £9 per year and with a Scottish address the price is £6. If you don't need full membership an 'international welcome stamp' system means that you pay £1.50 extra per night, each night collecting a stamp, and once you have six of them you are a fully paid-up member. Other YHA organisations around the world also issue these stamps.

The SYHA provides dormitory accommodation only, with some having family rooms. Every SYHA hostel has a self-catering kitchen, and breakfast is not included in the price except at Glasgow, Stirling and Edinburgh's Eglinton hostels (where the price then goes up). Sleep-sheets are included in the price. No sleeping bags can be used, except in Grade 3 and unclassified hostels.

These 'official' hostels have a few drawbacks. They are often used by large school groups, and there is nothing quite so hellish as a bedroom filled with screaming eleven-year-olds. Many hostels also have a strict lights-out policy, usually 11pm or 11.45pm, although some of the Grade 1 hostels are fortunately more liberal, allowing guests back in up until 2am (latest check-in at 11.30pm). A daytime lockout (10.30am-5pm) is imposed in Grade 2 & 3 hostels. In bad weather you *might* be able to stay inside, but sometimes there is a charge. You are also required to do a chore, chosen by the warden, in Grade 2 & 3 hostels. You are not allowed to drink alcohol on the premises of a SYHA hostel.

Fax bookings can be made between larger hostels. Phone bookings are only accepted the day before, and they will only keep beds until 6pm, sometimes not at all in summer.

Note that this organisation is particularly difficult about giving refunds even in the most straightforward circumstances, so only pay for a night's accommodation if you're certain you're staying. If you do want a refund they'll tell you to contact their head office in Stirling - do it, it's your money.

***If you have a Youth Hostel card, you can get half-price entry into any National Trust for Scotland (NTS) property.

1998 prices:

Grade 1 (or 'Superior') - in Glasgow, Stirling, Edinburgh (Eglinton) - £11.50-£12.50, includes continental breakfast.

Grade 1 - for Inverness, Aberdeen, Aviemore, Glen Nevis, Kyleakin, Oban and Loch Lomond - £8.60-£9.60.

Grade 2 (or 'Standard') - £6.10-£7.75

Grade 3 (or 'Simple') - £4.65.

If you are not a YHA member you pay £1.50 on top of these prices. For this reason all SYHA listings in this guide have the maximum and minimum prices. For anyone under 18 years, the prices are cheaper by about £1.

You can book beds in YHA hostels worldwide through the Edinburgh, Glasgow, Stirling, Inverness and Carbisdale Castle SYHA hostels. The SYHA National Office is at 7 Glebe Street, Stirling, FK8 2JA, tel:(01786) 891400. The SYHA's central booking telephone number is 0541-553255.

Independent Hostels

Basically the difference between these and SYHA hostels is that there is no membership fee required, there are fewer rules and they are usually open all year. Independent hostel owners are also aware that if it rains ALL day you might not like to be locked outside in it - they're open through the day so if you want, you can stay in and read a good book.

These hostels are privately run and each in its own way which leads to a greater diversity in the general atmosphere of each hostel and in the facilities provided. Some are almost luxurious and five minutes' walk from the train station, while others are basic and miles from anywhere. It's a good idea to phone ahead so you know what to expect, especially for the more remote areas. Although not a regimented organisation, the Independent Backpackers Hostels of Scotland do produce a brochure providing addresses, phone numbers and pertinent information. It is available at all Tourist Information centres for 20p and is free from all independent hostels throughout Scotland or write to Pete Thomas, Croft Bunkhouse and Bothies, Portnalong, Isle of Skye, Scotland, IV47 8SL.

Each independent hostel has a self-catering kitchen and breakfast is sometimes available (at a price). You're expected to clean up after yourself in the kitchen. Hot showers are almost always included in the price. In some hostels the bed-linen is included while in others you are expected to bring your own sleep-sheet or sleeping-bag. In almost all these cases if you do not have your own bed-linen you can hire it from the hostel. The rare exception to this would again only be in remote areas. Most have dormitory accommodation, some have twin or double rooms and a few have a style of bedding called 'alpine'. This is essentially a shared platform which anyone can sleep on and common in mountaineering areas only (sleeping on a hard surface is all part of the suffering). Prices range from about £10 (for a dormitory bed) in the larger towns to about £5 in some country areas.

Eight of these Independent Hostels form a chain which provide a reliable quality of service in a pleasant atmosphere. They are the Edinburgh High Street Hostel, Edinburgh Royal Mile Backpackers, Edinburgh Castle Rock Hostel, Inverness Student Hotel, Skye Backpackers (in Kyleakin), Fort William Backpackers and Oban Backpackers. Their Glasgow Backpackers Hostel is only open in summer. They are all in convenient locations for public transport and take bookings for each other.

BED & BREAKFAST

B&Bs offer comfortable private accommodation of twins, doubles or family rooms. Full bedding and a full hearty breakfast is included in the price and they are usually between £13 and £18. These small businesses are scattered all over the country and as they're so easy to find; there are just a few necessary (or cheap) B&Bs included in this book. The local Tourist Information will always have a list of B&Bs and can even book accommodation for you. Keep in mind that most, but not all, B&Bs are registered with the Tourist Information, so it's quite possible you could find a cheaper room looking for yourself.

CAMPING AND CARAVAN PARKS

There are hundreds of parks to choose from around the country, some in the most scenic spots you could hope for. Campers' fees range from £3 to £7 per tent, with some facilities costing extra. Not all caravan parks allow tents, but some of them rent out caravans on a nightly basis. It's worth asking about because this can prove more economical than a youth hostel. You can camp in the wild if you like, but if it's privately owned land you should ask for permission from the landowner first and leave no trace that you were ever there.

BOTHIES

Scattered around the Highlands, providing shelter for mountaineers, are a number of bothies. They are very small stone mountain huts, with no facilities at all except, usually, a fireplace (but often with no source of fuel). They sometimes have earth floors which soon turn to mud with too many wet boots, and by and large they should be treated as a last resort - camping is usually more comfortable when the weather is good.

Bothies are free, often deserted, and usually located in beautiful areas. Due to a few senseless acts of vandalism by some bothy users, the various bothy owners are somewhat reticent to publicise their locations. However, most appear on Ordnance Survey Maps. Word of mouth amongst other hill-walkers is another good source of this information.

Some hostels in central London

On your way to or from Scotland you may find it hard to avoid the busy metropolis of London. For your convenience here are a few reasonably priced independent hostels -

Quest Hostel, 45 Queensborough Terrace, W2, tel:(0171) 2297782.

Museum Hostel, 27 Montague St, WC1, tel:(0171) 5805360.

Victoria Hostel, 71 Belgrave Rd, near Victoria Station, tel:(0171) 8343077.

O'Callaghan's Hotels, 205 Earl's Court Rd, SW5, tel:(0171) 3703000, or 92 Ebury St, SW1, near Victoria Station, tel:(0171) 7306776.

Ceilidh Dances

Scotland is one of the few western countries where traditional dancing is still alive, probably because it's such good fun. You can, of course, find plenty of clubs playing boring old run-of-the-mill grunge, reggae, disco, techno, rave, etc, etc, but for a true world experience you must find a ceilidh (pronounced kay-lee).

Ceilidhs vary a lot of course with the best usually being in mid-winter in the Highlands and islands but the more frequent ones in the city can be great fun too. You might at first think that you don't know the steps to the dances, but another whisky or two should bring your memory back. Failing that, copy the guy in the kilt.

19. General Information

The population of Scotland is about 5 million - 800,000 in Glasgow, 500,000 in Edinburgh, 200,000 in Aberdeen and the other 3.5 million scattered elsewhere, but mostly in the central region. The capital city is Edinburgh. Geographically, Scotland is divided into the Highlands and the Lowlands. The line roughly marking the beginning of the Highlands runs from near Glasgow, north-east to Aberdeen, then north-west to Inverness. With magnificent hills and scenery throughout, this is where most visitors head. The Lowlands, however, are by no means flat and many parts are picturesque. The islands of Scotland consist of several groups. Off the west coast are the Inner and Outer Hebrides (the latter also known as the Western Isles), and to the north, Orkney, and beyond that, Shetland.

A few hundred years ago the landscape would have looked very different. Deforestation in the Highlands has left only 1% of the original Caledonian or Scots pine forest. Low growing heather covers a great deal of the land - most noticeable when the hills turn purple in August. In the fertile Lowlands the landscape is predominantly agricultural.

Religion

Despite the many church steeples on view, Scotland is no longer overtly religious. The country is mainly Church of Scotland (Protestant) but there are many religious groups who live happily side-by-side, with only a few areas of minor conflict. The northern islands of the Western Isles are strictly Protestant and their total observance of the Sabbath causes problems with both the more liberal mainland and their Roman Catholic neighbouring islands. Recently introduced Sunday ferry services caused an uproar. If you're going to be on Lewis, Harris or North Uist on a Sunday you'll need to get provisions beforehand. Prepare yourself for a very quiet day - you can't even hang your washing on the line.

Glasgow's proximity to Ireland (many Irish settled around here) has resulted in slight Protestant/Catholic friction, yet without any real violence. Going to a football match between the local teams Celtic and Rangers will probably highlight the worst of the hostilities.

Business Hours

Mainly 9am-5pm, Monday to Friday. Banks however, often don't open till 9.15am and closing times vary from 4pm to 5.30pm. Major post offices are open all day Saturday.

Shopping Hours

Mainstream shops are usually open 9am-5.30pm, Monday to Saturday, with late-night (usually until 7pm) shopping on a Thursday in larger towns and cities. Small corner grocer shops, however, can usually be found open until 9pm or 10pm. On Sundays most shops are closed, except for the larger shops on Princes St and the occasional book or record shop, while some supermarkets and all corner shops are still open (perhaps with shorter hours).

Money

All three Scottish banks (Bank of Scotland, Royal Bank of Scotland and the Clydesdale Bank) produce their own bank notes. It has the same value as the English and the Northern Irish pound, and all can be used throughout the UK but you might have trouble spending Scottish £1 notes outside Scotland. The English £1 note is obsolete, so English shopkeepers tend to view £1 notes with suspicion - just take them to a bank, however, and they can be exchanged. If you're taking money over to the continent, it's best to change your Scottish notes for English ones.

Public Telephones

In a coin phone, 10p will get your line connected but will only last a certain length of time. High-pitched beeps will tell you when to put more money in. Not all payphones are the same. British Telecom (BT) phones usually ask you to insert money before you dial, others want your coins after you dial, while an occasional phone requests you to press a button upon an answer. It's a bit confusing and mistakes can cost, so read the instructions.

Phone card telephones are frequent in towns and cities, and cards can be purchased from many shops, which display the phone card sign. Cards come in £2, £4, £10 and £20 denominations.

All local, national and international phone calls (to all countries) are at their cheapest on weekdays between 6pm and 8am and all weekend. If you want to phone 'reverse charges' (call collect) there's usually an exorbitant operator fee - so be kind to your family at home - phone them direct and get them to call you straight back. It's much cheaper for them this way.

BRITISH TELECOM NUMBERS: (free from payphones but sometimes you have to put money in which is returned at the end of the call).

100 - UK operator   **153** - International directory enquiries
192 - UK directory enquiries   **155** - International operator

As a very rough guide, take 30p with you for a local call, a pound or two to phone London, £5 for the continent and £10 or more for anywhere else. Any number that starts with 0800 or 0500 is a free call. 0345, 0990 or 0645 numbers are charged at a local rate from wherever you are in the U.K.

As the BT payphone prices for international calls are very high you should consider using the services of Swiftcall. This company offers very cheap rates for international dialling and you can phone from any BT payphone in the U.K. Swiftcall prices and BT prices per minute in January '98 were:

	Swiftcall	British Telecom pay-phone
Canada	14p	72p
U.S.A	24p	72p
Australia	20p/24p	£1.02
New Zealand	20p/30p	£1.02
South Africa	39p	£2.33/£2.72
Germany	14p	65p
Ireland	14p	56p/75p

To join Swiftcall you need to buy with a credit card a minimum of £25-£50 of units, which are refundable if you don't use them. Telephone 0800-7690000. The alternative is to buy a disposable Swiftcall card which are on sale at various outlets, telephone 0800-2790800 to find out where they can be purchased.

POSTAL SERVICES

Post offices will collect mail for you if your friends and relatives write 'Poste Restante' on the envelope, however, they will only hold your mail for 14 days. It might be better to get your mail sent to the hostel you will be staying at. Postcards and mail (under 60g) cost 26p (first class) or 20p (second class) to send inside the U.K. and 26p to send throughout Europe. Postcards being sent outside Europe cost 37p. Heavier items and letters being posted outside Europe should be weighed at a post office. For any postal enquiries telephone 0345-223344.

Highland Games

At a Highland Games you can expect to see just about every Scottish stereotype on view. Tossing the caber, hammer-throwing, shot-putting, highland dancing and bagpipe competitions usually feature. Though there are always many tourists present, these games are an ancient tradition laid on for the locals. They are of course a bit ludicrous but are great fun. Don't forget your umbrella, midge repellent and half bottle of whisky. And here's a hot tip - after the games follow the pipe band to the pub - a few drinks later it takes minimal encouragement to get them to play.

FOOD

Sadly, Scotland was at the wrong end of the queue when national culinary expertise was being handed out. And for those on a limited budget, sometimes it's as important to know what to avoid as well as what to look for.

The Chippie

Starting at the lower end of the scale is the ubiquitous fish and chip shop, known as 'the chippie'. The chips, though they can be cumbersome, greasy and soggy, are hearty and delicious and are probably Europe's last remaining chips that are not pre-frozen, half-cooked or artificially preserved. As your chips are about to be wrapped, you will be asked this poignant question - "salt and vinegar?", or on the east coast "salt and sauce?". You must answer this question directly and confidently, or you will be found out as a tourist.

Any subsidiary items on the menu should be approached with extreme caution. If you've ever wanted deep-fried pizza (that's in 10 inches of oil) - then Scotland's chippies are the place for you.

Warning - Haggis is a tasty dish, but must not be purchased from a chip shop. Refer to sentence on pizza.

Pub Lunches

Of course it depends on the pub in question, but a pub lunch is usually good value. Between about midday and 2pm many pubs offer a satisfying range of food. It is often the best place to try the famous haggis (on the other hand, pretend you're a local and ask for another delicacy - mince 'n' tatties). If you're on a budget but want to eat out, lunch in the pub is the way to do it, as your only choices in the evening will be more expensive restaurant meals.

Restaurants

The few truly Scottish restaurants are usually expensive, but are of a high standard, serving salmon, trout, venison, lamb, etc. Of the non-Scottish restaurants, Indian food is the most notable.

Almost all restaurants are licensed to serve alcohol, so you cannot bring your own drinks. A main meal price generally doesn't come much cheaper than £5.

Tipping

Tipping is not compulsory, but if you do tip, 10% of the bill is usual. Check, however, that a service charge hasn't already been included.

PUBS, CLUBS AND ALCOHOL

Whether it's a cheap and spartan public bar or an expensive highly decorated lounge bar, the pub is the social hub of any community in this country. As such it is important that you know the etiquette.

It's usual for just one person amongst a group of friends to order and pay for the whole round of drinks, knowing that the favour will more or less be returned by everyone eventually, although no-one really keeps track. If you are bought a drink by a local under such circumstances don't over thank them, just offer them one back later when you feel it's your turn to buy. If you really can't afford to enter into this situation just tell them so.

While in the pub, you should always have a drink in front of you - your friends simply won't be able to relax and enjoy their own drinks if you are empty-handed. And none of this buying half a pint and sitting pretty on it all night either. Generally, pubs are multi-generational. Young people tend to dominate but in a real pub there are usually middle-aged to elderly people drinking, plus the occasional dog. Unlike some countries, if you walk into a pub with only old people in it, you are not in the wrong place - just order your drink.

Opening hours are not as strict as in England. They're open all day - always until 11pm, and often later. If you want another bar after the pub's closing time, ask the barman or some revved-up locals.

Sundays can cause confusion - a pub that's open late every other night of the week can in some areas close early on a Saturday night. The theory being, the earlier to bed on a Saturday the earlier you'll be in church on the Sunday. This can be annoying, especially when you're travelling, and don't know what day of the week it is. However, none of the pubs will close before 11pm. On the Sunday morning, you'll be hard pressed to find a drink before noon (if you can hold out that long) - and again the pubs will be open till 11pm. These restrictions are always more strictly enforced in the small towns - exceptions will be found in the big cities and some tourist centres.

Clubs/Discos

Entrance prices range from nothing to £6, with Sundays to Thursdays being less busy and less pricey. Once inside, alcohol prices aren't much more than in pubs. Check local magazines (like 'The List' for Glasgow and Edinburgh) or ask Tourist Info where to find club listings. Best to avoid clubs with strict dress codes - unless you're up to it - so ask around before you choose one. There are many clubs with many kinds of music, but they probably won't stay open as late as you'd like them to (usually until 3am). Good advice is to start your night out earlier - around 8 or 9pm.

Buying Alcohol in the Shops

A shop that sells alcohol is an 'off-licence'. Off-licences, pubs and virtually all supermarkets sell 'booze' to 'carry-out' (but buying a 'carry-out' from a pub is the most expensive option).

Whisky

World-renowned for its quality, whisky has been an important part of Scottish life for centuries.

When choosing a whisky the first thing you should do is forget any famous whiskies you have heard of back home. Johnnie Walker, Chivas Regal and Glenfiddich are famous mainly because of the amount of money they spend on advertising.

Next you need to know there are two main types, malts and blends. Malt whiskies are the pure ones (generally more expensive but smooth), while blended whiskies are a mixture of malt and grain whiskies (cheap and rough). If you simply ask for 'a whisky' you'll get one of the cheaper blends. If you want a malt whisky you need to be more specific. A good way to help you decide on a brand is to ask one of the old guys perched up against the bar. If they won't help you, or you can't understand them, ask the bartender to recommend one. Always remember, never put Coca-Cola in your whisky. This is a crime in Scotland. Water or ice is an acceptable mixer for a cheap whisky as is dry or green ginger, but not much else. Numerous whisky distilleries throughout Scotland provide free or cheap tours which explain the whisky making process, and a nice treat at the end is a free sample.

Beer

Traditionally, ale (as opposed to lager) has been the common man's favourite refreshment. This has a variety of names, usually Heavy, 80, 70 or 60 Shilling, or Special. If you are unsure, ask for 'a pint of Heavy'. (Incidentally, in England this would be called 'Bitter', but not here.)

Though Scottish brewing is dominated by two main companies - Tennant Caledonian and Scottish & Newcastle - there are smaller companies with some interesting brews. Look out for beers such as Belhaven Best, Deuchars IPA, Golden Promise, Old Jock, Sandy Hunter's and Dark Island. And if that vastly advertised Irish Stout is to your liking, try Scotland's little known alternative - Gillespie's - you'll never look back.

Wine

Scottish wine is yet to have an impact internationally, or even at home. However, a real surprise is the Silver Birch wine (made from trees) produced by Moniack Castle - for an extra special treat, get the sparkling version.

Soft Drinks

Irn Bru. Made from girders.

Tap Water

Yes you can drink it - in fact it's lovely. In the Highlands it's quite often a slightly brown colour. This is just the peat which contributes to the water's softness and makes it even more drinkable.

Famous Scots

It is not commonly known that Sean Connery started his illustrious career as a milkman in Edinburgh, and that his first career move was to become a model at the art college. Stan Laurel of Laurel and Hardy fame was born in Glasgow as was Billy Connolly, Robert Carlyle and Robbie Coltrane. David Byrne of Talking Heads was born in Dumbarton, the actor Ewan MacGregor grew up in the country town of Crieff and the singer Annie Lennox was brought up in Aberdeen (and desperate to escape it). Scotland did present the world with the tartan-clad band the Bay City Rollers but has been trying to compensate for this since with bands and performers like Texas, Simple Minds and the Proclaimers. (Bros, Sheena Easton and WetWetWet - mere blips on an otherwise spotless record.)

For a small country, Scotland has made an incredible contribution to modern technology. Scottish inventors include James Watt (steam engine and first copying machine), Robert Watson-Watt (radar), R.W. Thomson and John Dunlop (rubber tyre), Alexander Graham Bell (telephone), Alexander Bain (fax machine, in the 19thC no less) and, last but not least, John Logie Baird (television). In the world of science, Alexander Fleming discovered penicillin, John MacLeod discovered insulin and James Young Simpson first realised the value of chloroform as an anaesthetic. Explorers include David Livingstone (Victoria Falls) and Alexander Mackenzie (Mackenzie River, Canada). Not forgetting the founder of the American navy, John Paul Jones, who was born near Dumfries and the philanthropist Andrew Carnegie. If you add to this Kirkpatrick MacMillan (bicycle), Charles Macintosh (Macintosh waterproof), James Chalmers (first adhesive postage stamp) and Alexander Shanks, the inventor of the lawnmower, you have a very impressive list.

Some famous people who are not Scottish but who sometimes think they are - Rod Stewart, Mel Gibson, Prince Charles.

Books

We have mentioned in the text several famous authors, however, if you are looking for something a bit more up-to-date to peruse over while you're on holiday here, why not try any of the following.

Iain Banks is one of Scotland's most prolific writers and you are most likely to enjoy his novels, 'The Crow Road', 'The Bridge' or 'Complicity'. He also writes science-fiction novels under the name Iain S.Banks. Irvine Welsh's 'Trainspotting' is excellent or you could read his book of short stories 'Maribou Stork Nightmares'. The novels 'Lanark', 'The Rise and Fall of Kelvin Walker' and 'Poor Things' written by Alasdair Gray are quite different from each other but all recommended.

Other notable authors to look for are A.L. Kennedy, James Kelman, Jeff Torrington, Muriel Spark and Janice Galloway.

For well-written, entertaining historical novels you really cannot surpass Nigel Tranter who has written about almost every period in Scottish history.

WORKING IN SCOTLAND

Unskilled summer jobs are pretty easy to come by. The influx of tourists in these months creates a lot of opportunities for budding chambermaids, dishwashers, waiters, etc, but don't expect to save a fortune. The experience will be your main reward and will provide you with the best way to understand the locals' idiosyncrasies. An easy way to get such a job is to pick up a tourist brochure and phone a selection of hotels. Most country hotels provide live-in accommodation and food which is convenient until cabin fever sets in or you fall out with the chef. Obviously the best time to apply is from June onwards, although just before Easter is another good time. Most small hotels and restaurants hire you on the spot or with only a few days' thought so writing to them months in advance is perhaps unnecessary. Farm work, especially fruit-picking, is another summer possibility particularly in the east. Phone rural Job Centres or the vast list of farmers in the Yellow Pages.

If you're not fussy you can work year-round. Country jobs are hard to come by but the cities keep rolling along - especially Edinburgh which always seems to have work. Glasgow, Inverness and Aberdeen have year-round opportunities, too. In any city don't expect much over £3-£4 an hour.

If you have a manual skill you're laughing. Secretaries are spoilt for choice - put your name down at temp agencies. Construction workers, too, are almost always in demand somewhere. If you have a specialised skill it is generally hard to get the particular job you want. You should write in advance to as many likely employers as possible.

National Insurance Number

You might be asked at a job interview what your National Insurance number is - to this you should reply that you've applied for one and your number will be allocated in a few weeks. Then, if you haven't already done so, run off and apply for one from the local Department of Social Security (take your passport along). Once you've got the job you will get asked for a 'P45' (a record of your previous pay and tax). You can't get a P45 until you've had a job in the UK so tell them this is your first UK job, unless of course it isn't, in which case contact your previous employer.

Tax

Having secured your dream job you'll doubtless be dismayed (unless it's casual work) at your first pay cheque/packet. This will be because you will probably be on temporary 'Emergency Tax' (which is excessive). This should rectify itself after a few weeks. At the end of your job be sure to claim back your tax. You won't get it all back as some is National Insurance and some may be due to the taxman legitimately, but you'll probably be due a good bit. Ideally phone the Inland Revenue, Centre 1, East Kilbride, Glasgow, G79 1AA; tel:(013552) 75009, three weeks before you stop work for the relevant form and return it when you finish work. Photocopy everything you send to them as they tend to conveniently 'lose' things. You might be lucky and get your money back in the first few weeks, otherwise persist - phone and/or write to them regularly, and you will get your money eventually.

HEALTH & EMERGENCIES

If you become ill or have an accident in Scotland your treatment, either in hospital or by a doctor is FREE (although you will have to pay for any medicines prescribed), so don't hesitate to get yourself treated.

However, should you bring your illness into the country you will, in theory, be charged for treatment.

If you have medical insurance, wait until they ask you about it.

If you need to phone for an Ambulance (STRICTLY EMERGENCY ONLY) the number is 999. (The operator will say 'Emergency, which service please'. Reply 'Ambulance', then wait for the next operator who will ask for details of the problem and your location. Give as much information as you can.)

The other emergency services on this number are the Police, Fire Brigade, Coastguard and Mountain Rescue. (NO coins are required to make an emergency call at a payphone.)

If you need treatment which is not an emergency, either look up the Yellow Pages - 'Doctors' or 'Hospitals' - or phone Directory Enquiries (192) and ask for the local doctor or a hospital with an Accident and Emergency Department. Note that a local doctor is usually more sympathetic than a hospital doctor.

If you have something valuable lost or stolen, always report it to the Police so that at least you have a chance of it being recovered. The Police in Scotland are, by and large, friendly and helpful towards tourists (and peaceful locals) so don't be apprehensive. The emergency number for the police is 999; for their local number look up the business section of the White Pages or phone Directory Enquiries (192).

HILL-WALKING SAFETY

Summer

The serenity of the Scottish mountains and glens is a magnet to a vast multitude of hill-walkers. Sadly every year hundreds of people are injured or killed on these mountains and you must make every effort to ensure this does not happen to you or your companions. For example, lack of proper footwear might cause a sprained ankle - this might not normally be a disaster but with night falling, a storm brewing, a demoralised and exhausted friend, temperatures dropping to freezing (even though it's summer) you're soaked through and miserably cold - this is when things are looking grim.

Before you set out, imagine the worst, then make sure you have done and will be doing your best to ensure the worst doesn't happen. Follow the weather reports for a few days before your trip, appreciate that the temperature will be about 10°C lower if you rise 1000m, and remember that wind speeds increase phenomenally with altitude. Assume that if something goes wrong that you won't be rescued and plan accordingly. Take responsibility for your own actions. Scotland's mountains are not that high but they are remote, the terrain is often difficult and the weather can change suddenly and dramatically.

You must take with you a map, compass and the knowledge of how to use them. Track your route on the map, continuously checking landmarks with your compass (this is fun anyway). Don't assume you're going the right way, constantly confirm this with your map. Beware that some mountains are magnetic and might produce wonky compass readings.

Proper boots are absolutely essential, your clothes must be wind-proof, water-proof and very warm. In cold conditions a survival/Bivi bag is essential. Take more than ample food, particularly chocolate, a torch or camera flash (some way of attracting attention in the dark), lightweight cooking stove and pan for warm drinks. Don't let your map or hat blow away. Don't go alone - companions can save your life. Check the weather forecast (there is a telephone forecast service, 0891 500441 for the west, 0891 500442 for the east, 50p per minute), and don't hesitate to abandon the walk if the forecast is bad. Be certain that the route and distance you are going are consistent with your fitness, don't overestimate your or your companions' abilities, and take nightfall into account. Leave your route plan back with your friends/ hostel/B&B or someone sensible, stating the time that you expect to get back (don't forget to inform them of your safe return). Be quite prepared to turn back if your instincts tell you to - don't look at your outing as a challenge which you must overcome.

If someone in your party is injured make sure they are warm and comfortable, mark their exact location on your map, find a telephone (easier said than done), dial 999 and give the emergency services full details, including the map grid reference of the injured person. The distress signal is six blasts of a whistle/shouts/or anything followed by a minute's silence, then repeated. If a helicopter is involved in the rescue, once you have attracted its attention don't keep waving, they may just wave back and fly away. Stand with your arms stretched outwards and upwards - Y-shaped - this is the distress signal. Before you venture into the hills, drop into a Tourist Information and pick up these leaflets; 'Enjoy the Scottish hills in safety', 'Learn to read or get lost'. They are also available (free) from the Scottish Sports Council, Caledonia House, South Gyle, Edinburgh, EH12 9DQ, tel:(0131) 317 7200.

Winter

In winter there is no such thing as hill-walking, it is **MOUNTAINEERING** and the only advice to give to the inexperienced is that you should join a mountaineering club. Most universities have one or the very helpful Mountaineering Council of Scotland can provide you with a list. Send a stamped addressed envelope to:-

Mountaineering Council of Scotland, National Officer,
IR 71 King St, Crieff, Perthshire, PH7 3HB.

EVENTS 1998

MARCH

2-6	GLENSHEE	Snow Fun Week, Competitions, fun and Apres Ski
3-8	PERTH	Scottish Curling Championship

APRIL

2-6	SHETLAND	Folk Festival
4-19	EDINBURGH	International Science Festival
9-12	EDINBURGH	Folk Festival
9-15	ARRAN	Folk Festival
11	MELROSE	International Rugby Sevens
15-20	KIRKCALDY	Links Market, Europe's largest street fair
18	AYR	Scottish Grand National, horse racing
24-26	ISLE OF MULL	Mull Music Festival
24-26	STROMNESS	Jazz Festival
30	EDINBURGH	May Day Beltane Celebration - Calton Hill
30-May 4	ISLE OF BUTE	Jazz Festival

MAY

3	GOUROCK	Highland Games
21-24	ORKNEY	Folk Festival
22-31	PERTH	Festival of the Arts
22-Jun 6	THE HIGHLANDS	Highland Festival
23-31	ISLAY	Traditional Music Festival
23-24	INNERLEITHEN	Beer Festival
24	BLAIR ATHOLL	Highland Gathering
30	BLACKFORD	Highland Games

JUNE

6	STRATHMIGLO	Highland Games
6-7	EDINBURGH	Meadows Festival
6-7	HAWICK	Common Riding
7	GIRVAN	Lowland Gathering
8-14	ARRAN	Folk Festival
11	INVERNESS	North of Scotland Highland Games
11	LANARK	Lanimer Day
13	KILMORE,OBAN	Highland Games
14	ARDROSSAN	Highland Games
14	FORFAR	Highland Games
14-20	PEEBLES	Common Riding
19-21	KILLIN	Traditional Music and Dance Festival
19-24	ORKNEY	St Magnus Festival
20	CAMPBELTOWN	Highland Games
20	OLD MELDRUM	Highland Games
20	NEWBURGH	Highland Games
21	ABERDEEN	Highland Games
25-28	INGLISTON	Highland Show(near Edinburgh)
26-28	DINGWALL	Traditional Music Festival

Events 1998

26-Jul 5	GLASGOW	International Jazz Festival
27	DRUMTOCHTY, KINCARDINESHIRE	Highland Games
28	BEAULY	Highland Games

JULY

1	KENMORE	Highland Games
4	FORRES	Highland Games
4	INVERGARRY	Highland Games
5	CUPAR	Highland Games
5-12	TIREE	Gaelic Festival
5-17	BARRA	Gaelic Festival
6-18	SKYE and LOCHALSH	Skye and Lochalsh Festival
8-9	FORT AUGUSTUS	Highland Gathering (I)
8-11	LUSS	Loch Lomond Golf Championship
10-12	STONEHAVEN	Folk Festival
11	DINGWALL	Highland Games
11	INVERNESS	Highland Games
mid-July	KINROSS	T in the Park Rock Concert
12	STIRLING	Highland Games
12	ARBROATH	Highland Games
15-18	STORNOWAY	Hebridean Celtic Music Festival
16-21	PITLOCHRY	Atholl Festival
17	NORTH UIST	Highland Games
17-26	TROSSACHS	Highland Festival
18	BALLOCH	Loch Lomond Highland Games
18	ELGIN	Highland Games
18	LOCHCARRON	Highland Games
18	TOMINTOUL	Highland Games
18	ISLE OF LEWIS	Highland Games
19	EDINBURGH	Highland Games
19	STONEHAVEN	Highland Games
21	INVERARAY	Highland Games
22	LUSS	Highland Games
22	SOUTH UIST	Highland Games
23	TOBERMORY	Highland Games
23-27	ISLE OF BUTE	International Folk Festival
25	SOUTHEND	Highland Games
25	LOCHEARNHEAD	Highland Games
25	TAYNUILT	Highland Games
25	FORT WILLIAM	Highland Games
25	DUFFTOWN	Highland Games
25-26	CALLANDER	World Highland Games
26	ST ANDREWS	Highland Games
26	ROTHIEMURCHUS, AVIEMORE	Highland Games
29	ARISAIG	Highland Games
29-30	FORT AUGUSTUS	Highland Gathering (II)
31	DURNESS	Highland Games
31	LANGHOLM	Common Riding

31-Aug 9	EDINBURGH	International Jazz Festival
end July	SKYE	Folk Festival

AUGUST

1	STRATHCONON	Highland Games (Muir of Ord)
1	ABERLOUR	Highland Games
1	ABOYNE	Highland Games
1	NEWTONMORE	Highland Games
1	TAIN	Highland Gathering
2	EDINBURGH	Highland Games
2	MONTROSE	Highland Games
2	PARTON near	Alternative Games -
	KIRKCUDBRIGHT	World Gird'n'Cleek championships,
		Hurlin' the Curlin' Stane
		Skipping Races, Tossin' the Sheaf,
		Flingin' the Herd's Bunnet,
		Hopscotch, Snail Racing.
2	BRIDGE OF ALLAN	Highland Games
3	MALLAIG	Highland Games and Music
5	PORTREE	Highland Games
5	KILLIN	Highland Games
7	DORNOCH	Highland Gathering
7-8	ABERFELDY	Highland Gathering
7-11	ST ANDREWS	Lammas Fair
7-16	SANQUHAR	Riding of the Marches
7-29	EDINBURGH	Military Tattoo
8	BRODICK	Highland Games
8	STRATHPEFFER	Highland Gathering
8	NORTH BERWICK	Highland Games
9	PERTH	Highland Games
9-31	EDINBURGH	Festival Fringe
12-13	FORT AUGUSTUS	Highland Gathering (III)
13	BALLATER	Highland Games
14	LOCHINVER	Highland Games
15	GLENFINNAN	Highland Gathering
15	HELMSDALE	Highland Games
15	GLASGOW	World Pipe Bands Championship
15	NAIRN	Highland Games
15	SOUTH	Festival of the Horse and Boys Ploughing
	RONALDSAY	Match
15-31	EDINBURGH	Book Festival
16	CRIEFF	Highland Games
16-30	EDINBURGH	Edinburgh Film Festival
16-Sept 5	EDINBURGH	International Festival
21	BLAIRGOWRIE	Glenisla Highland Games
21-23	STROMNESS	Beer Festival
22	ISLE OF BUTE	Highland Games
22	INVERGORDON	Highland Gathering
22	KIRKMICHAEL,	Highland Games
	BLAIRGOWRIE	
22	STRATHDON	Highland Gathering & Games

Events 1998

23	EDINBURGH	Highland Games
23	GRANTOWN-ON-SPEY	Highland Games
26-27	OBAN	Highland Games
27	EDINBURGH	Fireworks Concert
28-29	DUNOON	Highland Gathering
29	DUNBEATH,	Highland Games
29	BIRNAM/DUNKELD	Highland Games
29	DRUMNADROCHIT	Highland Gathering & Games
29-6 Sep	LARGS	Viking Festival, battles, concerts and fireworks

SEPTEMBER

2	FORT WILLIAM	Ben Nevis Race
2-3	FORT AUGUSTUS	Highland Gathering
5	BRAEMAR	Highland Gathering
5	MULL	Fiddler's Rally
6	BLAIRGOWRIE	Highland Games
12	PITLOCHRY	Highland Games
12	LEUCHARS	Airshow
13	PEEBLES	Highland Games
18-20	TARBERT	Music Festival
19	BONAR BRIDGE	Highland Games

OCTOBER

2-11	EDINBURGH & SPEYSIDE	International Scotch Whisky Festival
8-17	ABERDEEN	Alternative Festival
9-16	SKYE and LOCHALSH	Royal National Mod 1998
26-8 Nov	EDINBURGH	Scottish International Storytelling Festival

NOVEMBER

5	EDINBURGH	Fireworks
7	DUNVEGAN	Castle Fireworks
30	SCOTLAND	St Andrews Day

DECEMBER

25	KIRKWALL	Christmas Ba'
28-Jan 1	EDINBURGH	Edinburgh's Hogmanay
31-Jan 1	COMRIE	Flambeaux Procession
31	ABERDEEN	New Year Spectacular
31	GLASGOW	Hogmanay Celebrations
31	INVERNESS	Hogmanay Celebrations

JANUARY 1999

1	KIRKWALL	New Year's Day Ba'
15-3 Feb	GLASGOW	Celtic Connections Festival
25	SCOTLAND	Burns Night
last Tues in Jan	LERWICK, SHETLAND	Up-Helly-Aa

244

INDEX

246

ORKNEY

Kirkwall

John o'Groats

Wick

Thurso

Helmsdale

Durness

Tongue

Lochinver

Ullapool

Gairloch

Dingwall

Strathpeffer

Kyle of Lochalsh

Mallaig

SKYE

WESTERN ISLES

Huntly

ABERDEEN

Elgin

Dufftown

Nairn

Aviemore

Ballater

Kingussie

INVERNESS

Loch Ness

Fort Augustus

SHETLAND

Lerwick

248

KEY
Rail Lines

And finally....

We hope that you have enjoyed using Scotland for Backpackers and, more importantly, we hope that you have had a memorable Scottish holiday.

We research, update and re-publish this book every year so we would like to ask you, the reader, to tell us of any discoveries that you have made and would like to share. Also please let us have your comments, criticisms or suggestions regarding the book. Write to :-

Scotland for Backpackers
Reel Publishing
Suite 17, 28 North Bridge
Edinburgh   EH1 1QG
Scotland

Thanks

Erica Brock

House for an Art Lover

inspired by the original drawings of *Charles Rennie Mackintosh*

Bellahouston Park
10 Dumbreck Road
Glasgow
Telephone 0141 353 4770

£1 OFF

full-price entry ticket

Voucher expires on 28 February, '99

Auld Reekie Tours

Haunted, Underground City Tours
Depart from Tron Kirk, Royal Mile,
Edinburgh
Tel:(0131) 557 4700

£1 OFF
full-price ticket

Voucher expires on 28 February, '99

RENTALS   *REPAIRS*

EDINBURGH CYCLE HIRE

Blackfriars Street
(off Royal Mile near Holiday Inn)
Tel:(0131) 556 5560

10% OFF
bicycle rental

Voucher expires on 28 February, '99

CASTLE ROCK HOSTEL
HOLIDAY ACCOMMODATION

15 Johnston Terrace, Edinburgh
Tel:(0131) 225 9666

£1 OFF
first night's accommodation

Voucher valid until 28 February, '99

OBAN BACKPACKERS

Breadalbane Street
Oban
Tel:(01631) 562107

£1
OFF
first night's
accommodation

Voucher expires on 28 February, '99

Gordon Grant Marine

Boat trips from Oban
Railway Pier
Oban
Tel:(01631) 562842

10%
OFF
full price
tour ticket

Voucher expires on 28 February, '99

BALNAIN HOUSE
Home of
HIGHLAND MUSIC

40 HUNTLY STREET, INVERNESS
Tel 01463 715757

10%
OFF
exhibition
price

Voucher expires on 28 February, '99